The Sound of Storytime

Tiara Dixon and Paula Blough

Neal-Schuman Publishers, Inc.

New York   London

Published by Neal-Schuman Publishers, Inc.
100 William St., Suite 2004
New York, NY 10038

Printed and bound in the United States of America.

The paper used in this publication meets the minimum requirements of American National
Standard for Information Sciences—Permanence of Paper for Printed Library Materials,
ANSI Z39.48-1992.

Library of Congress Cataloging-in-Publication Data

Dixon, Tiara.
  The sound of storytime / Tiara Dixon, Paula Blough.
      p. cm.
  Includes bibliographical references and indexes.
  ISBN 1–55570–552–9 (alk. paper)
 1. Children's libraries—Activity programs—United States. 2.
Storytelling—United States—Audio-visual aids. 3. Children's
literature, American—Bibliography. I. Blough, Paula. II. Title.
  Z718.3D59 2006
  027.62'51—dc22   2006001299

Contents

PART V TAMBOURINES

PART VI VOCAL CHORDS

PART VII   ENCORE MEDLEY

THE SOUND OF STORYTIME RESOURCES

Preface

Most libraries run some version of a successful "story hour." Why do children universally enjoy the experience? Is it the pleasure of learning to read? Maybe it is the excitement of the group sharing an interesting story. Perhaps it is simply the timeless fact that children love adult interaction, compelling books, and appealing activities. *The Sound of Storytime* embodies those positives and adds the magic of music. Each of the programs in this book features original songs to sing as well as simple instruments to play. We have created the programs as a way to present children with superior books to read, connect children in quality activities, encourage singing, introduce playing instruments, and, most of all, have fun!

We have organized the forty-two programs of *The Sound of Storytime* into seven parts, each part offering six programs. Each part highlights a different, easy-to-play instrument: bells, rhythm sticks, sand blocks, shakers, tambourines, vocal chords, and an encore medley. Every program features an everyday part of life such as cookies, birthdays, bathtime, dinosaurs, and farm life.

The forty-two complete programs all offer:

- at least one featured book with recommendations for the best ages to use the books with;
- a summary of the featured book;
- an activity related to the featured book;
- optional book suggestions;
- a music and movement sing-a-long activity and a music activity with an enticing prop—complete with directions, lyrics, and the actual song to play on the companion CD-ROM;
- a storyboard—complete with directions, lyrics, and Ellison die-cut templates; and
- a "make and take" activity.

The Program Presentation Tips on page xxiii provide complete instructions and guidance for making the most of *The Sound of Storytime*.

We created these interesting activities and they have been "road tested" to encourage audience participation. We can guarantee that they are all tried and true and work well.

We expect novice and veteran storytellers alike will glean a wealth of fresh material for sharing picture books in ways that will enthrall and enchant. We hope professionals can use *The Sound of Storytime* to foster a love for reading by bringing a playful and interactive spin to everyday activities. Most importantly, busy librarians need not have a musical background or even be able to sing a single note. We include a companion CD-ROM sound recording of forty-eight original songs, sung to traditional tunes.

The Sound of Storytime offers a full repertoire of interactive adventures ready at a moment's notice. It provides tools to leverage resources to best effect, to help educate, and to entertain with no more than a few good picture books, trouble-free musical instruments, and a handful of inexpensive props.

We have designed *The Sound of Storytime* to inspire and ignite the novice storytime presenters' passion for children's literacy programs. For seasoned librarians, we anticipate that it will refresh and renew the excitement that may have faded over the years. It will offer even the most industrious individuals an uncomplicated chance to enrich and enhance storybooks in a way that fully engages young audiences.

Most importantly, these programs are intended to help children learn. Early childhood is a time of tremendous brain development. Learning potential is stimulated by everything in the child's environment. These programs are designed to increase the critical interplay between music and early literacy. We hope librarians will enjoy giving young children the opportunity to combine learning the rhythm of music and playing instruments with reading good books and participating in vital activities as much as the kids love the story hour experience.

Acknowledgments

TIARA

Thanks to my parents for faithfully taking me each week in a bicycle basket to Chicago Library Story Hour.

Thanks to my husband TJ for making our lives better than a Nicholas Sparks romance novel.

A special thanks to my favorite story characters, my children: Anna, Joey, Laura, and the new baby too.

I am grateful for my sister Sarah for years of side-splitting laughter over stories we will always remember, cherish, and share.

I would like to thank my Grandmother Eva for sharing the Bible—the most important book ever written—with me.

Thank you to my Grandma Edie for sharing our family heritage—the best stories I've ever heard.

Make your life a story worth telling.

PAULA

I would like to thank my loving family and friends for proudly embracing this journey with me.

I am eternally grateful to my remarkable parents, Roscoe and Gladys Walker, whom I deeply love and respect.

I am equally grateful to my loving husband of twenty-five years, John. He supported and encouraged me every step of the way—not to mention sacrificing months of home-cooked meals.

To my beautiful daughters, Shelly, Melanie, Summer, and Autumn, a special thank you for donating precious mother/daughter time to this endeavor.

Thanks to Patty G. Walker and Phyllis O'Neill, my talented sisters. You have always been there for me and came through again. Love to you both.

TIARA AND PAULA

Thanks to:

Keith Kaster, Low Key Productions

Ben Campbell, keyboardist

Autumn Blough, TJ Dixon, Phyllis O'Neill, Sarah Speck, Patty G. Walker, vocalists

Charlotte Barkley, special friend and babysitter extraordinaire

Joy Behrens, Mom, for all your help with this project

Mid-Continent Public Library, Liberty Staff

Gail Benton, Anitra Steele, and Myra Unger, for their supportive advice and encouragement

Neal-Schuman Publishers and Michael Kelley, Editor

Special thanks to Sheryl Skeie and Lisa Corcoran of the Ellison Die-Cut Company for the use of the wonderful patterns. Note: The patterns are copyrighted by and trademarks of Ellison. All rights reserved.

Introduction

HOW TO USE THE CD-ROM

We recorded an original chant or song for each of the forty-two programs in the book. Without any practice at all and with virtually no planning time, you can pop in the CD and add this fun, interactive element to any program.

Before you begin, you may want to listen casually to the chants and songs at home, in your car, or while walking. You will discover that many of the tunes are based on lifelong favorites.

Also included on the CD-ROM are Ellison die-cut patterns that can be used to prepare the quick and easy Make and Take Activities and Storyboards.

PROGRAM PRESENTATION TIPS

Featured and Optional Books

- Select any program that suits your needs.
- Once you have decided on a program, choose a text from the *featured book*. There is usually more than one featured book for each lesson to allow for individual preferences. The recommended titles are widely available.
- Avoid presenting two featured books at the same story hour. If you want to share a second featured book, eliminate the instrument activity from one of the two stories. In other words, plan to use the instruments with one book and one song or storyboard. You can provide multiple story hours from each of our programs with just a simple change in the featured story.
- Pick your featured title, read through the rest of the list, and choose a couple of books you like from the "Additional Books to Share" section.
- "Gather four books and read three" is a good rule of thumb. You should read a total of two to four books at a thirty- to forty-five-minute session.
- Gauge how many books you will actually read on how long or complicated the stories are and the age of your audience. There is a tremendous difference in the attention span of a younger three-year-old and an older four-year-old, so try to be responsive to your particular audience, changing your plans on the fly if necessary.
- Read your longest or most involved story first while the children are fresh. If the story is particularly challenging, take a movement and music break immediately after the close of the first narrative. If they are still attentive, go on to read the second book. As long as your audience seems to be engrossed, continue reading!
- Respect the unique threshold for attention of every child in your audience. Even if the children remain actively engaged after the second book, be sure still to insert a movement and music break, to preempt any wiggles that might arise.
- Liven up your presentation and tell a great story with supplementary ideas. If you were not born with a talent for story telling, these simple tips may be all the help you need. If, by contrast, you are a seasoned storyteller, it is great fun to swap ideas and put a fresh slant on your repertoire.

MUSIC AND MOVEMENT WITH INSTRUMENTS AND PROPS

- Play a song a few times before singing. Most of the songs on our CD are one to two minutes in length and will not disrupt the flow of the program.
- Transition from reading to music by demonstrating how and when to play the instrument. Before passing out instruments, ask the children if they would like to play an instrument with you. When they agree, pass out the instruments.

• Give clear instructions on how you want the children to behave with the instruments *before* you pass them out. Establish clear rules, such as "keep your instruments quietly in your lap until I point to you."

JUST FOR FUN

• Enhance your storytime or display area with these ideas. For example, always try to create an area where all the titles from the "Additional Books to Share" list can be displayed. These should be readily available for a book talk. Encourage your children to check them out to read and share at home.

ADDITIONAL SONGS TO SHARE

• Use an established song not available on our CD-ROM once in a while. We have listened to countless hours of children's music over the years, searching for the "perfect" song. We recommend our very favorites in this section.
• Check out CDs from your local library before deciding to include them in your personal collection.

STORYBOARD/FLANNEL BOARD

Making storyboards with common office equipment is inexpensive, quick, and versatile. Use a traditional flannel board or try the following convenient storyboard ideas:

• Make use of felt pieces cut with the Ellison die-cut machine. Put the pieces on the flannel board.
• Use clip and copy art available on computers. Employ photocopying and laminating equipment. Make storyboards with laminated paper pieces, whether Ellison die-cut shapes or clip art. It's a snap.
• Locate an Ellison die-cut or clip art picture of a character or object you need.
• Copy the picture on appropriately colored paper, laminate it, cut it out, and attach whatever you are using to affix it. Laminated paper storyboard pieces are versatile, inexpensive, and quick to make with the common office equipment.
• Use double-sided tape to attach pieces to a dry erase board.
• Use thumb tacks or double-sided tape to attach pieces to a bulletin board.
• Attach tape to a magnetic cookie sheet or the flannel board using double-sided tape or Velcro.

MAKE AND TAKE ACTIVITY

• Reinforce the fun events at storytime with an art activity. It supports the "Curriculum Topics" and provides the children with a simple hands-on activity. Some of these crafts allow the children to role-play the story or music from storytime with someone at home. Always make a sample of the craft ahead of time. Display it to give the children something with which to build their own ideas.

Index of Ellison Die-Cuts

We use the Ellison die-cutting machine to cut out crafts in a snap. For anyone unfamiliar with what the Ellison machine is, it is a hand-operated, die-cutting machine. When die shapes are inserted into the machine it cuts numerous sheets of paper at one time into a perfect shape. It is similar to using a cookie cutter, with much faster results. To see demonstrations and learn more about Ellison die-cuts, visit their Web site at www.ellison.com.

Many libraries, schools, and daycares will be familiar with and have access to the Ellison die-cutting machine. For those who do not, we have been able to cooperate with Ellison for the permission to provide the shapes on our CD-ROM. Simply download the pattern that you need for the craft and copy the pattern on a copy machine. Most patterns will need to be enlarged by an additional 50 percent or more. Use your judgment with this. After you select your desired size, simply cut out the shape and use it as a template to cut out as many as needed.

Alphabet Set 11151-5	Ant, small 12072	Apple 12078	Baseball, small 12186
ABC			
Bathtub 12202	Beagle 18151	Bear #1 12516	Beaver 12220
Bee, small 12226	Beetle 12228	Bell 12332	Bicycle 12234
Bird #3 12264	Birthday Cake 12270	Blue Jay 12280	Bone, small 12288
Book, Open 12300	Boy #2 12470	Butterfly #1, small 12490	Camel 12520
Candles, 6-Up 12522	Car #1 12550	Cardinal 13914	Cat #3 12620
Chick 12776	Chipmunk 17641	Circles 3" 15656	Clam Shell 17743

Clock Face & Hands   15914

Clouds   20556

Cow   12939

Crocodile   12970

Deer   13001

Dinosaur Set #1   16688

Donkey   13138

Door Hanger, Plain   13145

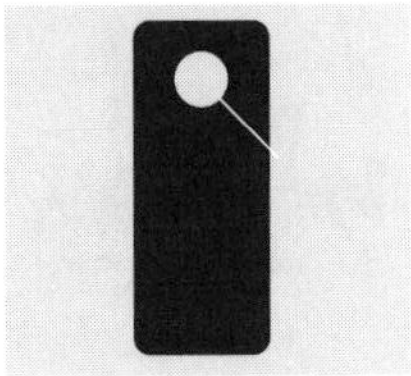

Duck   13164

Dump Truck   15131

Elephant #1   13204

Farmer   13246

Feather   13252

Firefighter   13284

Firetruck   13288

Fish #2   13298

Fish, Tiny   13330

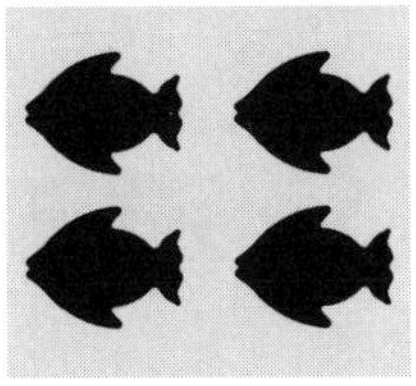

Fly   13386

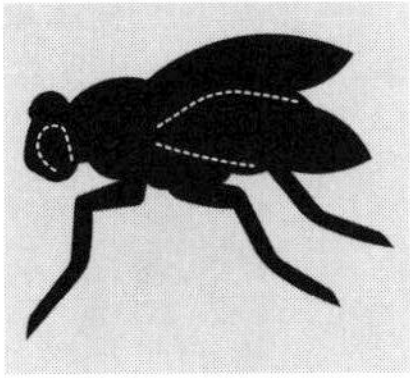

Fox   13420

Frog #2   13422

Giraffe #1   13474

Girl #2   13482

Goat   13492

Grasshopper   13526

Hammer   13550

Heart #1B   13604

Hen #1   13626

Hippo   20570

Horse #1 13650

Horse, Colt 13654

House 20572

Ice Cream Cone #1 13676

Jeep 13719

Kite 13745

Lamb #1 13767

Lion #2 13853

Lizard 13866

Man 13896

Monkey #2 13977

Moose 13981

Motorcycle #1 17958

Mouse 13989

Mutt 13108

Paint Brush #2 14138

Panther 14148

Paper Bag Puppet—Duck 14162

Pencil 14218

Pick Up 17484

Pie 14285

Pig #2 14289

Rabbit #1 14446

Rhinoceros 14482

Rooster 14508

School Bus #1A 14555

Sea Horse 14582

Shark 14608

Sheep   14610

Shell #3   17741

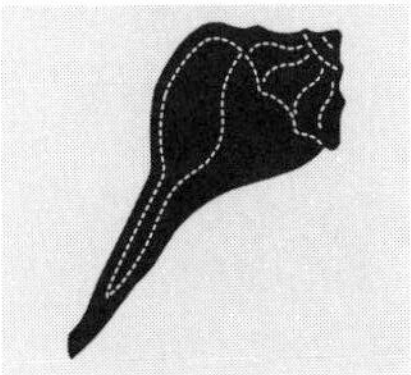

Skip Loader   15135

Snake #1   14650

Spider   14704

Sun #1C   14993

Sunflower   13351

Teapot   15029

Telephone   15055

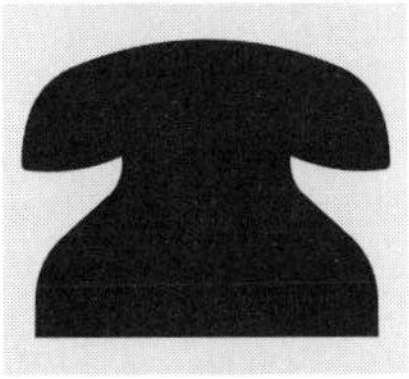

Tiger #1   17971

Toddler   15089

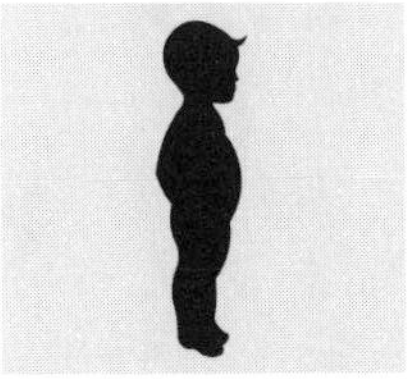

Tool Set   16766

Toothbrush & Tooth   15103

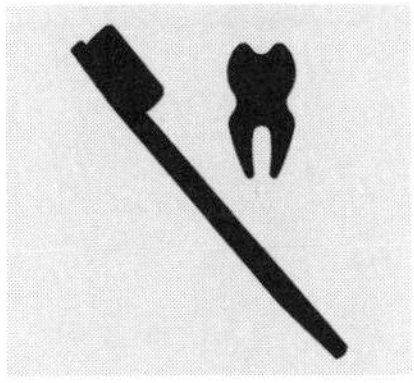

Toothpaste   15101

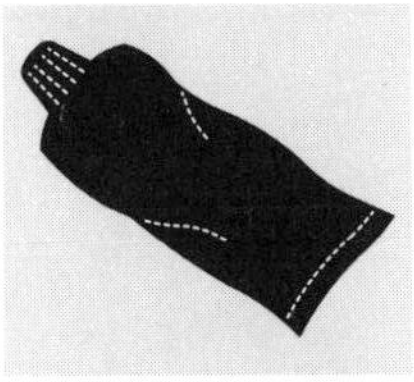

Tow Truck   15137

Toy Boat   12284

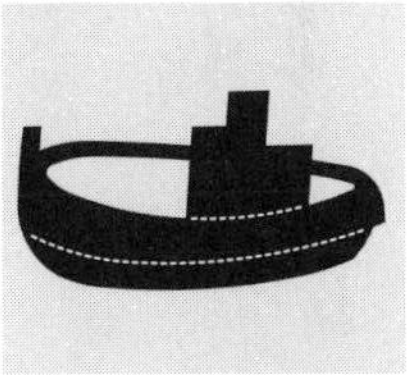

Tractor   15139

Train Set   16686

Tree   15145

Truck   15127

T-Shirt   15119

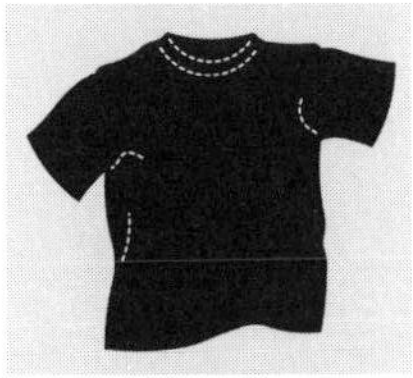

Turtle #1B   15121

Umbrella   15174

Wolf #1   15274

Woman   15278

Worm   13256

Zebra   15372

PART I

BELLS

LESSON 1

❧❀❧

CATS AND BIRDS

CURRICULUM TOPICS
Cats, Birds, Feathers, Mice

FEATURED BOOK
Ehlert, Lois. 1990. *Feathers for Lunch.* New York: Trumpet Club.

SUMMARY
An escaped housecat encounters twelve birds in the backyard but fails to catch any of them and has feathers for lunch. Ages 2–7

ACTIVITY
This is a great book to use the bells. The cat that is trying to catch the birds in the backyard is wearing a collar with jingle bells. The most effective way to use the bells with this story is to let the children ring their bells ever so lightly every time the page is turned. Toward the end of the story, there is a page with the cat lunging upward to catch the hummingbird. On this page, allow the children to ring their bells loud and long to warn the bird of the cat's sinister intentions.

ADDITIONAL BOOKS TO SHARE
Anello, Christine. 1990. *The Farmyard Cat.* New York: Scholastic. A hungry farm cat is eyeing the chickens when she accidentally upsets all the farm animals. This story has a repeating line, "I'll get you!" Let the children chant this line with you. Ages 2–7

Harris, Lee. 1999. *Never Let Your Cat Make Lunch for You.* Berkely, CA: Tricycle Press. The cat makes gruesome lunches for the little girl to take to school. This story is adorable and humorous, with a surprise ending. Ages 3–7

Horn, Emily. 2003. *Excuse Me . . . Are You a Witch?* Watertown, MA: Whispering Coyote. Herbert, the black cat, is lonely until he reads that witches love black cats. When he tries to find one though, it becomes much harder than he anticipated. Ages 3–7

James, Simon. 2002. *The Bird Watchers.* Cambridge, MA: Candlewick Press. Granddad tells Jess of the peculiar things that the birds do when he goes to the woods to observe them. His stories arouse her curiosity. When Jess decides to accompany him on one of his bird-watching excursions, she comes home with some peculiar stories of her own. Spectacular illustrations and a strong storyline combine to make this a great book. Ages 4–8

Miller, Virginia. 1997. *Be Gentle!* Cambridge, MA: Candlewick Press. When Bartholomew gets a little black kitten, he must learn to take care of him and be gentle with him. This book has a repeating line, "Be gentle!" Let the children repeat this line with you as they stroke the back of their own hand while saying "Be gentle" in a very soft and tender voice. The story has a satisfying ending and is a great learning tool for the very young. Ages 2–5

Newman, Lesléa. 2001. *Cats, Cats, Cats!* New York: Simon & Schuster Books for Young Readers. At night, when Mrs. Brown begins to snore, her sixty cats have fun galore. Ages 3–7

Ward, Cindy. 1997. *Cookies Week.* New York: Penguin Putnam Books for Young Readers. Each day of the week, Cookie the cat crashes, knocks over, or tears something up. This story could also be used with tambourines as well. Ages 2–7

MUSIC AND MOVEMENT WITH BELLS

Sing Along: "Poor Little Kitty"

Sung to the Tune: "Rock-a-By Baby"

Poor little kitty wherever she goes,
Her collar will jingle, so everyone knows.
Poor little kitty can't even creep,
Her collar will jingle, so birdie won't sleep!
Jing-jingle-jingle, jing-jingle-jing!
Jing-jingle-jingle, jing-jingle-jing!
Jing-jingle-jingle, jing-jingle-jing!
Jing-jingle-jingle, jing-jingle-jing!
MEOW!

Directions

Pass out the bells and play song #1 from the accompanying *The Sound of Storytime* CD. Each time the word jingle is used in the song, have the children jingle along with their bells, keeping to the rhythm of the tune. Let them sound out a big MEOW at the end of the song.

MOVEMENT ACTIVITY WITH FEATHERS

Feather Fun

Supplies Needed

Ellison die-cut, natural or craft feather, one feather for each child

Directions

Pass out one feather to each child. Play song #2 from the accompanying *The Sound of Storytime* CD by following the chant and leading in the movement. Tell the children to listen to the CD and follow your lead in this movement activity.

Raise your feather way up high,
Write your name up in the sky.
Take your hand and move it slow,
Bring your feather way down low.
Drop your feather, and don't make a sound.
Pick it up, and spin around!
Now stop! Hold it tight!
Shake it to the left, and shake it to the right.
Guess what! We're almost done!
Has everyone had lots of fun?
Now there's one last thing before we end,
Take your feather and tickle your chin!

This movement activity is one the children will love to do again and again. It is important to repeat activities as time permits. This allows children to participate fully while they are learning to follow directions. It is more important to have less variety and let the children truly enjoy themselves than it is to try to cram too much into a lesson and rush the children.

STORYBOARD

What's for Lunch?

Supplies Needed

Paper plate, standard size, one

Paper triangles for ears, two

Felt-tip marker, black

Ellison die-cut bird(s) #3, five in a variety of colors

Ellison die-cut feathers, five in matching colors

Glue stick

Scissors or safety razor blade

Tape or adhesive material to attach the items onto the storyboard

Directions

To make the cat, glue ears to the paper plate. Using a marker, draw the eyes, nose, and mouth on the cat. Cut a slit in the mouth large enough to slide five feathers inside. You may want to hand older children the feathers to slide into the cat's mouth. Use the storyboard with the cat and the five birds already attached. Begin by saying:

Five little birds pecking at the ground,
Looking for seeds lying around.
Along comes Mrs. Kitty wanting to munch,
But all she got was feathers for lunch!
Four little birds pecking at the ground,
Looking for seeds lying around.
Along comes Mrs. Kitty wanting to much,
But all she got was feathers for lunch!
Three little birds . . .
Two little birds . . .
One little bird . . .
NO little birds pecking at the ground,
Looking for seeds lying around.
Poor Mrs. Kitty wanted a bird lunch,
But all she got was feathers for lunch!

After each verse, take away one bird from the storyboard, while adding one feather to the kitty's mouth.

MAKE AND TAKE

Paper Plate Cat

Supplies Needed per Child

Paper plate, standard size, with a pre-cut slit for the cat's mouth

Two paper triangles for ears

Glue stick

Washable marker in black, one for each craft table

Ellison Die-cut feather or craft feather

Directions

Have each child create a cat like the one prepared for the storyboard activity.

MAKE AND TAKE 2

Feather Art

Supplies Needed per Child

Feathers, craft or real ones gathered from a field trip, one each

Construction paper, 9" × 12" in size, in light colors, one each

Crayons, paper wrapping removed

Washable tempera paint, any color

Directions

Feather Rubbings: Put the feathers under the paper and have the children use crayons to roll over the paper to create a feather imprint.

Quill Writing: Dip the quill into the tempera paint and direct the children to imitate how writing was done before the invention of the ballpoint pen.

Feather Paint Brushes: Use the feather end to dip into the paint and paint beautiful pictures. Have the children compare and contrast the three styles of feather art.

LESSON 2

COOKIES

CURRICULUM TOPICS
Cookies, Baking, Mathematics

FEATURED BOOK
Hutchins, Pat. 1986. *The Doorbell Rang*. New York: Mulberry Books.

SUMMARY
Ma makes a batch of cookies for her kids to share, but every time they sit down to eat them, the doorbell rings, announcing the arrival of another visitor. The children welcome each new guest and continue to divide the cookies evenly. When there are no more cookies left to divide, the doorbell rings once again. Luckily, it is Grandma with a tray of cookies! Ages 4–8

ACTIVITY
Pass out the bells. Instruct the children to play the part of the doorbell. This story lends itself well to this activity. The repeating line, "as the door bell rang," directly cues the children to participate. Children are to ring their bells each time a new visitor arrives at the door. If you have twelve or more participants, this story can also be acted out and extended using the storyboard. To add this element, make twelve brown paper or felt circles to represent the cookies. Begin by placing the twelve cookies on the storyboard. Count the cookies out loud with your listeners. Explain that this story begins with twelve cookies and two children. Call for two volunteers to come up and play the part of Ma's children, Sam and Victoria. When Ma tells the two children to share the twelve cookies, ask your audience how many cookies they think Sam and Victoria should get. As you continue reading, call up children from your audience to represent the number of guests that arrive. With the arrival of each new friend, turn to your listeners and encourage them to figure out how many cookies each child should get if the cookies are divided equally. If the participants do not know the correct answers, it is okay. With a turn of the page, the solution is given. Pause long enough for the actors to correctly redistribute the cookies. Redistribute each time a new guest arrives. While this additional activity may be inappropriate for some preschool groups, it is lots of fun for kindergarten and first-grade children.

ADDITIONAL BOOKS TO SHARE
Carter, David A. 2002. *Who Took the Cookie from the Cookie Jar?* New York: Scholastic, Cartwheel Books. This book is a fun version of the well-known children's rhyme. There are large flaps that lift to reveal one of six suspects. Ages 2–5

Fletcher, Colin. 2003. *Count Your Cookies*. Ontario, Ohio: Gingham Dog Press. Every Saturday, Mom bakes yummy treats for Laura and Harry. Mom tells her children to share the treats and be fair, but older sister Laura always finds a cunning way to trick her naive brother out of his half. When Mom overhears one of Laura's tricks, she concocts a cunning idea of her own and helps Harry get his just desserts! Cheerful illustrations and solid storyline make this a good choice for reading aloud. Laura plays four tricks on her brother. As you read, make sure your young audience has the chance to assimilate what is going on in the story. Each time Laura misleads her brother, pause for a moment. Ask your listeners to explain what was unfair about how Laura divided the cookies. For even more impact, use the storyboard to demonstrate. Before story hour, glue paper cookies onto eight paper plates, arranging them exactly as Laura allocated the cookies for her and her brother in each of the four examples in the story. You do not need to be an artist to make the simple cookie shapes from construction paper. Freehand the shapes or trace cookie cutters to make the storyboard pieces. As you read each one of the four examples, place the two representative plates on the storyboard to discuss and compare. Ages 3–7

Hanson, Mary. 2002. *The Difference Between Babies and Cookies*. San Diego, CA: Silver Whistle/Harcourt. Mom prepares big sister for the new baby. Mom says that babies are as sweet as cookies and as playful as tiger cubs. Big sister interprets Mom's ideas quite literally, and when the new baby arrives, things are not exactly as she expected. Despite the conflicting impressions, big sister is happy helping to care for the new baby. Sizable illustrations and clear details brilliantly portray the amusing yet conflicting perspectives. Ages 3–7

Lass, Bonnie, and Philemon Sturges. 2000. *Who Took the Cookies from the Cookie Jar?* Boston, MA: Little, Brown. Read this book and help skunk solve the mystery of the missing cookies. This Building Block Nominee is complete with notes for singing the tune and instructions for clapping and playing an accompanying circle game. Vivid characters and brilliant desert landscapes make this adaptation unique and interesting. Ages 2–7

Lin, Grace. 2004. *Fortune Cookie Fortunes*. New York: Alfred A. Knopf. After opening fortune cookies with her family, a young Chinese American girl observes that the fortunes all seem to come true. From then on, she sees the whole world in fortune cookie fortunes. Children love fortune cookies and will enjoy the notion of viewing their own world from this unique perspective. We know a young family of four that made a family tradition of reading their fortunes out loud to each other after a dinner out at their favorite Chinese restaurant. As they went around the table, Dad read his, Mom read hers, and big sister painstakingly sounded hers out. Finally, their rambunctious two-year-old son, having no intention of being left out of the fun, held his fortune up as if he could indeed read, and very matter-of-factly stated, "Someone is going to get a spanking." Share this inspirational book with children, and you are sure to conjure up some fun stories of your own. For an extra special storytime treat, consider passing out fortune cookies to eat and read. Often, local restaurants are generous to donate these novelty items. Ages 3–7

Moffatt, Judith. 1996. *Who Stole the Cookies?* New York: Grosset and Dunlap. This book is another adaptation of the popular playground rhyme. All the animals deny taking the cookies, but a trail of cookie crumbs reveals a clue leading into a cave and straight to the culprit. The story has a satisfying ending and teaches the value of sharing and forgiveness. Because the characters are common animals, and the text is repetitive and predictable, this particular adaptation is great for acting out with puppets. Ages 2–7

Munsch, Robert N. 2000. *Mmm, Cookies!* New York: Cartwheel Books, Scholastic. Christopher makes cookies from play clay and tricks his mom and dad into taking a bite. When Christopher's teacher hears of his antics, she knows just how to teach Christopher a lesson. This story is packed with repeating action words and onomato-poeia. Consider teaching the children to make the repeating "whap, whap, whap" sound of the clay by clapping their hands together. Act out the action of sprinkling the sugar by wiggling fingers on the words "chik, chik, chik." On the words "glick, glick, glick," make the motion of spreading icing with a knife by swiping your index finger back and forth over your hand. Finally, flick your hand with your thumb and middle finger to make the sound of the "plunk, plunk, plunk." (We omit the "swish, swish, swish" sound when we tell this story.) When the story reads that mom and dad are in the bathroom washing out their mouth for a long time, conjure up some giggles by really pretending to brush your teeth for an exaggerated amount of time. The book includes a recipe for play clay. Make some play clay cookies of your own at craft time. Ages 4–8

Numeroff, Laura Joffe. 1985. *If You Give a Mouse a Cookie*. New York: HarperCollins. A must-read, favorite, modern classic. A boy offers a cookie to a passing mouse and unintentionally begins a chain of requests that keep him busy waiting on the mouse for the rest of the day. After reading this story, try recreating the series of events with real props or pictures. You will need to make paper pieces or gather the following objects to represent the items listed in the story: a cookie, a glass of milk (use an empty plastic cup), a straw, a picture of scissors, a broom, a "mouse size" blanket and pillow, a storybook, paper and crayons, a pen, a roll of tape with a noncutting blade, another glass of milk, and a second cookie. Begin the activity by passing out the props or paper pictures to the children. Work as a group to reconstruct the story. One at a time, have children bring their pieces to the front and line up in the order of the story. This is a fun way to test memory, listening, and deductive reasoning skills. Ages 3–7

Rix, Jamie. 1997. *The Last Chocolate Cookie*. Cambridge, MA: Candlewick Press. When Maurice attempts to take the last chocolate cookie at the table, his mother tells him he must offer it to everyone else first. Maurice interprets his mother's request quite literally and takes a journey around the world and into space, offering the cookie to everyone he meets. Children relate sympathetically to Maurice's table manners faux pas, and the hint of disgusting humor makes them roar with laughter. Be sure to practice the nonsense words in this story before you present it at storytime. Ages 3–7

Wellington, Monica. 1992. *Mr. Cookie Baker*. New York: Dutton Children's Books. Mr. Baker spends his day making and selling cookies. The story demonstrates each stage of the cookie-making process. Use craft time to make paper cookies. Provide colored paper, a variety of cookie cutters, crayons, and safety scissors. Children trace around the cookie cutters and use safety scissors to cut out paper cookies. (Note: All children should be directly supervised when using safety scissors.) Extend this book for a whole day of play by opening your own cookie store. Before the children arrive, decorate a refrigerator box to make a simple store front. Or, if you already have one, a puppet stage also makes a wonderful store front. Use smaller boxes to create pretend ovens. Gather additional playtime props like mixing bowls, wooden spoons, spatulas, measuring cups, cookie trays, toy cash registers with play money, baker's hats, and aprons. Keep all of these things out of the children's sight until after story hour and craft time. Once children have completed their paper cookies, reveal the bakery and host a play group session. Encourage the children to arrange their paper cookies on cookie sheets and to bake, serve, and sell them in the shop. Ages 2–7

MUSIC AND MOVEMENT WITH BELLS

Sing Along: "Cookies to Share"

Sung to the Tune: "Twinkle Twinkle Little Star"

Ring! Ring! Ring! The cookies are done! *(Sing in unison)*
Let's pick up toys and have some fun!
They're so tasty and so good, let's share some with the neighborhood!
Ding-dong, ding-dong! Cookies to share!
I'll start here, if you'll start there.
Ding-dong, ding-dong! Cookies for you! *(Girls sing)*
Hot from the oven and tasty, too!
Ding-dong, ding-dong! Cookies for you! *(Boys sing)*
Hot from the oven and tasty, too!
Ding-dong, ding-dong! Cookies for you! *(Girls sing)*
Hot from the oven and tasty, too!
Ding-dong, ding-dong! Cookies for you! *(Boys sing)*
Hot from the oven and tasty, too!
Ding-dong, ding-dong! Cookies for you! *(Girls sing)*
Hot from the oven and tasty, too!
We gave lots of cookie away! *(Sing in unison)*
We'll bake more another day!

Pass out the bells and play song #3 from the accompanying *The Sound of Storytime* CD. Divide the storytime group into two sections. Separate boys in one group and girls in the other. Everyone will start out singing and ringing their bells in unison. At the chorus ("Ding-dong, ding-dong cookies for you! Hot from the oven and tasty, too!"), have only the girls ring their bells and sing. At the next line at the same cue, have the boys sing. Continue going back and forth until the song is over.

ADDITIONAL SONGS TO SHARE

Toddler Trio: Silly Favorites. Little Buddha Studios, 2000. Compact Disk. R2 76675. Song #18, "Who Stole the Cookies!" This song makes a great nonspeaking puppet show. Choose any puppets you like to represent the characters in the song. This is also a fun song to play as children are entering storytime and working on their crafts.

STORYBOARD

A Surprise Cookie Treat

Supplies Needed

Metal cookie sheet, large enough to hold two dozen average-size cookies (make sure a magnet will stick to the pan)

Construction paper, 9" × 12" in size, brown, five sheets, or a large brown paper sack

Washable marker, brown

Scissors

Peel-and-stick magnetic strips, approximately ½" per cookie used

Stickers, plain white, ½" by ½" in size, twelve

Bag of small candy treats, or individually packaged cookies, one per child

Directions

Cut approximately two dozen round circles from the brown construction paper or brown paper sack. You can make a round circle template or trace around a cookie cutter, but cookies do not need to be exactly the same shape, so it is easier to cut circles and not worry about the exact size or shape. If you work with Ellison die-cuts, use the circles. Use a brown marker to add a few dots on top of the cookies that resemble chocolate chips. Cut the roll of adhesive magnets into ½" strips and attach a magnet to the back of each cookie. Write the word "treat" on six white stickers and then place a sticker on the back of six of the cookies. Place all of the cookies in the pan. Pass out the bells before the activity and tell the children to place the bells in their lap and keep them very quiet until you instruct them to ring their bells. Let each child take a turn coming up to the cookie pan and removing a cookie as you recite the verse. Explain to the children that some of the cookies have a sticker on the back. If they select a cookie with the word "treat" on the sticker, they will receive a special treat from you; and everyone will get to pick up their bells and ring them. If the cookie does not have a sticker on the back, ask them to place the cookie back in the pan. When a child selects the cookie with a sticker, remember to take that cookie and hold it to the side until everyone has had a turn. When all of the children have turned over a cookie, you may add the treat cookies back into the pan and repeat, as time permits. If you repeat the activity, make sure the children are not watching as you slip the treat cookies back into the pan. At the end of the activity, give a piece of candy to the children who did not choose the treat cookie, so everyone is a winner.

Recite this verse as the children take a cookie:

Paper cookies are not to eat,
But turn one over and find a treat!

The children will quickly learn this little verse. Have them recite it with you!

MAKE AND TAKE

Cookie Decorating

Supplies Needed per Child

Sugar cookie, plain, nondecorated, commercially packaged if necessary

Canned frosting, one can per craft table

Decorative cookie sprinkles, one container per craft table

Craft sticks, small, one

Paper plate, small size, one

Plastic lined tablecloths, one per craft table

Moist paper towels or wipes for cleaning up fingers

Plastic sandwich bags, one

Directions

Let the children decorate their own cookie. Before the activity, talk to the children about what this activity entails. Explain to them that they need to clean their hands first, and when they use the craft sticks to decorate their cookies, they should not put the sticks in their mouths until they are totally finished frosting their cookie. Put a spoonful of icing on each child's plate and encourage them to use their craft stick to spread the frosting on their cookie. After the icing, let them shake the sprinkles onto the cookie. Keep moist paper towels or wet wipes handy to clean up sticky hands after the activity. When the children are completely finished with the cookie and have clean hands, help them place their cookie in a plastic sandwich bag to take home. If you prefer the children to eat the cookies at the craft table, feel free to do so. Grocery stores are often willing to donate cookies for activities such as this one.

LESSON 3

FIRE SAFETY

CURRICULUM TOPICS

Fire Safety

FEATURED BOOK

Yee, Wong Herbert. 1994. *Fireman Small*. Boston: Houghton Mifflin.

SUMMARY

Every time Fireman Small pulls up the covers to go to sleep, the fire alarm rings. Ages 3–7

ACTIVITY

Fireman Small is told in rhyming text, and the children will be cued to play their alarm bells each time the poem reads, "And pulls the covers over his head." *Fireman Small* and *Fire! Fire! Hurry! Hurry!* is similar in concept and design. Read the activity instructions for the previous book, *Fire! Fire! Hurry! Hurry!* for more detailed guidelines intended for leading these activities.

FEATURED BOOK

Zimmerman, Andrea, and David Clemesha. 2003. *Fire! Fire! Hurry! Hurry!* New York: Greenwillow Books.

SUMMARY

Captain Kelly and the firefighters are anxious to eat their delicious spaghetti dinner, but each time they sit down to eat, the fire alarm sounds. Ages 3–7

ACTIVITY

This story is designed very well for incorporating instruments. The text is predictable, and all the cues the children need to play their part are built right into the storyline. Begin by introducing the children to the book. Show them the cover and read the title. Show the audience the bell instruments, and demonstrate the sound they make. Encourage the children to suggest ideas about how the bells will be used to help tell the story. Most likely, your participants will quickly guess the truck siren or the fire alarm. Praise them for their great ideas, and explain that they will be using their bells to make the sound of the fire alarm. Pass out the bells, and begin the story. Each time the fire alarm is to sound, the book will read, "but suddenly—." The first time you read this phrase, pause, and see if your listeners pick up on the cue. If not, prompt them by asking, "What do you suppose is going to happen?" The group will certainly deduce the correct answer. Respond with, "You're right, it is the fire alarm! Sound your alarm bells!" Give the children a moment to enjoy their instruments, and resume the story. Children love to participate in this way, and they will intuitively know to chime in on the appropriate parts throughout the duration of the story.

ADDITIONAL BOOKS TO SHARE

Cuyler, Margery. 2001. *Stop Drop and Roll*. New York: Simon & Schuster Books for Young Readers. Jessica worries about everything, until she discovers that the best way to extinguish your fears is to learn what to do in an emergency. Share this story and practice the ten fire safety skills with the children in your class. Ages 4–8

Desimini, Lisa. 2001. *Dot the Fire Dog*. New York: Blue Sky Press. Dot, the fire dog, plays and sleeps in the firehouse. When the fire alarm rings, Dot and the firefighters race their fire truck to rescue people and animals. Packed with action, and adorned with bright, crisp illustrations, this story makes a great read-aloud. Ages 3–7

Fox, Christyan, and Diane Fox. 2001. *Fire Fighter PiggyWiggy*. Brooklyn, NY: Handprint Books. Whenever PiggyWiggy sees a fire truck race by, he dreams of all the brave and adventurous things that he could do as a firefighter. This story is sure to spur the imaginations of children, and spill ideas into their playtime adventures. This book is an excellent formula for a successful read-aloud, sporting bold print and large, colorful pictures. Ages 2–7

MacLean, Christine Kole. 2002. *Even Firefighters Hug Their Moms*. New York: Dutton Children's Books. Too busy at work for hugs, an inventive boy and his sister explore the world of rescue heroes through dramatic play. This story is a fabulous model for inspiring pretend play. Ages 4–7

Mitton, Tony. 2000. *Flashing Fire Engines*. Boston: Kingfisher. This colorful rhyming story takes the reader through the many duties of firefighters, and also shows how a fire is extinguished. Three friendly animal firefighters performing these tasks adds some extra character in this very informative, easy to understand story. Ages 2–6

Osborne, Mary Pope. 2002. *New York's Bravest*. New York: Alfred A. Knopf. The bravery and heroic life of a legendary New York firefighter, Mose Humphreys, is given tribute by this fascinating American tall tale. This story opens the door to further discuss American tall tales and history. Be sure to read the "historical note" written by the author so you can share this information with your listeners. Ages 4–8

Wilson-Max, Ken. 1996. *Big Red Fire Truck*. New York: Scholastic. With this interactive storybook go on a rescue mission and even raise the fire truck's ladder. We rarely recommend intricate lift-the-flap style books for story hour, but this book has a good balance, and the activities do not detract from the story. The large, easy-to-see moving parts reinforce impacting impressions. Ages 3–7

MUSIC AND MOVEMENT WITH BELLS

Sing Along: "Fire! Fire! Fire!"

Sung to the Tune: "Three Blind Mice"

Fire! Fire! Fire!
Fire! Fire! Fire!
Sound the alarm! Sound the alarm!
Ring, ring, ring, ring, ring, ring, ring!
Ring, ring, ring, ring, ring, ring, ring!
Ring, ring, ring, ring, ring, ring, ring!
Fire! Fire! Fire!

Directions

Pass out the bells and play song #4 from the accompanying *The Sound of Storytime* CD. The short song is repeated three times and allows the children to ring their bells throughout the chorus. This is another very easy song with few words, making it a perfect addition to enjoy with the lesson. A great tip to keep the children in sync with the rhythm is to sing along with the chorus as you lead with your bell. Often times we tend to sing the verses, but use only the instruments throughout the chorus. We have found that when we tried this technique, there was very little need to instruct the children. They will follow your lead without hesitation, making your task much easier.

Sing Along: "The Fire Truck"

Sung to the Tune: "Baa, Baa Blacksheep"

The fire truck's parked and all was well, until they heard the fire bell!
The firemen slid right down the pole, and shouted, "Fire! It's time to roll!"
The truck went ding, ding, ding, ding, ding!
Ding, ding, ding, ding, ding, ding, ding!

Directions

Pass out the bells and play song #5 from the accompanying *The Sound of Storytime* CD. This short song is repeated three times and allows the children to ring their bells throughout the chorus. Prompt the children to call out, "Fire! It's time to roll!" Use a deep voice on this line; the children will imitate you and will enjoy expressing themselves using a different tone.

ADDITIONAL SONGS TO SHARE

Piggyback Songs: Singable Poems Set to Favorite Tunes. Kimbo, 1995. Compact Disk. KIM 9141CD. Play song # 11, "Never Play with Matches." A lead singer sings the verse through once then a chorus of children echo. Have your audience sing along with the children. Act out the words of the song. Shake your head "no" on the words "never, never." When the song says, "you will burn your fingers," cry "ouch!" and blow on your fingers. Make the shame sign, cross one index finger over the other, on the words "shame on you." Point to yourself on the words "we are Smokey's helpers," and make the sign language for thank you at the end of the song by extending your hand from your chin out toward the audience.

JUST FOR FUN

National Fire Prevention Week is the Sunday through Saturday period in which October 9 falls. Arrange a guest visitor from your local fire department to come during storytime. There is nothing more exciting to children than the opportunity to meet firefighting personnel and explore a real fire truck.

STORYBOARD

Five Red Fire Trucks

Supplies Needed

Ellison die-cut fire trucks, red, five

Tape or self-adhesive material to attach fire trucks to storyboard

Directions

Add all five of the fire trucks in a row to the storyboard prior to the presentation. Remove a fire truck at each line the story prompts:

Five red fire trucks parked in a row,
The fire alarm rang, so one had to go! *(Remove fire truck)*
Four red fire trucks so shiny and bright,
The Chief said, "Let's go, we've got a fire to fight!" *(Remove fire truck)*
Three red fire trucks still waiting for a fire,
One needed repair, it had a flat tire! *(Remove fire truck)*
Two red fire trucks parked in the dark,
One took a test drive with Captain Clark! *(Remove fire truck)*
One red fire truck waiting all alone,
Hoping the other trucks would hurry back home! *(Leave fire truck)*
LOOK, here comes one! *(Add fire truck)*, Then two, three, and four! *(Add remaining three, keeping in a row)*
Five red fire trucks parked in a row,
Waiting for the alarm to ring for their turn to go!

MAKE AND TAKE

911 Refrigerator Magnet Reminders

Supplies Needed per Child

Ellison die-cut firefighter

Wooden clothespin, one

Cool glue gun (for adult use)

Magnets, one

Washable markers, two per craft table

Glue stick

Tape

Directions

Prior to the activity, preglue the magnets onto the clothespins. Let the children write 911 onto the Ellison die-cut firefighter and glue or tape it on the clothespin on the opposite side the magnet is attached. Make sure you talk to the children about the 911 emergency number, and tell them to place their magnetic clip on their refrigerator or other metal surface close to a telephone. In the event of an emergency, this will help them to remember the numbers to dial.

LESSON 4

PIZZA

CURRICULUM TOPICS

Pizza, Baking/Cooking

FEATURED BOOK

Walter, Virginia. 1995. *Hi, Pizza Man!* New York: Orchard Books.

SUMMARY

A girl and her mother play a game as they wait for their pizza dinner to be delivered. Ages 3–7

ACTIVITY

Children play the part of a pretend doorbell. Each time the mother asks, "What would you say?" the children say "ding dong!" and ring their bells. This activity is played much like a classic "knock, knock joke." Keep a set of bells for yourself, and cue the children to chime in. Do not turn the page and reveal the next imaginary character until the children ring the doorbell and then quietly return the bells to their lap. After the story, give your listeners an opportunity to play the game too. Encourage them to think of their own ideas about who else might come to the door.

ADDITIONAL BOOKS TO SHARE

Gelman, Rita Golden. 1999. *Pizza Pat*. New York: Random House. A cumulative account of the process Pizza Pat uses to make his famous pizzas. This story is told in a rhythmic rhyme similar to the classic folktale, *The House That Jack Built*. Ages 3–7

Katz, Karen. 2004. *Grandpa and Me*. New York: Little Simon. Help Grandpa find everything he needs to make a pizza under big lift-the-flaps. Ages 2–6

Holub, Joan. 2001. *The Pizza That We Made*. New York: Viking Books. Three friends demonstrate all the steps of making a pizza, from gathering the ingredients to eating with friends. Ages 3–7

Pieńkowski, Jan. 2001. *Pizza!: A Yummy Pop-Up Book*. Cambridge, MA: Candlewick Press. The king is coming for lunch and he is a very hungry lion. The animals decide to make him pizza. Inside the book is a rotating paper wheel that lets the reader make choices of tasty toppings they would like for their pizza such as like worms, snails, caterpillars, bugs, and tadpoles. In the end, the king enjoys the pizza and is roaring for more! This tasty pop-up book is sure to score high on the children's gross meters. Ages 2–6

Sierra, Judy. 2001. *Preschool to the Rescue*. San Diego, CA: Harcourt Brace. When a pizza van gets stuck in the "deeper-than-you'd-think" mud puddle, a series of rescue vehicles try to help, but also end up getting stuck in the mud. Read this story to find out how the preschool children were able to do what the mighty rescue vehicles could not. The author infuses an inventive twist to the end of this tale, and the result will be inspirational to pretend play. After hearing this story, children will never look at a mud puddle the same again. Large, distinct pictures, repeating lines, and descriptive words that are fun to mimic make this cumulative story an excellent choice for reading aloud. Ages 3–7

Steig, William. 1998. *Pete's a Pizza*. New York: HarperCollins. Have you ever heard a child squeal in delight at a grown up that slings them over their shoulder and plays like the little one is a "sack of potatoes?" In this story, a boy and his father play a similar game. When Pete is in a bad mood, his dad cheers him up by making him into a pizza. The dad puts Pete on the kitchen table where he stretches and whirls him like dough, greases him with oil, and sprinkles him with flour. This book is an inspirational and irresistible idea for pretend play. It takes a lot of forethought and planning to gather the supplies, but consider inviting a volunteer child and parent from your audience to come up and act out the story as you read. This is especially fun if you have a father in the audience. We suggest that you first read the entire story to all of your listeners. Secondly, follow up by choosing a parent/child team of volunteers. Conclude by repeating the book while adding the dramatic play demonstration. Ages 3–7

Sturges, Philemon. 1999. *The Little Red Hen Makes a Pizza*. New York: Dutton Children's Books. This story is a modernized adaptation spun from the classic tale of the little red hen that bakes bread and is *loaves* of fun to read. We have successfully presented this story two ways. One idea is a very simple puppet show that can be performed after just a few minutes of practice. Read the story with three puppets, a puppet stage, two or three puppeteers, and one storyteller. As one person reads the story, sitting on a chair in front of the stage, puppeteers play the part of the duck, dog, and cat by popping their heads through the curtain to say their one repeating line, "Not I!" The second idea is to divide the audience into thirds and coach each section to play the part of the duck, the dog, or the cat. Before storytime, prepare paper puppets by gluing Ellison die-cut ducks, beagles, and cats onto small craft sticks. Prepare enough for everyone in the audience to hold one of the three characters. One third of the group will play the part of the duck, one third will be the dog, and one third will be the cat. Each time the hen asks her neighbors for help, cue your audience by stating, "the duck said . . . , the dog said . . . , the cat said . . ." When it is their animal's turn to talk, the section holding the appropriate puppets should collectively hold up their puppets and say their line. All the characters repeat the same line, and are to reply, "Not I!" Ages 3–7

MUSIC AND MOVEMENT WITH BELLS

Sing Along: "Let's Make a Pizza Pie"

Sung to the Tune: "Alouette"

Pizza, pizza, I want pizza! Pizza, pizza, lets make a pizza pie!
Pepperoni, cheese and sauce, sausage and oregano!
Knead the dough? Knead the dough!
Need a pan? Need a pan!
OHHH! OHHH!
Pizza, pizza, I love pizza! Pizza, pizza, lets bake our pizza pie!
Put the dough in the pan, top it with tomato sauce!
Add the rest? Add the rest!
Bake it up? Bake it up!
OHHH! OHHH!
Pizza, pizza, I love pizza! Pizza, pizza, we made a pizza pie!
Ummm-ummm-ummm-ummm! Ummm-ummm-ummm-ummm-ummm-ummm!
Ummm-ummm-ummm-ummm! Ummm-ummm-ummm-ummm-ummm!
PIZZA!

Directions

Pass out the bells and play song #6 from the accompanying *The Sound of Storytime* CD. Have the children gently ring their bells throughout this song. When the "ummm's" begin, have the children rub their tummies and hum. In a very satisfied and full of delicious pizza voice, have the children say PIZZA!

MOVEMENT WITH BELLS

The Pizza Jingle!

Jingle for Cheese!
Jingle for Hamburger!
Jingle for Sauce!
Jingle for Onions!
Jingle for Rocks! *(A silly addition)*

Directions

Discuss with the children all of the delicious ingredients that might possibly be on a pizza. Encourage the children to help you to think of ingredients. After some discussion, have them stand up and ring their bells when you shout out an ingredient they would want on their pizza. Keep adding items that you previously discussed. To shake it up a bit, shout out a few silly items like rocks, soup, macaroni, soda, or potato chips. The kids love to stand up and jingle!

ADDITIONAL SONGS TO SHARE

Disney's Silly Songs. Walt Disney Records, 1988. Compact Disk. 60819-7. Play song #8, "Pizza Pie Song," while the children are entering storytime and during craft time.

Palmer, Hap. "Rhythms on Parade." Hap-Pal Music Inc., 1995. Compact Disk. HP102E-AC633. Play song #20, "Play and Rest." Pass out the bells. Play and rest instruments as directed in the song.

Raffi. *Let's Play!* Shoreline Records, 2002. Compact Disk. 11661-8108-2. Play song #9, "If You're Happy and You Know It," and let the children ring their bells in a fun and silly version of this traditional song.

STORYBOARD

The Disappearing Pizza

Supplies Needed

Paper plate, standard size, one

Construction paper, 9" × 12" in size, beige, one

Markers or crayons in assorted colors

Scissors

Tape or adhesive material to attach plate onto the storyboard

Directions

Make a paper pizza as in the "Make and Take" craft below. Divide and cut the paper pizza into five triangles. Attach tape to the back of each pizza slice. Add the paper pizza pieces onto the storyboard to form a whole pizza. As you read the story below, remove the pizza slices, one piece at a time until all slices are removed.

> Five slices of pizza hot in the pan!
> Dad grabbed one and burned his hand! Ouch!
> Four slices of pizza smelling up the room. *(Remove pizza slice)*
> Brother grabbed one, and away he zoomed!
> Three slices of pizza with lots of sauce and cheese. *(Remove pizza slice)*
> Sister asked for one and said, "pretty please?"
> Two slices of pizza, they're just about gone. *(Remove pizza slice)*
> Mother took one, and gave a tired yawn!
> One slice of pizza all tasty and hot! *(Remove pizza slice)*
> Brother took the last one so sister could not!
> No more pizza left in the pan!
> We'll bake two next time, now that's a better plan!

For an added surprise topping of excitement, you could spell out the word "pizza" on the paper plate. When the slices are removed, the word is a surprise on the plate.

MAKE AND TAKE

My Personal Pizza

Supplies Needed per Child

8" circle cut from beige construction paper (for crust)

Slightly smaller circle cut from red constructions paper (for sauce)

From colored construction paper, precut the following assorted paper toppings freehand in approximately ½" to 1" pieces

Green rectangles (for green peppers)

Pink circles (for pepperoni)

Yellow triangles (for pineapple)

Small brown circles (for hamburger or mushrooms)

Small black circles (for olives)

White paper shreds from a paper shredder, cut into approximately 1" strips (for mozzarella cheese)

Glue stick

Directions

Have the children create their own personal pizzas. Children will begin by pasting the red circle on top of the beige circle to resemble a pizza crust and sauce. Place the assorted toppings on the craft table. Allow the children to choose and glue their favorite ingredients on their pizza.

LESSON 5

SCHOOL

CURRICULUM TOPICS
School, Character Values—Patience, Waiting, Taking Turns, Sharing

FEATURED BOOK
Hines, Anna Grossnickle. 2001. *William's Turn*. New York: Children's Press.

SUMMARY
During recess, William sits on the steps anxiously waiting for his turn to ring the school recess bell. Ages 2–7

ACTIVITY
We recommend this simple lesson as an introduction to the techniques employed by this resource book if you, or the group of children you are working with, have not done an interactive storytime using instruments. Two skills crucial to successful participation in class and group activities, having patience and waiting one's turn, are introduced in this short story. Begin by reading the story. Afterwards, ask the children if they think they can demonstrate patience and taking turns like William did. Give them the opportunity to show their skills by passing out the bells and re-reading the story. Instruct the children to hold their bells perfectly still until it is time for William to ring the recess bell. They can do this by placing their bells on the floor beside them or by holding the bells tightly to their chest until it is time to ring. When the story reads, "William rang the bell!" children are to ring their bells, too. The fundamental concepts taught in this lesson can be employed anytime throughout the year, but we particularly enjoy sharing this story at the beginning of each new school year. In the "Additional Books to Share" section, you will find books that reinforce the skills of waiting patiently, sharing, and taking turns as well as books about going to school.

ADDITIONAL BOOKS TO SHARE
Bell, Babs. 2004. *The Bridge Is Up!* New York: HarperCollins. When the bridge goes up, it creates a terrific traffic jam in this cumulative tale. Each time the story adds a new motorist to the list of stuck vehicles, it repeats the line, "so everyone has to wait." Demonstrate the sign language for "waiting" by holding your palm up and wiggling your fingers. Throughout the story, encourage the children to chant this repeating line and make the waiting sign with you. The illustrations in this story are plenty colorful and bold, but for some added fun, use the storyboard to keep track of the vehicles. Pass out the pictures of a bus, car #1, bicycle, pick-up truck, motorcycle, skiploader, and tractor to seven of your listeners. Participants will bring up their pieces one at a time and place them in the order as their vehicle is added to the traffic jam in the story. Storyboard pieces can easily be made from Ellison die-cuts or magazine pictures and then laminated for durability. Ages 2–7

Carlson, Nancy L. 2004. *Henry's Show and Tell.* New York: Viking. Henry loves kindergarten except for one thing: show and tell. He becomes so nervous that every time it is his turn to share, he gets shaky in the legs and feels like he is going to "barf!" His teacher encourages him to practice at home using a mirror to help him overcome his fears. Henry gets his turn again and has a mild disaster, but he is able to speak and get through his show and tell. Another day Henry's turn comes, and the pet spider that he brought to share gets loose. Henry tells the teacher, and very quickly she declares recess! The illustrations in all of Nancy Carlson's books are animal-based and are lively and humorous. Ages 2–7

Danneberg, Julie. 2000. *First Day Jitters.* Watertown, MA: Whispering Coyote. There is not a child, or grown up, who can't relate to the "first day jitters" on the first day of school. This story is unlike all the other "first day of school" books because of the unique and humorous surprise twist at the end. One of our all time favorite stories, this book is a must read for every new student. Although the simplistic text and attractive illustrations would be appropriate for younger children, the plot of the story more accurately applies to school-aged children. Ages 5–9

Edwards, Becky. 2002. *My First Day at Nursery School.* New York: Bloomsbury Children's Books. On the first day of school, a little girl protests that she wants to stay with her mommy. Her objections incrementally subside as she, and the reader, is introduced to all the wonderful things you can do at school. Ages 2–5

Hazen, Barbara. 1998. *That Toad Is Mine!* New York: HarperFestival. Two best friends share everything until the discovery of a much-coveted toad. The boys try to employ the methods they have used to share other things, but decide they can't cut the frog in two or share it like a game or a book. Read this story to find out how the friends solve the problem. This fun rhyme reads effortlessly, and the cheerful illustrations depict the lively exuberance of two young boys. Ages 3–7

Lipniacka, Ewa. 2003. *Who Shares?* New York: Dial Books for Young Readers. When two brawling siblings are told to share, they continue to antagonize each other by sharing the things they should not. The story concludes when they are both sent to bed for unintentionally sharing chicken pox. As you read each page, ask your listeners to offer their thoughts about whether the characters are sharing nicely or not. Children enjoy the hysterical antics of theses two ornery bunnies. Ages 3–7

Mackall, Dandi Daley. 2003. *First Day.* New York: Harcourt. A little girl faces her fears on her first day of school and discovers that she can't wait to come back for her second day of school. The rhyming words, great pictures, and positive light the author casts on this subject is what makes this book shine. Ages 3–7

Meiners, Cheri J. 2003. *Share and Take Turns.* Minneapolis, MN: Free Spirit. A story about sharing and taking turns that weaves in specific examples of different ways to share. This book includes three pages of detailed discussion ideas and extension activities for teachers and parents. The large illustrations are ideal for reading aloud to groups. Ages 3–7

O'Neill, Alexis. 2002. *The Recess Queen.* New York: Scholastic Press. Mean Jean bullies everyone on the playground until a new girl moves into the class and shows Mean Jean it is much better to be friends than to push and bully. This tender lesson about bullying and friendship is great for school visits. Ages 5–8

Roth, Carol. 2002. *The Little School Bus.* New York: North-South Books. Large pages present cheerful illustrations of animal characters catching the school bus in this cumulative tale. Enrich this story with the storyboard. Pass out Ellison die-cuts, one each, of a goat, pig #2, fox, chick, bear #1, worm, and sheep to children in your audience. One at a time, let children add the characters as they are introduced in the story. Throughout the story there is a repeating line, "Riding the bus to school to school, riding the bus to school." When you read the line, bounce in your chair as if you were riding the bus and have the children repeat the lines and bounce along with you. Allow them to practice the line and the bounce with you before starting the book. Ages 2–6

Sturges, Philemon. 2004. *I Love School!* New York: HarperCollins. On brightly illustrated pages, school children describe everything they love about school. Ages 2–6

MUSIC AND MOVEMENT WITH BELLS

Sing Along: "Is It My Turn Yet?"

Sung to the Tune: "Mary Had a Little Lamb"

Tell me, is it my turn yet, my turn yet, my turn yet?
Tell me, is it my turn yet?
To ring, ring, ring the bell!
It's the *girls* turn to ring the bell, ring the bell, ring the bell!
It's the *girls* turn to ring the bell,
So ring, ring, ring, ring, ring!
Tell me, is it my turn yet, my turn yet, my turn yet?
Tell me, is it my turn yet?
To ring, ring, ring the bell!
It's the *boys* turn to ring the bell, ring the bell, ring the bell!
It's the *boys* turn to ring the bell,
So ring, ring, ring, ring, ring! Tell me, is it my turn yet, my turn yet, my turn yet?
Tell me, is it my turn yet?
To ring, ring, ring the bell!
It's the *girls* turn to ring the bell, ring the bell, ring the bell!
It's the *girls* turn to ring the bell,
So ring, ring, ring, ring, ring! Tell me, is it my turn yet, my turn yet, my turn yet?
Tell me, is it my turn yet?
To ring, ring, ring the bell!
It's the *boys* turn to ring the bell, ring the bell, ring the bell!
It's the *boys* turn to ring the bell,
So ring, ring, ring, ring, ring!
Close with:
Now everyone may ring their bells, ring their bells, ring their bells!
Everyone may ring their bells,
Let's ring, ring, ring, ring, ring!

Directions

Pass out the bells and play song #7 from the accompanying *The Sound of Storytime* CD. Ask the children to remain seated with their bells on the floor next to them. In this song the girls and boys will take turns ringing the bells. The song will prompt the girls to ring first, then the boys. The song ends with everyone ringing their bells again. Ask all the children to pick up their bells, stand up, and ring. This activity will reinforce the feature story, *William's Turn,* and will teach patience and obedience.

ADDITIONAL SONGS TO SHARE

Moricz, Michael. *Time to Sing!* Anything Audio Multimedia, 2000. Compact Disk. 113SING. For two- and three-year-old children, play song #1, *Wheels on the Bus,* and lead the actions. This is the perfect version for this age because the song is upbeat but the words are slowed down enough for young learners to be able to sing and play along.

Most Amazing Truck, Train & Plane Songs. Dragonfly Studio, 2004. Compact Disk. R2 76567. Play song #8, *Wheels on the Bus.* Lead the actions and play along to this song. This is one of our favorite versions because the lead singer gives prompts between verses for upcoming actions.

STORYBOARD

School Match Game

Supplies Needed

Index cards, 4" × 6" size, 16 total

Ellison die-cuts, bell, boy #2, girl #2, man, apple, open book, small baseball, school bus #1A, pencil, two of each

Felt tip marker

Glue stick

Tape to attach cards onto the storyboard

Bells (optional with this activity)

Directions

Glue each Ellison die-cut onto each index card, gluing the boy and girl onto the same index card. Use the marker to identify the item on the bottom of the card on the same side the picture is attached. Write what each Ellison die-cut stands for: bell/school bell, boy and girl/students, man/teacher, apple/snack, book/learning, baseball/recess, school bus/ going to school, pencil/writing. The cards can also be made by simple illustrations, stickers, magazine cut-outs, or any other picture, making sure to have identical matches. The list of school items are examples and can easily be modified or lessened to serve your needs. Add tape to both sides of the index cards so they will adhere when turned over. Randomly number the cards 1 through 16 and place the cards face down in order onto the storyboard. Explain to the children that they will "take turns" approaching the storyboard and trying to find a match for the first item they turn over. If the child does not select a match, they will need to turn both cards back over, face down, and return to their seats. If they turn the correct one over, let them take another turn, until they do not match. If you want to use the bells with this activity, the children could ring their bells in praise each time a child makes a match on the storyboard. Leave the matched items showing and continue the game until all the cards are paired together correctly. Most children are familiar with the matching game and love to play it. If the game ends before every child has had a turn, repeat the game. When finished with the game and all the cards are turned over, go through the items and talk about what each item is and how they relate to school. In this activity, pay close attention to the children taking turns. Throughout the discussion, ask them to raise their hands, and when they have spoken or had a part in the discussion, make sure to call on a different child. Taking turns in this activity will reinforce the feature book and will teach good manners and fairness as well.

MAKE AND TAKE

School Match Card Game

Supplies Needed per Child

Index cards, 4" × 6" size, 8 each

Ellison die-cuts (two of each, for a total of four different school items, totaling eight) using any of the same items used in the School Match Game in the "Storyboard" section

Glue stick

Washable markers, one or two per craft table (optional)

Directions

Let each child make his or her own set of School Match Game cards. Have the children glue two of each school items onto the cards, for a total of eight cards or four pairs. Let them number the back of the cards one through eight. Explain to the children that they, too, can play the match game with their friends at home.

LESSON 6

TELEPHONE

CURRICULUM TOPICS

Telephone Etiquette, Learning Your Telephone Number, Monsters

FEATURED BOOK

Hassett, John. 2004. *Mouse in the House.* Boston: Houghton Mifflin.

SUMMARY

A family of five moves into a messy old house and finds that a mouse lives there. Nana Quimby will not put up with a mouse, so Father rings the pet shop and orders an owl to rid the house of the mouse. With an owl in the house the mouse runs away, but Nana Quimby won't stand for an owl in the house, so Mother rings the pet shop and orders a dog. The dog runs the owl out of the house, but it has fleas. Another animal is ordered and delivered to get rid of the animal before, each time upsetting Nana Quimby even more. The last straw is when an elephant is called in. Nana Quimby orders the mouse back and runs away to Florida to live with her cousin. This is a hilarious book full of adventure and fun. Ages 3–7

ACTIVITY

Pass out the bells before this story and each time a family member telephones the pet store, prompt the children to ring their bells and make the sound of the telephone with their voices.

FEATURED BOOK

Jackson, Jean. 1998. *Big Lips and Hairy Arms: A Monster Story.* New York: DK Publishing.

SUMMARY

Two monsters get scared when they start receiving mysterious telephone calls from a deep, raspy voice. Ages 4–8

ACTIVITY

Entertaining and suspenseful, this story is great fun to tell. Pass out the bells. Each time the phone rings, children get to play the part of the telephone. Be sure to read this story before you present it. Most of the cues are direct, but be prepared to reverse some of the phrases to make the prompts clear and keep the progression of the storyline. When the story reads, "Brring-a-ling-ling! The phone rang a second time," omit the onomatopoeia and instead read, "The phone rang a second time." Pause to let the children ring the bells and make the sound of the telephone. The modifications are very simple, don't let it intimidate you.

FEATURED BOOK

Ljungkvist, Laura. 2001. *Toni's Topsy Turvy Telephone Day.* New York: Harry N. Abrams.

SUMMARY

Toni calls six of her friends and invites them to a potluck dinner. Toni instructs each person to bring a specific item for the potluck. The guests misunderstand her words, and arrive with all kinds of nonsensical things. (This story reads much the way the traditional game *Broken Telephone* plays.) The *Broken Telephone* game is also referred to in the book by Linda Grossman under the Additional Books to Share section. Ages 4–8

ACTIVITY

Pass out the bells. Each time Toni calls one of her six friends, pause and give participants time to ring their bells like a telephone. Brrring, brrring, brrring. When you are ready to move on with the story, signify this by pretending to pick up an imaginary phone and say hello. This step is not written into the book, but is a very simple modification. Resume the story and repeat as required. Before you present this book, take a few minutes to practice and decide exactly what point you want the children to play their instruments.

ADDITIONAL BOOKS TO SHARE

Ashley, Susan. 2005. *I Can Use the Telephone.* Milwaukee, WI: Weekly Reader Early Learning Library. This is a great book to use when introducing children to the proper use of a telephone. It explains to young children how and what to say when using a telephone, along with other important details such as emergency phone numbers. Ages 3–7

Denslow, Sharon Phillips. 1995. *Radio Boy.* New York: Simon & Schuster Books for Young Readers. In the 1870s, a young boy aspires to develop all kinds of new inventions. The appeal of this story is sure to entice children to further explore technology and their own dreams. Ages 6–8

Emberley, Ed. 1992. *Go Away, Big Green Monster!* Boston, MA: Little, Brown. If you choose *Big Lips and Hairy Arms* as your featured book, consider following with this favorite monster story. With each turn of the page, die-cut holes successively reveal and then conceal a big green monster. Involve the children in the story by encouraging them to call out the repeating line "go away." Ages 3–7

Gambrell, Jamey. 1996. *Telephone.* New York: North-South Books. The telephone rings off the hook in this whimsical nonsense poem as animal after animal phones in with peculiar requests. The text demands that you read slowly with attention to enunciation. Ages 3–7

Grossman, Linda Sky. 2001. *It's No Joke, My Telephone Broke.* Toronto: Second Story Press. A class plays the popular circle game of *Broken Telephone* and learns the importance of speaking clearly. After reading this book, try playing the game *Broken Telephone* with your class. Ages 6–8

Koski, Mary. 1998. *Impatient Pamela Calls 9-1-1.* Duluth, MN: Trellis Publishing. Pamela learns to use the telephone and when to call 911. Following the story, reinforce the lessons Pamela learned about calling for help in an emergency. Propose and discuss scenarios like the ones Pamela faced in the book. Do we call 911 if a cat is stuck in a tree? Do we call 911 if a person is choking? Ages 4–8

Lambert, Martha. 2003. *I Won't Get Lost.* New York: HarperCollins. When a young dragon gets lost, he learns that it is very important to know his full name, address, and telephone number. Help the children in your classes and programs to master these crucial skills by allowing them to practice during your craft session. Ages 4–8

Pleau-Murissi, Marilyn. 2003. *Caillou: The Phone Call.* Quebec: Chouette Publishing. Caillou has something important to tell his mommy, but the phone keeps ringing and interrupting him. For more fun pass out the bells and instruct the children to ring the bells each time the telephone rings in the story. Ages 3–5

Raschka, Chris. 2000. *Ring! Yo?* New York: Dorling Kindersley. Can you tell what the conversation is about when you only hear half of what is said? In this story, two friends are having a conversation on the phone, but the reader only hears one side. Before you begin to read this book, explain to your listeners that they are going to hear one side of a telephone conversation. Ask them to imagine what the person on the other side of the telephone might be saying. After the story, lead a discussion about their thoughts. The last few pages of this book reveals the whole conversation. Compare the ideas that your class has with what really was said. Ages 6–8

MUSIC AND MOVEMENT WITH BELLS

Sing Along: "The Ring-a-ling Song"

Sung to the Tune: "Pop Goes the Weasel"

All day long the telephone rings, ring-a-ling-a-ling-a!
I hid it under my bed one night to STOP all the ringing!
All day long the telephone rings, ring-a-ling-a-ling-a!
I hid it under the rug one night to STOP all the ringing!
All day long the telephone rings, ring-a-ling-a-ling-a!
Last night I hid it under my dog to STOP all the ringing!
All day long my little dog rang, ring-a-ling-a-ling-a!
Tonight I hope he finds a way to STOP all the ringing!
Ring-a-ling-a-ling-a-ling-ling! Ring-a-ling-a-ling-a!

Ring-a-ling-a-ling-a-ling-ling!
WOOF! WOOF! WOOF! WOOF! WOOF!

Directions

Pass out the bells and play song #8 from the accompanying *The Sound of Storytime* CD. Let the children ring their bells throughout each verse until they get to the phrase "STOP all the ringing!" At each additional verse, the amount of time to stop all the ringing is increased. Have the children come to a stop and freeze motion, until the beginning of the next verse. At the end of the song, when the dog barks, let the children let out some big "WOOFS," too!

JUST FOR FUN

What Do You Hear?

Select and play a sound effects CD, such as *100 Sound Effects,* Vol. 2. Premium Music Collection, 1998. Compact Disc. PMC60802. Choose some unique sounds from it. While the children are seated ask them to listen carefully and decide what sound they are hearing. As soon as they think they know the sound, have them stand up and jingle their bell. Then let them share what they think the sound was. Talk to the children about being very quiet and listening very carefully so everyone has an opportunity to hear. This activity will help develop listening skills and patience.

ADDITIONAL SONGS TO SHARE

Moricz, Michael. *Time to Sing!* Anything Audio Multimedia, 2000. Compact Disk. 113SING. Play song #24, "Five Little Monkeys." Since the music on this CD is engineered to give its young audience "time to sing," everyone can sing along to the lively tune. Lead the children to perform the action words of this traditional finger play about the five little monkeys jumping on the bed. Children can jump up and down on the appropriate lines, hold the number of monkeys up on their fingers, pretend to use the telephone, and scold with their index finger. With five stuffed monkeys and a character to play the doctor, this song can be used to host an easy puppet musical. The music is very upbeat, but the words have been slowed way down so there is plenty of time to manipulate puppets.

STORYBOARD

What Rings and What Sings

Supplies Needed

Ellison die-cuts—telephone, bell, clock face and hands, bird #3, woman, teapot, one each
Tape or self-adhesive material to attach items onto the storyboard

Directions

Talk to the children about noises. Ask them what ringing sounds like and let them jingle their bells. Ask them what singing sounds like, and discuss the song you just finished singing. Tell them that you are going to add some items to the storyboard, one at a time, and they are going to decide whether the item rings or sings. The ringing items are the telephone, bell, and clock. The singing items are the teapot, bird, and woman. Let the children ring their bells when they think you have chosen an item that rings. Ask them to keep their bells silent when you add an item they think sings. Discuss each one as you add them onto the board, and let the children make the sound of what they think each particular item might sound like.

MAKE AND TAKE

My Own Telephone Book

Supplies Needed per Child

Ellison die-cut telephones, six each

Hole punch, one per craft table

Yarn or ribbon, 12" strip, one

Washable markers or crayons

Directions

Have the children stack the Ellison die-cut telephones together and punch two holes across the top. The children may need help with this portion of the activity. After the holes are in, have them thread the yarn or string in holes. Even up the yarn or ribbon after threading through and tie a bow. The bow should be on the outside of the telephone book. Let the children color the outside of their telephone book any way they would like. Have the children write their name and telephone number on the inside page, if they know it. If they do not know their telephone number, be sure to suggest they find out so they can write it down in their telephone book later. Tell them they can take their telephone books home, and continue to add telephone numbers. A great addition to this idea is to have sticker emblems for safety, such as fire, police, and ambulance, available for the children to add to their telephone books. Check with your local police and fire department to see if they have stickers they would like to donate. Beside the stickers, have them put the emergency telephone number for fire and police. In most areas it is now 911, but be sure you have checked this out before you instruct the children that might live in rural areas.

PART II

RHYTHM STICKS

LESSON 7

APPLES

CURRICULUM TOPICS

Apples, Emotions/Feelings, Giants, Mice, Monsters, Smiles

FEATURED BOOK

Winer, Yvonne. 1987. *Mr. Brown's Magnificent Apple Tree.* New York: Ashton Scholastic.

SUMMARY

Mr. Brown goes to count the apples on his tree, but every day there are fewer apples than the day before. Who will get the last apple, Mr. Brown or the mouse family? Ages 3–7

ACTIVITY

Pass out the rhythm sticks. Throughout the story, children use the rhythm sticks to create the sound of the mouse "tip tapping up the tree."

ADDITIONAL BOOKS TO SHARE

Benjamin, A. H. 1998. *It Could Have Been Worse.* Waukesha, WI: Little Tiger Press. Mouse is on his way home from visiting his town cousin as he falls into a hole, sits on a thistle, and gets a dunking in the stream. Mouse is convinced things could not get any worse, but it is his clumsiness that is actually saving him. Things could have been much worse, but mouse is oblivious to the reality of the day and all of his narrow escapes. Mouse finally makes it home and is complaining to mother when the house cat has a little mishap and mother assures mouse, "It could have been much worse!" Ages 3–7

Benjamin, A. H. 2001. *Little Mouse and the Big Red Apple.* Wilton, CT: Tiger Tales. Just as he is feeling a bit hungry, Little Mouse finds a big red apple. As he is trying to push the apple back to his house, he runs into all kinds of obstacles. This is a colorful story of friendship and sharing. Ages 3–7

Carlson, Nancy. 2002. *Smile a Lot!* Minneapolis, MN: Carolrhoda Books. A frog explains how smiling is a great way to get through life's ups and downs. Point to the large letters on the pages that say "Smile a Lot!" and ask the children to help you repeat this line. Ages 3–7

Dann, Penny. 2001. *If You're Happy and You Know It!* New York: Barron's Educational Series. This is another version of the well-known song that offers great illustrations and oversized words. Ages 3–6

Emberley, Ed, and Anne Miranda. 1997. *Glad Monster, Sad Monster.* Boston: Little, Brown. Sometimes it is hard to tell someone that you are sad or happy, lonely or glad. This joyful and useful book enables children and adults to discuss feelings in an easy and nonthreatening way. Encourage your listeners to interact with the story and express themselves as the book prompts. Ages 3–7

Emmett, Jonathan. 2002. *A Mouse in the Marmalade.* Wilton, CT: Tiger Tales. Cook is asleep while all kinds of different animals make themselves at home in his kitchen. Cook finally wakes up and all he finds is crumbs. This is a fun pop-up book to read to the children because they love to see the creepy little creatures hiding under the food. Each page has one distinct delicacy just waiting to be opened for a big surprise. Ages 2–6

Faulkner, Keith. 2000. *The Mouse Who Ate Bananas.* New York: Orchard Books. A mouse loves to eat bananas but is not too tidy about where he throws his peels. Each banana peel thrown causes another jungle animal to fall. Elephant, rhino, lion, and giraffe all get bruised and banged up by mouse's careless habit. Together, they decide to give mouse a lecture about leaving his peels everywhere. Mouse just laughs and tells them they should watch where they were going. As mouse proudly scampers off, he lands on his own slippery banana peel. This is a great read-aloud with huge lift-the-flap pictures, as well as a lesson to be learned. Ages 2–7

Horăček, Petr. 2004. *A New House for Mouse.* Cambridge, MA: Candlewick Press. When a big, red, juicy apple appears outside her small hole/home, Little Mouse is eager to make a meal of it. She tries to bring it inside her house, but the apple is too big. Little Mouse decides that her house is too small and ventures out (with the apple) to find a new home. Every time she thinks she has found the perfect hole, another animal has already moved in and is enjoying their cozy home and has no room for her. She continues to look for a home as she nibbles and nibbles and nibbles on that big, red, juicy apple. She finally ends back where she started and now her nibbled down apple fits right into her cozy little hole/home. This brilliantly illustrated story has a die-cut hole looking into an animal's home that gets bigger at the turn of every page. The peek-a-boo effect of this book is perfect for all ages. Ages 2–7

Lewison, Wendy Cheyette. 1989. *Where Is Sammy's Smile?* New York: Grosset & Dunlap. Sammy came down to the breakfast table one morning without his smile. His mother asked him where his smile was, but Sammy didn't know. The whole family begins to look for Sammy's smile. This is an adorable lift-the-flap book that is fun to read aloud. Ages 3–6

Low, Alice. 2004. *Blueberry Mouse.* New York: Mondo Publishing. Blueberry mouse loves blueberries so much that she has decided to live in a blueberry pie house. Everything is going well until she decides to nibble a little blueberry from her blueberry house. She even sacrifices her blueberry blanket, sheet and bedclothes for another little blueberry nibble. Who needs them anyway, when you can turn up the heat and sleep on the floor? She finally eats herself out of house and home, but Blueberry mouse is tenacious and decides to make a much better house the next time, in the form of a blueberry cake. Ages 3–7

Ormerod, Jan. 2003. *If You're Happy and You Know It!* New York: Star Bright Books. A little girl and various animals sing their own versions of this popular rhyme. Choose either version. Ages 3–6

MUSIC AND MOVEMENT WITH RHYTHM STICKS

Sing Along: "I Spied an Apple"

Sung to the Tune: "Clementine"

I spied an apple, spied an apple, way up high in the tree!
It was red, and it was shiny, and it was smiling down at me!
Well, I climbed up—in the tree, and—I began to shake,
Because—I was afraid that the limb would surely break!
Well, the ole wind started blowing—and the tree began to sway!
I knew that shiny apple was going to blow away!
I was scared, yes AFRAID! I was frightened as could be,
So I gave up, and I climbed down—and I let that apple be!
Sometimes I think about that apple that was high up in the tree—
And I wonder, yes I wonder if it really smiled at me!

Directions

Pass out the rhythm sticks and play song #9 from the accompanying *The Sound of Storytime* CD. This song does not require any type of instruments, but the children will enjoy tapping. It is also good practice for the children to have the opportunity to listen and coordinate the tapping to the beat of the song. If you choose not to use rhythm sticks with this song, add some hand gestures to the song, such as cupping your hand over your brow and looking up high for the apple in the tree, and pretend to climb the tree and pointing to your cheek and smiling when the apple is smiling. This is a fun song and another easy one to learn after playing through it a couple of times.

MOVEMENT CHANT

Way Up High in the Apple Tree

Supplies Needed per Child

Ellison die-cut apples, two, green or red

Directions

Give each child two die-cut apples and ask them to hold one in each hand. Have the children stand and pretend to be an apple tree, with their body as the trunk and their arms as the branches. As they stand tall and hold the apples way up high, begin chanting:

Way up high in the apple tree, two little apples smiled at me.
I shook that tree as hard as I could, down came the apples,
Ummmm, ummmm, good!

As you recite the verse, have the children wave their arms like a tree blowing in the wind. At the line "I shook that tree," have them shake their arms and drop the apples. Repeat as long as the children are having fun.

ADDITIONAL SONGS TO SHARE

Palmer, Hap. *Rhythms on Parade*. Hap-Pal Music Inc., 1995. Compact Disk. HP102E AC633. Play song #10, "Tap Your Sticks." Pass out the rhythm sticks and play along.

Reid-Naiman, Kathy. *Tickles and Tunes*. Merriweather Records, 1997. Compact Disk. M9701. Play song #24, "I'm Passing Out the Sticks/Tap and Stop." Pass out the rhythm sticks and let the children tap as directed. End the activity by playing song #26, "Time to Put Away."

STORYBOARD

Sneaky, Squeaky Mouse

Supplies Needed

Ellison die-cut houses, seven to nine, in assorted bright colors

Ellison die-cut mouse, one

Tape or self-adhesive material to attach items onto the storyboard

Seven to nine different colored houses are placed on the storyboard, and a mouse is to hide behind only one of the houses. Children are to guess which house the sneaky, squeaky mouse is hiding behind by chanting:

I'm a sneaky, squeaky mouse,
Bet you can't catch me!
Knock on any door,
Then count to three!

Directions

Pass out the rhythm sticks. Each time you knock on the door of the house, let the children knock three times with their rhythm sticks, then count aloud to three. The best way to introduce the storyboard is for the leader to choose the colored house that the mouse will be hiding in and slip the mouse behind the house prior to the activity. Lead the activity by chanting the verse and choosing the color of house to look behind. Repeat this several times, selecting a different color house each round. This will keep you in control of when the mouse will be revealed. After you have knocked on a few houses with no success finding the mouse, let the children help decide which house they think the sneaky, squeaky mouse might be hiding. Continue to let the children take the lead until they choose the correct door. Use a lot of animation and enthusiasm as you knock and count, and especially when you remove the house. Act disappointed when the mouse is not found. When you finally find that sneaky, squeaky mouse, clap and express your excitement! Your enthusiasm will be contagious and the children will be even more excited to try this activity again.

MAKE AND TAKE

Mosiac Apple

Supplies Needed per Child

Ellison die-cut apple, one each, red or green

Glue stick

Construction paper, scraps, assorted colors

Directions

Give the children a few scraps of assorted colored construction paper and let them tear small pieces. Have them paste the torn scraps of paper onto the apple to form a mosaic pattern. If you have access to a small picture of each child you can add another dimension onto the apple by gluing their picture onto the mosaic apple and making a picture frame.

MAKE AND TAKE 2

Apple Faces

Supplies Needed per Child

Ellison die-cut apples, red or green, two

All or any of the following: Washable markers, stickers, stamp pads, smiley face rubber stamp, glue, sand, or glitter

Directions

For a simple art project, children can draw, stamp, or use stickers or glue with glitter or sand to make smiling faces on their apples. The children can use the apples they used in the movement activity, "Way Up High in the Apple Tree." In addition, there are countless different mediums that can be used to create faces on the apples. Set out a variety of craft items and let the children use their imaginations creating their happy faces. The decorated apples also look adorable on a fall bulletin board.

This project can easily be expanded to the subject of feelings. Make all kinds of moody fruits—happy, sad, scared, angry, and so forth. The perfect time to read these books and use these activities is in September. Apples are ripe and ready to be picked and harvested. School is beginning and for some children, it is their first time at school. Many children are very anxious about being away from home and in a new environment. Talking about emotions and feelings is a very important subject to share with the children.

LESSON 8

BIRTHDAYS

CURRICULUM TOPICS

Birthdays, Baking

FEATURED BOOK

Coffelt, Nancy. 2003. *What's Cookin'? A Happy Birthday Counting Book.* San Francisco: Chronicle Books.

SUMMARY

Ten cooks arrive at the door to help bake an extra special birthday cake surprise. Ages 3–7

ACTIVITY

With each turn of the page, there is a knock at the door. The cooks arrive one at a time. As each cook arrives, they knock on the door the same number of times as the order of their arrival. In other words, the second cook knocks twice, and the tenth cook knocks on the door ten times. Children use their rhythm sticks to make the knocking sound at the door. Before you turn each page, prompt the children to knock at the door by saying something like, "What's that sound? I hear two knocks at the door." Turn the page and point and say the word "knock" the number of times you want them to tap their sticks. Repeat this prompt for the first few pages. The children will soon be able to predict the number of times they are to "knock" their sticks together, corresponding with the number of cooks that have arrived. As you see they are beginning to figure this out, change your prompt by asking them to tell you how many knocks they hear at the door.

ADDITIONAL BOOKS TO SHARE

Beil, Karen Magnuson. 1998. *A Cake All for Me!* New York: Holiday House. Piggy bakes a cake all for himself. When friends unexpectedly show up at his door, he reluctantly decides it is best to share. Ages 3–7

Elya, Susan Middleton. 2002. *Eight Animals Bake a Cake.* New York: G. P. Putnam's Sons. Eight bilingual animals contribute the needed ingredients to bake a cake. Bilingual text impeccably crafts the two languages to tell one coalescent story. Even if you have never taken a single Spanish class, do not let the infusion of a few simple Spanish words intimidate you from presenting this ingenious book. Embrace the challenge! You do not have to possess an aptitude for languages to successfully share this story. The detailed pronunciation guide included at the front of the book and a few minutes of practice is all the preparation you will need. The benefits of being introduced to a second language in early childhood are well documented. As comically entertaining as it is linguistically as well as culturally edifying, this story has propelled the basic concept book into a whole new echelon. Share this book and seize the opportunity to introduce children to a second language. Reinforce the new vocabulary words by playing a fun game on the storyboard. Before storytime, prepare storyboard pieces that represent the characters in the story. Print both the animal's Spanish and English names on each character. You will need these Ellison die-cuts: mouse, cat #3, mutt, blue jay, frog #2, horse #1, cow, and pig #2. Make as many duplicates of the animals as you need so everyone has a character to play with. Pass out these pieces before the story. As you pass out the pieces, point to and pronounce, for the whole audience, the words on each character. Explain the animals have different sounding names in Spanish than in English. Challenge the children to remember their character's Spanish name for a game you will play after sharing the story. Let the children hold their character during the story. After reading the book, play the memory game. One at a time, call the animals by their Spanish name. Say, "Let's see how good your memory is. Who has la gato?" If the children forget, simply prompt them by saying, "la gato says meow." Encourage the children with the appropriate pieces to place their characters on the board. As each character is placed on the board, pronounce the name one more time. Ask your audience to echo the word back to you. Another good book to consult for animal pronunciation is Beaton, Clare. 1996. *Animals/Los Animales.* Hauppauge, NY: Barron's. Ages 3–7

Fox, Mem. 1989. *Night Noises.* San Diego: Harcourt Brace Jovanovich. Old Lily Laceby dozes by the fire, but her faithful dog keeps hearing strange noises in the night. The suspenseful tale builds until everyone is surprised to discover the creepy noises outside are Lily's friends and family gathering to surprise her for her ninetieth birthday party. Ages 3–7

Graham, Bob. 2005. *Oscar's Half Birthday.* Cambridge, MA: Candlewick Press. Oscar's family decides one year is too long to wait to celebrate his birthday, so they plan a half birthday celebration. Dad and mom, both in braids, sister Milly, wearing fairy wings and her favorite dinosaur hand puppet, and little Oscar enjoy a pleasant picnic in the park. At the park, Oscar's half-birthday is celebrated by onlookers joining in with the family in the traditional happy birthday song. This is a sweet story of love and celebration with an interracial family. A variety of sounds such as the tickety-clack, tickety-clack of the train on the overhead tracks are shared throughout the story. The ink and watercolor artwork is spectacular. Ages 2–7

Riddell, Chris. 2003. *Platypus and the Birthday Party.* Orlando, FL: Harcourt. Platypus and his friend plan an elaborate birthday party for their mutual friend. The end of the story reveals the friend is a stuffed toy, and all the preparations for the party were pretend play. We love stories that give children ideas for playtime. Encourage your listeners to go home after storytime and plan a party for their favorite stuffed animal! Ages 3–7

Rose, Deborah Lee. 2002. *Birthday Zoo.* Morton Grove, IL: Albert Whitman. The whole zoo hosts a birthday party for one lucky boy. In this cleverly written rhyming story, the children will enjoy seeing bats passing out the hats, lynx pouring the drinks, and the sloth spreading out the tablecloth, to name a few. What child wouldn't love this fantasy birthday party? Ages 2–7

Stadler, Alexander. 2004. *Duncan Rumplemeyer's Bad Birthday.* New York: Simon & Schuster Books for Young Readers. Your birthday is supposed to be your special day. Isn't everything supposed to go your way? Duncan is turning seven and can't wait for his birthday. But when he has trouble sharing with his party guests, he finds out there are some things you can't do, even on your birthday. Ages 3–7

Warnes, Tim. 2003. *Happy Birthday, Dotty!* Wilton, CT: Tiger Tales. Dotty is excited about her birthday but cannot find her friends to celebrate. Instead, Dotty finds a path of arrows that lead her to several wonderful gifts. In the end, the arrows lead her to the very best gift of all—her friends. Ages 3–7

Willard, Nancy. 2003. *The Mouse, the Cat, and Grandmother's Hat.* Boston: Little, Brown. When an uninvited guest sneaks into the birthday party in Grandmother's hat, all sorts of havoc ensues. Ages 3–7

MUSIC AND MOVEMENT WITH RHYTHM STICKS

Sing Along: "The Birthday Knock"

Sung to the Tune: "Yankee Doodle"

My birthday is my favorite day of the whole year!
I've invited all my friends, OH WAIT! I think they're here!
Knock, knock, knock, knock, knock, knock, knock!
They're knocking at my dooooor!
Knock, knock, knock, knock, knock, knock, knock!
OH WAIT! Here comes some more!

I love my birthday, yes I do!
It's so much fun to plan!
I'd invite 100 friends, if mom would say I can!
Knock, knock, knock, knock, knock, knock, knock!
They're knocking at my doooor!
Knock, knock, knock, knock, knock, knock, knock!
I still have room for more!

Directions

Pass out the rhythm sticks and play song #10 from the accompanying *The Sound of Storytime* CD. Have the children tap each time there is a knock at the door. Repeat the song a few times so the children have plenty of opportunity to tap their rhythm sticks.

Sing Along: "My Birthday Wish"

Sung to the Tune: "Old MacDonald Had a Farm"

I made a wish on my birthday, and it came true!
I wished for lots of friends to play, or maybe just a few!
Now there's a knock, knock here, and a knock, knock there!
Here a knock, there a knock, everywhere a knock, knock!
Birthday wishes do come true! So make a BIG wish, too!

Directions

Pass out the rhythm sticks and sing this song a cappella to the familiar tune while letting the children tap their sticks together every time there is a knock at the door. Repeat the song a few times so the children have plenty of opportunity to use the instrument.

ADDITIONAL SONGS TO SHARE

Birthday Party! Singalong. Little Buddha Studios, 2001. Compact Disk. R2 74261. This whole CD is packed with fun birthday party celebration songs and games.

Reid-Naiman, Kathy. *Tickles and Tunes.* Merriweather Records, 1997. Compact Disk. M9701. Play song #25, "When You're One." Pass out the rhythm sticks and play along as directed.

STORYBOARD

How Many Candles?

Supplies Needed

Ellison die-cut birthday candles in coordinating colors, one per child

Construction paper, 9" × 12" in size, light color, one

Markers, assorted colors

Glue stick

Scissors

Double-sided clear tape, 8" strip

Tape to attach items onto the storyboard

Directions

To make the birthday cake, cut the long side of the construction paper in half. Next, take one half of the paper and cut away three inches on the length. Stack the two sheets together, centering the smaller sheet on the top. Attach the two pieces together with glue or tape, making it look like a double-layer birthday cake. Round the top edges, if you desire, use your markers to decorate the cake. A few examples of decorations are flowers, zigzags, scallops, or hearts. Print "Happy Birthday" on the bottom layer of the cake. Place the eight inch strip of clear, double-sided tape across the very top layer of the cake. This provides the paper candles a way to stick onto the cake. Using tape, attach the birthday cake to the storyboard.

Prior to this activity, talk to the children about birthdays and ask them what they enjoy about their birthday. Birthday presents, friends, games, and birthday cake might be a few responses. Point at the words "Happy Birthday" on the cake, and ask the children if they know what the words spell. Follow up by spelling out the letters in unison. Spelling gives the children a chance to exercise their letter recognition skills. Explain to the children they are going to come to the storyboard and add a candle to the top of the cake until the cake is full. Prior to the activity and if you have a very small group, you may want to draw an X or make a dot with a marker where each candle should be placed. For larger groups, this is a great exercise all the children can participate in. As the children take turns coming to the board, hand them a paper candle. Let them stick it on and give them the opportunity to count. The first child will add one and say "one." The second child will add one candle and say "two," the third will add one candle and say "three," and so on. When the children have counted past ten, you may need to help by letting everyone begin to count in unison. If you have a very young group, you may want to count out loud from the start. Make sure you have plenty of candles!

Begin the activity by repeating this verse:

How many candles will it take to top this yummy birthday cake?

Complete the activity with the following verse:

[Amount] candles it did take, to top this yummy birthday cake!

JUST FOR FUN

Supplies Needed

Tablecloth or floor covering

Assorted candy, individually wrapped and age-appropriate

6" rings (remove the plastic lids from large coffee cans and cut out the center leaving about one inch of the outer ring), three

Spread a tablecloth on the floor and add a generous supply of individually wrapped and age appropriate candy on top. Let the children take three turns tossing the rings onto the candy covered tablecloth. The children can keep the candy their rings encircled. Continue to spread the candy around as areas become sparse. (Children could decorate a small lunch bag with birthday stickers, markers, stamps, and so forth to put their candy in as a take-home goody bag.)

MAKE AND TAKE

Make Your Own Birthday Cake

Supplies Needed per Child

Construction paper, 9" × 12" in size, assorted colors, one

Ellison die-cut birthday cakes in assorted colors, one

Ellison die-cut candles in assorted colors, one for each year each child is old

Glue stick

Washable markers or crayons in assorted colors

Birthday themed stickers or rubber stamps (optional)

Directions

Let the children glue a birthday cake onto the sheet of construction paper and decorate with markers, crayons, stickers, and/or rubber stamps to create their own birthday cake. Tell them they can glue on one candle for each year of age they are. Encourage them to write their name on their cake or the paper. Suggest to the children that they can draw balloons, gifts, or whatever they want on the construction paper to make it their own sensational birthday creation.

LESSON 9

CLOCKS

CURRICULUM TOPICS

Clocks, Telling Time, Shadows

FEATURED BOOK

Anderson, Lena. 1998. *Tick-Tock*. New York: R & S Books.

SUMMARY

At one o'clock, Will takes Hedgehog, Pig, Elephant, and Duck to the park for a playdate. The story accounts their fun-filled day one hour at a time. After their action-packed adventures you would think the little tikes would fall fast asleep at bedtime, but a weary Will is still reading bedtime stories at midnight. The concept of telling time mystifies many young children, but this story demonstrates the concept so simply that even preschoolers can comprehend the idea. Coupled with adorable characters and events children relate to, this story appeals to a wide age range. Ages 3–7

ACTIVITY

With every turn of the page, the story reads "tick-tock" and gives the new time of day. The author associates each hour of the afternoon and evening to the everyday activities children relate to and enjoy. Ask the children to help you read this book. Show them the bold title words, "Tick-Tock," on the cover of the book. Explain that these words are the first words on every page of the story. Ask the children to read these words with you each time you turn the page. As they say their part, children are to simultaneously tap their rhythm sticks together two times to make the sound of a clock's tick tock. Pass out the sticks and read the story.

ADDITIONAL BOOKS TO SHARE

Appelt, Kathi. 2000. *Bats Around the Clock*. New York: HarperCollins. Bats boogie the night away in this rhyming, rollicking tale. This story begs to be acted out. Show the children how to do some of the silly dances you know in this story. As you read, give them time to stand up and show you their best moves! Ages 3–7

Browne, Eileen. 1993. *Tick-Tock*. Cambridge, MA: Candlewick Press. Two bouncy squirrels disobey Mom by jumping on the furniture. When Mom's prized cuckoo clock is knocked to the floor and broken, the squirrel children go on a frantic quest to have the clock repaired before Mom returns. Every child can sympathize with the regret the squirrels suffer and the comical consequences that ensue. Ages 4–7

Dunbar, James. 1996. *Tick-Tock*. Minneapolis, MN: Carolrhoda Books. This imaginative presentation of the concept of time is sure to captivate young grade-school children. Topics presented are the measurements of seconds, minutes, hours, days, weeks, months, seasons, years, decades, and centuries. When you introduce this story, don't give away the subject matter. The story begins with a riddle that will draw the children in and really get them thinking. Introduce the story by reading the riddle to the children and asking them to raise their hands and guess what the story will be about. This book can be extended through all sorts of math and science projects. After the book, show-and-tell a variety of stop watches, timers, calendars, and clocks. Use a stop watch and tell the children you are going to time how long it takes them to perform different tasks. Get them up and moving. Time the children doing eight jumping jacks or touching their toes ten times. When you're ready for them to settle down and get ready for the next story, tell them you are going to start the stop watch and see how long it takes them to get seated quietly. For fun, set an alarm clock that will go off sometime during the story hour. Tell the children of something extra special you plan to do when the alarm clock rings. The alarm clock can signify something as simple as it's time to pass out the instruments or even a more elaborate treat. Ages 5–8

Harper, Dan. 1998. *Telling Time with Big Mama Cat*. San Diego: Harcourt Brace. Mama Cat has a scheduled routine that she follows everyday. Each page features a different clock displaying the appropriate time. The sturdy cardboard cover folds out to reveal a clock face with moveable plastic hands. Keep time on the clock as you tell the story of Mama Cat's day. Set the book on an easel so you have both hands free to move the toy clock. Ages 3–7

McCaughrean, Geraldine. 2002. *My Grandmother's Clock*. New York: Clarion Books. A granddaughter wonders why her grandparents have not fixed their broken grandfather clock. The grandmother teaches her granddaughter that there are other ways to measure time than just on a clock. The warm illustrations are large enough to share with a large group. Ages 5–8

Moon, Nicola. 2002. *Mouse Tells the Time*. London: Pavilion Children's Books. Mouse asks all his forest friends if they can teach him to tell time. Mouse gets a lot of varied explanations, but still is not satisfied. This story introduces some really great science concepts like how a shadow is created and how to use an hour glass. Intrigue your listeners by showing them a real hour glass or by setting up an overhead projector and letting them take turns making shadow puppets. Ages 4–8

Moon, Nicola. 2004. *Tick-Tock, Drip-Drop!* New York: Bloomsbury Children's Books. All the noises in the house are keeping Rabbit awake. All of Rabbit's complaining is keeping Mole awake. Will anyone be getting any sleep tonight? The list of bothersome noises gets successively longer and longer. You may consider reading this book as a feature book with instruments. If so, children tap sticks together on the repeating words "tick-tock." Ages 3–7

Perl, Erica S. 2005. *Chicken Bedtime Is Really Early*. New York: Harry N. Abrams. This book describes how different animal mothers and fathers get their young ones ready for bed on the farm. Chickens are the earliest to go to bed, because they are the earliest risers. They begin their bedtime ritual at five o'clock, and then it's lights out at six o'clock. At seven o'clock the cows and sheep begin to call their young into the barn. Throughout the story, the hours get later and later as all of the animals go down for the night. This story is a fun read-aloud, and a clock could be easily introduced. As you read the story, and turn the pages where the time changes, turn the hands on the clock to match the time in the book. Ages 3–8

Walton, Rick. 2002. *Bunny Day*. New York: HarperCollins. This story accounts a bunny family's activities every hour from breakfast to bedtime. If your audience consists of older children, ages five to seven, consider adding the following activity. Before the session, make up paper clocks and laminate for each participant so they can use them to keep time during the story. These clocks can be simply made from the same craft materials the children will later use to make their own paper clock during craft time. Pass out the clocks and let the children keep time on them while you read. Collect the clocks to reuse. Ages 3–7

MUSIC AND MOVEMENT WITH RHYTHM STICKS

Sing Along: "My Tick-Tocking Clock"

Sung to the Tune: "Grandfather's Clock"

I wanted a clock to learn how to tell time,
And my Grandfather gave me one!
It has a big face and two hands, one is small,
And I hung it on my wall!
It goes tick-tock, tick-tock, tick-tock, tick-tock!
Tick-tock, tick-tock, tick-tock, tick,
And I love my tick-tocking clock, hanging on my wall!

Directions

Pass out the rhythm sticks and play song #11 from the accompanying *The Sound of Storytime* CD. Ask the children to sing through the verse as the song leads, and when they get to the tick-tock lines, they can tap their rhythm sticks following the distinct beat of this song. This song is short enough that you might want to repeat it a few times through so the children can enjoy the rhythm sticks.

ADDITIONAL SONGS TO SHARE

Arnold, Linda. *Make Believe*. Ariel Records, 1986. Compact Disk. YM–121–CD. Play song #2, "Tick Tock." Let the children join in the chorus. Children can also use rhythm sticks to make the "tick tock" sound.

STORYBOARD

Mr. Clock

Supplies Needed

Paper plate, standard size, white, one

Scissors

Hole punch

Small round stickers (optional), twelve

Index card stock in black, one

Large brad fastener, one

Black felt tip marker

Directions

Make a paper plate clock by first adding the numbers onto the clock. You could write the numbers one through twelve onto round stickers, sticking them onto the paper plate. Or you could write the numbers directly onto the plate using a working clock as a guide. Cut out two clock hands using the black index card stock paper. The larger hand should measure approximately 3" × ½", and the smaller hand should measure approximately 2" × ½". On each hand, cut one end, in the shape of a point. On the short, straight ends of each hand, punch a hole so that the brad will fit. Find the center of the paper plate and poke a small hole through by using the sharp point on the end of the large brad. Slip the large hand into the brad, then the small hand, push the brad with the hands attached into the center of the paper plate. Fold back the brads on the back of the plate and the clock is ready to tell time. Attach the clock to the storyboard, or simply hold it and recite the following:

> Tell me Mr. Clock for goodness sake,
> What time is it when I wake? *(Place hands at 8:00)*
> Tell me Mr. Clock, so I can follow the rule,
> What time is it when I go to school? *(Place hands at 10:00)*
> Tell me Mr. Clock, I have a hunch,
> What time is it when I eat lunch? *(Place hands at 12:00)*
> Tell me Mr. Clock, I made a big mess,
> What time is it when I take recess? *(Place hands at 2:00)*
> Tell me Mr. Clock, my mind is starting to roam,
> What time is it when I get to go home? *(Place hands at 4:00)*
> Tell me Mr. Clock, I'm feeling thinner,
> What time is it when we have dinner? *(Place hands at 6:00)*
> My homework's all done, and my tummy's been fed,
> What time is it when I have to go to bed? *(Place hands at 8:00)*
> Tell me Mr. Clock, do you ever sleep?
> "No!" said Mr. Clock, "I have *time* to keep!"

MAKE AND TAKE

Paper Clocks

Supplies Needed per Child

Paper plate, standard size, white, one

Small round stickers, (optional), twelve each

Index card stock in black, one

Large brad fastener, one

Washable black felt-tip marker, two or three per craft table

Washable markers or crayons in assorted colors

Directions

Use the same directions for making the clock as in the Storyboard Activity, "Mr. Clock." Because the children are still developing their fine motor skills and the index paper is very thick, precut the hands of the clock for the activity, cutting points for the hands and using the hole punch at the opposite end. Let the children draw or color anything they would like on the face of the clock, but make sure they write their numbers and are written or attached in the correct order. If you have a very young group, the round stickers work best. You could put the numbers on the stickers yourself, if needed. If children are older, let them add their own numbers with the markers. This is a very traditional preschool activity the children will remember for years to come.

LESSON 10

❧❀❧

GOATS

CURRICULUM TOPICS
Goats, Trolls

FEATURED BOOK
Carpenter, Stephen. 1998. *The Three Billy Goats Gruff*. New York: HarperFestival.

SUMMARY
Three goats trick the mean, ugly troll into letting them cross the bridge. Vivid pictures, not too fierce characters, and a storyline designed for children to chime in makes this book our favorite version of the classic tale. Ages 3–7

ACTIVITY
Read the title of the book to your listeners. Ask them for their ideas about what part or sound the rhythm sticks might play in the telling of this story. Some of the children are sure to have heard the story before, so encourage them to use those critical thinking skills. Conclude the discussion by demonstrating how to use the rhythm sticks to make the sound of the goat's hooves "trip trapping" over the bridge. Children can either drum sticks on the floor or tap the two sticks together. Pass out rhythm sticks to everyone. No matter how many times you share this time-honored tale, children are always enthralled by it. Adding the element of instruments only heightens their enthusiasm.

ADDITIONAL BOOKS TO SHARE
Alakija, Polly. 2002. *Catch That Goat!* Cambridge, MA: Barefoot Books. Ayoka, a young Nigerian girl, has been left in charge of the family goat. Within minutes of her new responsibility, the goat disappears. Ayoka searches the streets of the town and stops to ask each market vendor if they have seen her goat. No one has seen her goat, but she begins to realize that all the vendors are missing items as well. As she stops by each market stall, she asks the same question, ". . . have you seen my goat?" Encourage the children to repeat the line with you. At each place the goat stops and steals, the vendors take inventory of the remaining items. Feel free to pause on each page and count aloud with the children the items that are left. This is an additional learning feature the author has cleverly incorporated in the text. In the end, the goat beats Akoya home, and so does her mama! She has some explaining to do, but the illustrations of the goat's final adventures are self-explanatory. This is a playful and exciting book with a happy ending. Ages 2–7

French, Vivian. 1999. *Big Fat Hen and the Hairy Goat*. London: David & Charles Children's Books. Big Fat Hen lives in the farmyard and always thinks she knows best. So when Hairy Goat says, "I want a juicy, green cabbage for my breakfast!" she happily opens the gate to Farmer Tile's garden where lots and lots of cabbages grow. Big Fat Hen does her best to always be "helpful." She is a little too helpful this time and gets herself into quite a predicament. She looks to Wise Old Dog for help. He will help her for a price. Big Fat Hen pleases everyone and in the end pleases herself with the results. The illustrations are bright and colorful and will be very pleasing to the young eye. Ages 2–7

Gugler, Laurel Dee. 2003. *There's a Billy Goat in the Garden*. Cambridge, MA: Barefoot Books. When an escaped billy goat wrecks havoc in the farmer's garden, bigger and bigger barnyard animals successively offer to help chase out the troublesome goat. In the end it is the tiny bee that gets the job done. Composed of vivid and discernable illustrations, rollicking rhyme, and repeating lines, this book has all the ingredients of a great read-aloud. As with most stories told in succession, this story can be easily adapted into a storyboard. Adding the element of the storyboard makes the story more interactive with the audience. The Ellison die-cuts you need are a small bee, rooster, goat, beagle, pig #2, donkey, cow, and horse #1. To begin, place the billy goat on the board, and read the title from the cover of the book. Enlist the audience to help you tell the story. Pass out the rest of the pieces to your participants. As you read the story, each time an animal offers to help, the participant with the appropriate animal will add his or her piece to the board. Ages 3–7

Hoberman, Mary Ann. 2002. *Bill Grogan's Goat.* New York: Little, Brown. A pesky goat has an appetite for clothes that gets him in all sorts of trouble! When his owner, Bill Grogan, attempts to get rid of him, the goat ends up on a wild train adventure with an engineer and some rowdy barnyard animals. This adaptation is the perfect complement to this well-known children's chant. Past renditions of this folk tale can be too dark for young children, but the team that created this version appropriately infused cheery and optimistic conclusions. The illustrations are colorful, animated, and playful. After reading the story, teach the children the tune provided on the inner jacket cover of the book. Ages 2–7

Newton, Jill. 2002. *Gordon in Charge.* New York: Bloomsbury Children's Books. Gordon is a proud goat and loves being in charge of the farm. He bosses the sheep, he bosses the cows, and he bosses the chickens. All the farm animals obey Gordon just to keep him quiet. One day on the farm a new arrival waddles into the yard, Gordon the Goose! Gordon the goat is not at all amused. They begin bickering as each wants to be in charge. They decide to compete to see who will be in charge of the farm. Several competitions take place, some a bit destructive, until both Gordon's get in over their heads. They are rescued by a third Gordon. Gordon the farmer takes over, and Gordon the goat and Gordon the goose both agree it is a lot of work being in charge. But will it last? This story will keep the children's attention with its large, colorful illustrations and adventuresome text. Ages 2–7

Polacco, Patricia. 2003. *G Is for Goat.* New York: Philomel Books. Children will enjoy this book as it takes them through each letter in the alphabet, "goat style." From "F" for flower eating, to "M" for clothes munching, to "R" for head ramming, and many more antics taking place in a goat's life. The children will enjoy reciting each bold letter of the alphabet throughout the pages. The illustrations are very vivid and large enough for a group of children to view clearly. Ages 2–7

Polacco, Patricia. 2004. *Oh, Look!* New York: Philomel Books. Three little goats find an open gate and get into mischief. Lead the children to act this story out as it is told in the same style as the classic adventure romp, "We're Going on a Bear Hunt." Ages 3–7

Tompert, Ann. 1999. *The Hungry Black Bag.* Boston: Houghton Mifflin. This is a story about Ole Goat of Grede Mountain, who, on market day, wants everything everyone else has. He wants it all for free, and wants it whether he needs it or not! With his black bag dragging behind, he begins his threatening, stealing rampage. Each stop he makes at the different animal stands, he keeps taking, and his bag continues to get bigger. There is a repeated line in the book you can have the children say with you, "And the bag grew bigger." Each page adds an additional bigger, "And the bag grew bigger and bigger." Ole Goat of Grede Mountain finally tangles with the wrong animal and bites off more than he can chew. Bear recovers all the stolen merchandise and returns it to the other animals. This whimsical jaunt clearly shows that in the end, greedy goats get only what they deserve. Ages 3–7

MUSIC AND MOVEMENT WITH RHYTHM STICKS

Sing Along: "The Billy Goats Ballad"

Sung to the Tune: "Did You Ever See a Lassie"
There once was a billy goat, a billy goat, a billy goat,
There once was a billy goat who crossed over a bridge!

He went trip trap, and trip trap, and trip trap, and trip trap!
There once was a billy goat who crossed over a bridge!
There was a second billy goat, a billy goat, a billy goat,
There was a second billy goat, who crossed over a bridge!
He went trip trap, and trip trap, and trip trap, and trip trap!
There was a second billy goat who crossed over a bridge!
There was a third billy goat, a billy goat, a billy goat,
There was a third billy goat, who crossed over a bridge.
He went trip trap, and trip trap, and trip trap, and trip trap!
There was a third billy goat who crossed over a bridge!
The mean, ugly troll, he wanted a billy goat,
The mean, ugly troll, he tried every time!
They'd go trip trap, and trip trap, and trip trap, and trip trap!
The mean, ugly troll, he tried every time!
The mean, ugly troll, he fought with the billy goat,
The mean, ugly troll got tossed off the bridge!
He went glub-glub, and glub-glub, and glub-glub, and glub-glub!
The mean, ugly troll got TOSSED off the bridge!

Directions

Pass out the rhythm sticks and play song #12 from the accompanying *The Sound of Storytime* CD. Let the children make the "trip-trap" sound every time it is sung in the song. At the end of the song, when the troll gets tossed off of the bridge and goes glub-glub, have the children plug their nose and get quieter and quieter as they sing it, as if the troll is sinking farther and farther into the water.

ADDITIONAL SONGS TO SHARE

Disney's Silly Songs. Walt Disney Records, 1988. Compact Disk. 60819-7. Play song #17, "Bill Grogan's Goat," and lead a sing along. A chorus of children echo the lead singer in this song. Ask the children in your audience to echo along with the CD as well.

STORYBOARD

The Naughty Billy Goat

Supplies Needed

Ellison die-cut T-shirt, in red, green, blue, yellow, white, black, orange, or any assorted colors, one per child

Ellison die-cut goat, one

Tape or self-adhesive material to attach items onto the storyboard

Directions

Pass out the assorted colored shirts giving each child at least one, and more if you have a small group or extra time for this activity. Add the goat onto the storyboard and tell the children that the naughty goat is looking for clothes to eat. Explain to them that when they hear the goat ask for their colored shirt, to come up and add it to the storyboard. Another way to play this activity without any paper clothing is to have the children stand up when you call out the colored shirt that they are wearing. Ask them to continue to stay in the front until all of the children have been called up. Continue chanting and changing clothing colors until every child has had their turn:

I'm a naughty billy goat, I'm as hungry as can be!
I'm looking for a *red shirt*, can you help me?
I'm a naughty billy goat, I'm as hungry as can be!
I'm looking for a *green shirt*, can you help me?

You may have to give the same color out to more than one child so that a couple can come up at the same time and add their articles of clothing.

MAKE AND TAKE

Three Billy Goats Gruff Retold

Supplies Needed per Child

Construction paper, 12" × 18" in size, in a light color, one

Ellison die-cut goats, three

Glue stick

Washable markers or crayons in assorted colors

Directions

This activity will reinforce the feature story, *The Three Billy Goats Gruff,* in this lesson. The children will recreate the story by making their own story through art. Review the story with the children before this activity, asking a few simple but important questions as to the placement of the billy goats and troll. Ask the children if the troll lived under the bridge or over the bridge? Ask them again what the billy goats were trying to do. After the short review, explain to the children what they will be doing for this activity. Have the children draw or color a big bridge on the construction paper. Next, have them glue the goats onto the paper in their respective places. Let them use their imagination, and draw the mean, ugly troll. They can add grass, sun, flowers, rocks, and other item they think would be present in the setting as well. Remember to have a sample craft available for the children to view. At the top of your sample page, write the title of the story, *Three Billy Goats Gruff.* The children who are old enough to write should be encouraged to add the title to their creation. Always remind the children to put their names and date on their art projects as well. It is a good habit for any child to practice, and it helps the parents who keep and cherish their little artists' masterpieces for future identification.

LESSON 11

MARCHING ANTS

CURRICULUM TOPICS

Ants, Aunts, Marching

An ant farm makes a great, inexpensive library or school display and is guaranteed to generate a lot of interest and circulation from your juvenile nonfiction collection. Set up the display area by draping your surface with green grass style carpeting or mat. Place the ant farm in the center of the mat at the eye level of the children. Around the ant farm, arrange colorful and attractive books about insects and garden creatures for the children to check out and take home. Place creepy, plastic, and rubbery bugs, snakes, frogs, turtles, and lizards around the display and invite children to touch. Make sure the toys you choose are recommended for children under age three. We have also had great success with a similar butterfly display. Butterfly caterpillars in an attractive display container can be ordered from the company Insect Lore. Over a few weeks' time, patrons really enjoy observing the caterpillars change into butterflies and learning more about the insects from library books. Generate great enthusiasm by hosting a grand butterfly release party.

FEATURED BOOK

Manning, Maurie. 2003. *The Aunts Go Marching.* Honesdale, PA: Boyds Mills Press.

SUMMARY

There are no ants in this story, but there are a whole lot of aunts! In this unique version of the popular children's song, "The Ants Go Marching," a young girl dressed in her raincoat marches through the rain while beating on a drum. She is followed by aunts dressed in raincoats and black umbrellas. In this version the aunts march one by one, but the little aunt stops to bang her drum, then "they all go marching down to the town, in the rain, in the rain." One loud boom sends all of the aunts running to get out of the rain. Once they are safe inside, the little girl cries, "Let's do it again?" This is a very fun and energetic version of the story. The clever illustrations are bright and perky even on a dreary day. Ages 3–7

ACTIVITY

Read the story to the children. After you have read it once, pass out the rhythm sticks and let the children stand up, march, sing along, and tap through the story this time while you lead them back through the march while turning the pages of the book.

FEATURED BOOK

Owen, Ann. 2003. *The Ants Go Marching.* Minneapolis, MN: Picture Window Books.

SUMMARY

A depiction of the traditional song illustrated in storybook form. Ages 3–7

ACTIVITY

There are numerous activities and ways to interact with this book. One way is to pass out the rhythm sticks and encourage the children to keep the marching beat by drumming on the floor or tapping rhythm sticks together as you read or sing the book. Another way is to encourage the children to keep track of how many ants have joined the march by holding up the appropriate number of fingers as you read. On each page of the book, the illustrator has superimposed a symbol of a hand holding up the number of fingers that represents how many ants have joined the march. After reading the story, pass out the rhythm sticks. Play a musical version of the song on the CD player, and lead the children to play their sticks and march in place or on a parade around the room. We recommend the song titled *The Ants Go Marching* in the *Toddler Action Songs* CD listed below in the "Additional Songs to Share" section. Lastly, if you have tambourines, you can divide the group into two. Give half the group rhythm sticks and the other half tambourines. The children with rhythm sticks can tap to the beat, and the children with tambourines can strike their instruments on the words "Boom! Boom! Boom!" This last suggestion can be used to accompany the book or the musical CD previously mentioned. Children also love to shout "hurrah!" Encourage all of these fun "ant"ics.

ADDITIONAL BOOKS TO SHARE

Hoose, Phillip. 1998. *Hey Little Ant.* Berkeley, CA: Tricycle Press. A boy is about to squish an ant when the ant begins to talk and plead for his life. The story concludes open-ended and asks the listeners to decide what should be the fate of this ant. This book can be read or sung. A tune is provided on the back cover. Giant-sized images fill up whole pages, giving the reader a sense of the ant's micro-perspective. Ages 3–7

McElligott, Matthew. 2004. *Absolutely Not.* New York: Walker. Being a tiny ant, Frieda worries there is danger in everything. Frieda's friend, Gloria, is a brave and who is not afraid of anything. Gloria takes Frieda on a walk and tries to convince her there is nothing to fear. Both girls end up learning to balance their extreme ideas. Ages 3–7

McGrath, Pam. 1998. *Pam McGrath's Hungry Ants.* Columbia, SC: Summerhouse Press. Ten ants work together to carry home a feast in this counting storybook. Before the story, pass out ten ants to be added to the storyboard as you read. Each time an ant joins the other workers in the story, choose a child to bring their ant character up and add it to the board. Ages 3–7

Mould, Wendy. 2001. *Ants in My Pants.* New York: Clarion Books. Jacob wants to stay home and play, but mom wants Jacob to get dressed and go shopping. When Jacob protests there are animals in his clothes that are keeping him from getting dressed, Mom claims she doesn't see them. Are the animals imaginary or not? Parents and children alike will relate in amusement to this charming story. Ages 3–7

Numeroff, Laura Joffe. 2004. *What Aunts Do Best; What Uncles Do Best.* New York: Simon & Schuster Books for Young Readers. This is an endearing story that, if turned over one way, is a book about aunts, and if turned over the other way, is a book about uncles. For the purpose of this lesson, read the story about aunts. From roller coaster rides to late-night television to convertible rides, aunts are lots of fun. The illustrations are packed with watercolor cartoons of sheep, cats, and squirrels posing as aunts. The true message in this story is what aunts do best and that is "give you lots and lots of love." The children will enjoy listening to the story and many will relate to the fun times they have had with their own aunts. Ages 3–7

Prigger, Mary Skillings. 1999. *Aunt Minnie McGranahan.* New York: Clarion Books. Aunt Minnie McGranahan is a small and tidy lady who lives alone in a small little house. She is very set in her ways. She does not care for children and never had any of her own, and the neighbors say that that is a good thing. She has a system for doing everything a certain way. One day, Aunt Minnie McGranahan gets the message that her nine nieces and nephews are orphaned. She does what any self-respecting aunt would do and takes in all nine of them. With some adjustment of Aunt Minnie's system for doing everything, she devises a way to make things work in a fun and loving way. She finds out that she does love kids after all. Set in the 1920s, the illustrations are whimsical and fresh and are filled with nostalgic charm. This story is actually based on the life of the real Aunt Minnie from Kansas, a member of the author's family who adopted nine children in 1920. Ages 3–8

Rattigan, Jama Kim. 1994. *The Aunt Farm.* New York: Houghton Mifflin. A young boy named Truman receives a package from his Aunt Fran for his birthday. It is instructions for sending away for an ant farm. Truman follows the instructions and mails off for the ant farm. Much to his surprise, he gets aunts instead of ants! He makes the best of a bad situation and establishes his own aunt farm so he can train them to be the best they can be at flying kites, really listening when children speak, and doing back flips with their eyes closed! This is a cute read-aloud with an interesting spin. Ages 4–8

Sayre, April Pulley. 2002. *Army Ant Parade.* New York: Henry Holt. What should you do if you find yourself in the path of an army of ants? Step out of the way, of course! Adorned with beautiful illustrations of the rainforest and packed with onomatopoeia, read this suspenseful tale of one camper's eerie encounter in the rainforest of Panama. Ages 3–7

MUSIC AND MOVEMENT WITH RHYTHM STICKS

Sing Along: "Tap with Me 1-2-3"

Sung to the Tune: "When Johnny Comes Marching Home"

March with me . . . 1—2—3 . . . March, *(rest)* March!
March with me . . . 1—2—3 . . . March, *(rest)* March!

March with me . . . 1—2—3,
I'll march with you if you'll march with me, and we'll all go marching . . . 1—2, 3!
Tap with me . . . 1—2—3 . . . Tap-tap, tap-tap!
Tap with me . . . 1—2—3 . . . Tap-tap, tap-tap!
Tap with me . . . 1—2—3,
We're as happy as we can be, to Tap, tap, tap, tap . . . 1—2, 3!
March and tap . . . 1—2—3 . . . March-tap, march-tap!
March and tap . . . 1—2—3 . . . March-tap, march-tap!
March and tap . . . 1—2—3
We're in perfect harmony, as we march and tap, and march (rest) and tap!

Directions

Pass out the rhythm sticks and play song #13 from the accompanying *The Sound of Storytime* CD. Line the children up in single file with sufficient space between them to join in a marching and tapping activity. Explain to them you are going to be the leader, and while remaining in single file, they will be asked to follow specific instructions. Ask how many know how to march. Ask how many know how to tap. Of course, most of them will, but you can show them if they don't. Then, ask them how many can tap and march at the same time. Again, let them show you they know how. Talk about rhythm and ask them if they can follow the beat. Test them by tapping out the beginning of the song without the music. Tell them to listen closely to your tapping, as you are going to ask them to tap out the same beats they just heard. By explaining this first and giving them the opportunity to practice, the children will be more in tune to the rhythm of the song and will easily understand your directions. If you have a large space to march around, take full advantage and march the children all around the room. If your space is limited, you may have to march in a small circle and continue circling throughout the song. For the young child, this is an intense coordination activity. It will benefit their listening and fine motor skills, as well as teach them to learn to follow directions while enjoying every moment!

Sing Along: "Two Sticks"

Sung to the tune: "Jingle Bells"

Take two sticks, just two sticks! Tap them one, two, three!
Take two sticks, just two sticks, and march and tap with me!
Take two sticks, just two sticks, and turn yourself around!
Take two sticks, just two sticks, now play them on the ground!
(Plays through again, while children tap sticks)
Take two sticks, just two sticks! Tap them one, two, three!
Take two sticks, just two sticks, and march and tap with me!
Take two sticks, just two sticks, and turn yourself around!
Take two sticks, just two sticks, now play them on the ground!
(Plays through again, while children tap sticks)
Take two sticks, just two sticks! Tap them one, two, three!
Take two sticks, just two sticks, and march and tap with me!
Take two sticks, just two sticks, and turn yourself around!
Take two sticks, just two sticks, now lay your two sticks down!

Directions

Pass out the rhythm sticks and play song #14 from the accompanying *The Sound of Storytime* CD. Let the children take their two rhythm sticks and follow along with the song.

ADDITIONAL SONGS TO SHARE

The Ants Go Marching. Macacy Entertainment, 2002. Compact Disk. MK2 5083. Play song #3, "The Ants Go Marching." This CD has our favorite version of this song. Lead the children on a parade. March around the room to this fun song.

Cedarmont Kids Singers. *Toddler Action Songs.* October Sound and Mattinee Studio, 2002. Compact Disk. 84418-0137-2. Play song #2, "The Ants Go Marching." Lead the children on a parade. March around the room to this fun song.

Chapin, Tom. *Great Big Fun for the Very Little One.* Sundance Music, 2001. Compact Disk. R2 78361. Play #6, "The Parade Came Marching." Lead the children in a march around the room and follow the song making the silly movements along the way. This is a very appropriate song to share during this lesson because this is a squishy, soggy march through the pouring rain, as in the featured book.

STORYBOARD

Aunts or Ants?

Supplies Needed

Five index cards, 5" × 7" in size

Ellison die-cut animals—monkey #2, goat, hippo, lion #2, and a woman, one of each (attach these onto the index cards)

Ellison die-cuts—one small ant and one additional woman

Tape or glue stick to attach items onto card

Directions

Tape or glue each of the five Ellison die-cut items onto the index cards prior to the storyboard activity. Attach the Ellison die-cut ant onto the storyboard and beside it, attach the woman. Talk to the children about aunts. Tell them aunts are always ladies, they are a female relative, their daddy's sister or their mother's sister. Discuss how many aunts the children have, what they like to do with their aunts, where they live, and other general conversation about aunts. Next, talk to them about an ant. Tell them some easy facts about ants. Ants have six legs, with each leg having three joints. They use their antennae not only for touch but for smelling too. An adult ant cannot chew and swallow its food. Instead, they swallow the juice that they squeeze from pieces of food. They usually live about forty-five to sixty days. When you discuss their legs, count the legs of the ant on the storyboard along with the children. Show them the antanae and tell them about them. This would also be a good time to introduce homonyms. Explain to the children that some words sound alike but have a different spelling and meaning. They will not necessarily understand this, but homonym is a fun word to try to pronounce. Let the children try to pronounce the word. After you have talked about both types of ants/aunts, explain to the children that you have some questions to ask them. Let the children guess which aunt/ant is the correct answer on the storyboard by saying aloud the lady aunt, or the bug ant. Ask them the following questions:

Which aunt/ant has six legs?
Which aunt/ant might use an umbrella when it rains outside?
Which aunt/ant chews her food and swallows it?
Which aunt/ant has two legs?
Which aunt/ant might live in a house? *(both)*
Which aunt/ant might wear a hat?
Which aunt/ant might drive a car?
Which aunt/ant might enjoy a picnic? *(both)*

There are a number of questions you can ask the children, depending on how long you want this activity to last. When you are finished with this part of the activity, introduce them to this little song:

"The Aunt Song"

Sung to the Tune: "London Bridge"

I love my aunt, she loves me too, loves me too, loves me too!
I love my aunt, she loves me too, she's a *monkey!* (Turn monkey card over)

I love my aunt, she loves me too, loves me too, loves me too!
I love my aunt, she loves me too, she's a _billy goat! (Turn goat card over)_
I love my aunt, she loves me too, loves me too, loves me too!
I love my aunt, she loves me too, she's a _hippo! (Turn hippo card over)_
I love my aunt, she loves me too, loves me too, loves me too!
I love my aunt, she loves me too, she's a _lion! (Turn lion card over)_
I love my aunt, she loves me too, loves me too, loves me too!
I love my aunt, she loves me too, she's a _LADY! (Turn lady card over)_

Directions

Make sure you have the cards in the order you are going to sing them, leaving the lady card to turn over last. As you sing the song acappella and turn the card over, act shocked and surprised that it is an animal you just revealed. The children will love to watch you with a confused and funny expression on your face, as they become engaged in this song. Continue singing until you get to the last card with the picture of the lady, and then act very satisfied and happy you finally found the correct one.

MAKE AND TAKE

The Aunts/Ants Go Marching!

Supplies Needed per Child

Construction paper, 9" × 12" in size, any color, one each

Ellison die-cut small ants, black, seven each

Ellison die-cut woman, four each

Flat toothpick, one each, cut into two equal parts

Glue stick

Washable markers, assorted colors

Directions

Have the children turn their construction paper horizontally. Ask the children to glue the black ants onto one side of the paper, marching in a straight line towards the middle of the paper, and the lady aunts on the other side of the paper all in a row marching towards the ants and meeting in the middle of the page. They can draw small drums in front of the lady aunts and glue the toothpicks to the drums. Have a sample of the finished "make and take" activity available for the children to see and follow. You could also have your sample titled "The Aunts/Ants Go Marching." Let the children who know how to print copy the title. Before you end the activity, ask the children if they remember what the word is for two words that are spelled differently but sound alike? They might just fool you!

LESSON 12

❧

WOODLAND ANIMALS

CURRICULUM TOPICS

Woodland Habitats, Woodpeckers, Bears, Skunks, Love, Friendship, Owls

FEATURED BOOK

Faulkner, Keith. 2003. *Tap! Tap! Tap!* New York: Barron's Educational Series.

SUMMARY

There is a tapping sound echoing through the forest. Lift the large flaps to help the mother animals check on their babies and figure out which critter is making all the noise. Ages 2–7

ACTIVITY

Introduce the cover of the book to your listeners. Encourage the group to sound out the title. Discuss how exclamation points are used in the title to tell the reader to add emphasis. Ask the children to contribute ideas about how they could add emphasis to the words "Tap! Tap! Tap!" during the story. Suggest using the rhythm sticks to make the sound. Pass out the rhythm sticks. Ask the children to tap their sticks together and chant the words each time you point to the phrase "Tap! Tap! Tap!" This book is very easy to read and lends itself well to the activity. Even so, make sure you always preread the book. You can very simply rearrange the wording to better prompt the children to play their part. With each turn of the page, add a phrase like, "Then again—the sound was heard all through the forest." At the end of the story, right before you reveal the woodpecker's project, add a few extra series of taps. Read the words and play the instruments like a crescendo in music. Then, just like a musical conductor, abruptly halt the activity. After everyone is quiet, bring the story to a mysterious and intriguing climax by whispering, "Then there was silence!" Resume the story as it is written.

ADDITIONAL BOOKS TO SHARE

Alborough, Jez. 1992. *Where's My Teddy?* Cambridge, MA: Candlewick Press. Eddie has lost his teddy bear in the woods. He bravely sets off to find his faithful companion, but instead happens on someone else's lost teddy bear. This second lost teddy bear is absolutely enormous. What sort of giant must have lost this teddy bear? Eddie is in for a frightening surprise when he comes face-to-face with the owner of the gigantic teddy bear. Ages 3–7

Cotton, Cynthia. 2002. *At the Edge of the Woods*. New York: Henry Holt. Early in the morning, at the edge of the deep, dark woods, the forest creatures play until the big bear comes out to get some fresh air. Use the storyboard and let the children help you tell this story. Before you begin the story, pass out Ellison die-cut pieces to represent ten ants, nine butterflies, eight sparrows, seven mice, six blue jays, five bees, four lizards, three foxes, two fawns, one chipmunk, and one bear. Vertically number the storyboard from one to ten. Leave space for the children to line up the animals across the board after the appropriate number. Ages 3–7

Crum, Shutta. 2005. *The Bravest of the Brave*. New York: Alfred A. Knopf. Little skunk is alone in the woods at night. All sorts of ghostly, ghoulish, and fierce creatures send prickles up little skunk's furry back. Skunk manages to muster up brave thoughts and finds his way home. Great, full-size illustrations and a rhyming text with lots of action words that can be performed or mimicked make this a good choice for reading aloud. The intriguing and mysterious language provokes the children's imagination, while the pictures draw a reassuring conclusion. When the story reads, "I called my call as clearly as I could," make sure to interject skunk's plea for his mother. The picture depicts this part, but it's easy to miss. Ages 3–7

Duffy, Dee Dee. 1996. *Forest Tracks*. Honesdale, PA: Bell Books/Boyds Mills Press. Can your listeners guess which forest animals made the tracks in this book? Read this story and go on an imaginary adventure through the woods. Enlist the children to help act out the story with you. Hold your hand to your forehead like you're shading your eyes and point to the ground like you really see some interesting tracks every time the book repeats the word "Look!" Encourage the children to copy your actions in a "monkey see, monkey do" fashion. When the book reads, "Listen!" hold your hand to your ear and pretend to hear a sound far in the distant woods. Draw the kids in by asking them if they too, heard anything. Ages 2–7

Fleming, Denise. 1996. *Where Once There Was a Wood*. New York: Henry Holt. A housing development replaces the woodland habitat of many living creatures. Inspired by a true story, this very short story is long on intrigue and complete with a conclusion that makes an impact. Discussion ideas and ways children can create backyard habitats to help protect displaced creatures follow the story. Ages 3–7

Koeppel, Ruth. 2005. *Owen's Way Home*. Pleasantville, NY: Reader's Digest Children's Books. Owen Owl lived in a hole in a big old tree. He went out at night but always returned home early the next morning. One morning, Owen Owl got ready to go home but found himself lost. He could not find his tree hole anywhere. Owen flew all over looking for his hole as he seemed to have some added urgency that day. He kept finding holes, but every hole he found was not his. Finally, he found the right hole and in time for him and Mrs. Owl to welcome their new baby owl cracking out of its shell. There is an adorable lift-the-flap. The last page allows the reader to help the new arrival come out of the egg. This large board book has been cleverly constructed with a die-cut hole on every page. Ages 2–7

Whatley, Bruce. 1996. *The Teddy Bears' Picnic*. New York: HarperCollins. Teddy bears gather in the woods for a secret teddy bear picnic. Read or sing this book for a sneak peek of this magnificent clandestine event. There are several versions of this story, but this particular one has full-sized illustrations and can be purchased with an accompanying musical cassette performed by Jerry Garcia. Share this book at storytime and invite your participants to bring along their own favorite teddy bears, too! Ages 2–7

MUSIC AND MOVEMENT WITH RHYTHM STICKS

Sing Along: "Woodpecker Tap!"

Sung to the Tune: "Mary Had a Little Lamb"

Woodpecker, will you tap a tune?
Tap a tune? Tap a tune?
Woodpecker, will you tap a tune?
Then we will tap one back!
Tap, tap, tap, tap—tap, tap, tap!
Tap, tap, tap! Tap, tap, tap!
Tap, tap, tap, tap—tap, tap, tap!

Tap, tap, tap, tap, tap!
Thank you for that tapping tune, tapping tune, tapping tune!
Thank you for that tapping tune, now we will tap one back!
Tap, tap, tap, tap—tap, tap, tap!
Tap, tap, tap! Tap, tap, tap!
Tap, tap, tap, tap—tap, tap, tap!
Tap, tap, tap, tap, tap!

Directions

Pass out the rhythm sticks and play song #15 from the accompanying *The Sound of Storytime* CD. Let the children tap their sticks together each time they hear the word "tap," following the distinct rhythm of the song.

ADDITIONAL SONGS TO SHARE

Baby's First Playtime Songs. St. Clair Entertainment Group, 1999. Compact Disk. BFM44472. Play song #4, "We're Going on a Bear Hunt." Lead the children on an imaginary bear hunt. This version is unique because you, the leader, can echo the lead singer on the CD. The lead singer is a male voice, and a woman's voice repeats every line. Act out the song with the children and encourage them to echo the words.

Palmer, Hap. *Rhythms on Parade.* Hap-Pal Music Inc., 1995. Compact Disk. HP102E AC633. Play song #3, "Woodpecker." Pass out the rhythm sticks and encourage the children to echo the woodpecker in the song.

STORYBOARD

Picture Tappin' Woodpeckers

Supplies Needed

Construction paper, 12" × 18" in size, brown, or one large brown sack
Ellison die-cut cardinals, five (substitute cardinal for woodpecker)
Washable marker, brown
Tape to attach items onto the storyboard

Directions

Tear or cut brown construction paper or a brown paper sack into the shape of a large tree trunk. Use the brown marker and from left to right draw an eye, a heart, and the letter U toward the top of the tree trunk. This is an illustrated version of "I Love You!" Using tape, attach the tree trunk to the storyboard with the top of the trunk butting up against the top of the storyboard, as if the tree were hanging over the top. Number the woodpeckers with your marker, one through five, large enough for the children to see. Tape all five woodpeckers, one through five, in a row at the top of the trunk, covering the eye, heart, and U. Follow the story below:

Five woodpeckers tapping on a tree,
Tap! Tap! Said woodpecker number one,
"Let's draw, shall we?" *(Point to woodpecker #1)*
Tap! Tap! Said woodpecker number two,
"Let's put our beaks together and tap I Love You!" *(Point to woodpecker #2)*
Tap! Tap! Said woodpecker number three,
"Is there enough room to tap that on the tree?" *(Point to woodpecker #3)*
Tap! Tap! Said woodpecker number four,
"There's room for that and even more!" *(Point to woodpecker #4)*
Tap! Tap! Said woodpecker number five,
"Won't our friends be surprised?"
(Point to woodpecker #5)
So they tap, tap, tapped all day on the tree!
Tapping for all their friends to see!
Five tired woodpeckers left one by one!
(Remove all woodpeckers and reveal the picture while saying the last verse)
Let's take a look at what they have done!

The picture will be the eye, heart, and the U together, which stands for "I Love You" in woodpecker language! The children love this storyboard activity. When you are finished, take time to teach them "I Love You" in American Sign

Language! The easiest way to teach this is to have them hold up their hand with all five finger stretched out, now pull down the middle finger and the ring finger, leaving the pointer, pinky and thumb stretched out. This is the sign for "I Love You!" Let then practice this a few times.

MAKE AND TAKE

Tree Tapping Art

Supplies Needed per Child

Brown construction paper, 12" × 18" in size, or one large grocery sack

Ellison die-cut cardinals, two (substitute cardinal for woodpecker)

Washable markers or crayons in assorted colors

Glue stick

Directions

Tell the children they get to make woodpecker art. Have the children tear brown construction paper or a brown paper sack into the shape of a large tree trunk. Let them draw any picture they would like to draw on the trunk using the washable markers. After they are satisfied with their drawings, have them glue their woodpeckers onto the tree. Glue one woodpecker on one side of the trunk, and the other woodpecker onto the other side of the trunk. This is a cute, quick creation that the children love to make. Anytime there is an opportunity to tie the art project into the lesson, it is beneficial for everyone.

PART III

SAND BLOCKS

LESSON 13

BATHTIME

CURRICULUM TOPICS

Farm Animals, Healthy Habits, Bathtime

FEATURED BOOK

Cowley, Joy. 1999. *Mrs. Wishy-Washy*. New York: Philomel Books.

SUMMARY

Cow, pig, and duck are playing in the mud when along comes Mrs. Wishy-Washy. The farm animals are loving the mud, but Mrs. Wishy-Washy will not stand for it. She scrubs them clean in her large metal tub, "wishy-washy, wishy-washy!" When she turns her back on the trio of mud loving animals, the fun starts all over again. Ages 3–7

ACTIVITY

When Mrs. Wishy-Washy begins to scrub the animals, "Wishy-Washy, Wishy-Washy," ask the children to rub their sand blocks together making the washing sound. Have children continue throughout the story.

ADDITIONAL BOOKS TO SHARE

Bedford, David. 2003. *Mo's Stinky Sweater*. New York: Hyperion Books for Young Readers. Mo the monkey always wore his rainbow sweater. No matter where he went or what was going on, he wore his rainbow sweater. One day Mo's mother decided she was going to wash Mo's stinky, dirty sweater. She pulled it right off of Mo, but Mo pulled back. Other mother animals began to help Mo's mother pull the sweater, while their young helped Mo tug back. After some humorous tugging adventures, Mo finally washed his rainbow sweater himself. When it was dry and ready to put back on, Mo realized it was way too big. He made the best of a bad situation and turned it into a hammock. The illustrations are big, bright, and playful. The children will love the tug-of-war game that the animals play. Ages 2–7

Christelow, Eileen. 2000. *Five Little Monkeys Wash the Car*. New York: Clarion Books. Five little monkeys wash the family car before trying to sell it. But that is only the beginning of their adventures with the old heap. Ages 3–7

Edwards, Frank B. 2000. *Mortimer Mooner Stopped Taking a Bath*. Kingston, Ontario: Pokewood Press. When Mortimer Mooner decides to stop wearing his tie on Monday, his appearance goes downhill the rest of the week. Ages 3–7

Jarman, Julia. 2004. *Big Red Tub*. New York: Orchard Books. Dad fixes Stella and Stan a big bubble bath in their big red tub. They enjoy splashing one another and playing with the bathtub toys, and they have a great time playing in the water. The dog comes in and asks if he can take a swim. They say yes, so the dog dives right into the tub with a big splash. Next comes a lion who asks if he can take a wash in the big red tub; they say yes! Next comes duck looking for some water action, and they let him join in. More and more animals join in the big red tub until it carries them out of their house and around the world twice. After worlds of fun and adventure in their big red tub, they are finally towed home by a flock of flamingos. In the end, mom enters the bathroom and Stella and Stan begin to tell her of their wonderful water adventures! Ages 3–7

MacDonald, Betty Bard. 1997. *Mrs. Piggle-Wiggle's Won't Take a Bath Cure*. New York: HarperCollins. Patsy, a young girl, will not take a bath. She continues to get dirtier and dirtier until one day Patsy's mom calls for help. Mrs. Piggle-Wiggle suggests the "radish cure," and the fun begins. You can use a lot of animation when reading this story, especially when the mud is dried on Patsy's face. Keep your mouth and lips pursed together as if you were the one wearing the dried mud on your own face as you read the page. Ages 3–8

Mayer, Mercer. 1987. *Just a Mess.* New York: Golden Book. A boy cleans up his messy room to find his baseball mitt. Ages 3–7

O'Garden, Irene. 2003. *The Scrubbly-Bubbly Car Wash.* New York: HarperCollins. When faced with a "crusty, dusty, dirty car," two enthusiastic siblings and their father know just where to go. Once inside the car wash, the children describe the sights and sounds. For a fun activity, let the children wash small toy cars and trucks in a tub of water. Ages 3–7

Roth, Carol. 1999. *Ten Dirty Pigs.* New York: North-South Books. Pigs from one to ten take baths to clean up and then get dirty again. Ages 3–6

Slangerup, Erik Jon. 2000. *Dirt Boy.* Morton Grove, IL: Albert Whitman. A boy runs away from home to avoid taking a bath and is befriended by Dirt Man, a filthy giant who lives in the woods. After a big scare, the boy decides to go home and clean up. Ages 3–8

Williams, Mo. 2004. *Knuffle Bunny: A Cautionary Tale.* New York: Hyperion Books for Children. Daddy and his young toddler, Trixie, along with her favorite stuffed bunny, take a trip to the Laundromat. Trixie helps her daddy stuff clothes into the machine and adds the coins. As they head back home, Trixie realizes she has left her stuffed bunny at the Laundromat. Trixie has an alarmed look on her face and begins to speak in jibberish, trying to communicate to her daddy what is wrong. Daddy cannot understand anything she is trying to tell him. The frustration builds and Trixie begins to cry uncontrollably. When her daddy tries to pick her up and calm her, "she went boneless." Trixie is very unhappy and tries in every way to get her daddy to understand her. Finally, they arrive back at home and Mother knows exactly what is wrong. The whole family runs back to the Laundromat to rescue the stuffed bunny. After several tries, Daddy rescues the bunny, and Trixie exclaims, "Knuffle Bunny!!!" This is an adorable story of frustration and misunderstanding from the parent's view as well as that of a child. Most parents and children will relate to this book. The illustrations are real photos with cartoon characters superimposed. This is a unique book that will be enjoyed by all. Ages 2–7

Zion, Gene. 2002. *Harry the Dirty Dog.* New York: HarperCollins. In this classic book, a white dog with black spots runs away from home and gets very dirty. His own family does not recognize him as a black dog with white spots. Ages 3–7

MUSIC AND MOVEMENT WITH SAND BLOCKS

Sing Along: "I Love to Scrubba-dub"

Sung to the Tune: "The Farmer in the Dell"

I love to scrubba-dub! I love to scrubba-dub!
I love to scrubba-dub, in my little metal tub!
Scrubba-dubba-dub! Scrubba-dubba-dub!
Scrubba-dubba-dubba-dubba! Scrubba-dubba-dub!
Will you help me scrub? Will you help me scrub?
Will you help me scrub, in my little metal tub?
Scrubba-dubba-dub! Scrubba-dubba-dub!
Scrubba-dubba-dubba-dubba! Scrubba-dubba-dub!
There's nothing left to scrub! There's nothing left to scrub!
There's nothing left to scrub, in the little metal tub!
NO scrubba-dubba-dub! NO scrubba-dubba-dub!
NO scrubba-dubba-dubba-dubba in the little metal tub!

Directions

Pass out the sand blocks and play song #16 from the accompanying *The Sound of Storytime* CD. Let the children rub the sand blocks back and forth making the scrubbing sound throughout each "scrubba-dubba-dub."

ADDITIONAL SONGS TO SHARE

Arnold, Linda. *Make Believe.* Ariel Records, 1986. Compact Disk. YM 121-CD. Play song #7, "Bathtub Song." Children rub their sand blocks together to make the scrubbing sound on the chorus. Clap them together for two beats on the words, "Ha! Ha!"

Chenille Sisters. *1-2-3 for Kids.* Red House Records, 1989. Compact Disk. Play song #1, "Singing in the Tub," as the children enter storytime and during craft time.

JUST FOR FUN

Fine Motor Skills: Bathing Animals

Supplies Needed

Small wash tubs

Water

Liquid detergent

Small plastic animals

Nail brushes and toothbrushes

Directions

Fill the small tubs with water and liquid detergent and let the children scrub small plastic farm animals with toothbrushes and nail brushes. This is an ideal activity for learning centers. Note: If small tubs are not available, use moistened wipes to scrub the animals.

STORYBOARD

Mrs. Wishy-Washy Cleans Up!

Supplies Needed

Ellison die-cut animals—cow, pig #2, duck—one each

Ellison die-cut bathtub or small plastic container to use as a bathtub, one

Crayon, brown, one

Tape or self-adhesive material to attach the items to the storyboard

Directions

Color one side of each animal with the brown crayon, making them look dirty. When presenting the storyboard activity pass out the sand blocks and ask the children to help you make the scrubbing sound by rubbing their sand blocks together. When adding the dirty animal to the tub, pretend to scrub, then turn the animal over and make him appear clean. Display the clean animal on the board. Continue the chant with each animal:

Mrs. Wishy-Washy she was lookin' to scrub,
Made her dirty cow jump in the tub!
Wishy-washy, wishy-washy, cow's in the tub,
Wishy-washy, wishy-washy, scrub-a-dub dub!
Mrs. Wishy-Washy she was lookin' to scrub,
Made her dirty pig jump in the tub!
Wishy-washy, wishy-washy, pig's in the tub,
Wishy-washy, wishy-washy, scrub-a-dub dub!
Mrs. Wishy-Washy she was lookin' to scrub,
Made her dirty duck jump in the tub!

Wishy-washy, wishy-washy, duck's in the tub,
Wishy-washy, wishy-washy, scrub-a-dub dub!

MAKE AND TAKE

Mrs. Wishy-Washy Goes Home

Supplies Needed per Child

Ellison die-cut farm animals—cow, pig #2, and duck—one each

Ellison die-cut bathtub

Glue stick

Construction paper, 9" × 12" in size, light colors

Crayons, brown and other assorted crayons

Directions

Have each child draw a picture of Mrs. Wishy-Washy on their sheet of paper. To make the farm animals appear dirty, use the brown crayon to color one side of each animal. Glue the Ellison die-cut bathtub onto the paper next to Mrs. Wishy-Washy, leaving the top of the tub open to form a pocket. Children can take home and retell the story of Mrs. Wishy-Washy, by lifting the animal in and out of the bathtub and turning them over.

LESSON 14

❦

CROCODILES AND MONKEYS

CURRICULUM TOPICS

Crocodiles, Wild Animals, Monkeys

FEATURED BOOK

Brown, Jo. 2002. *Where's My Mommy?* Wilton, CT: Tiger Tales.

SUMMARY

Little crocodile hatches from an egg and goes searching for his mother. Ages 2–7

ACTIVITY

Pass out the sand blocks. Explain to the children the only word Little Crocodile knows is "snap." Every time he opens his jaws, it is the only word that comes out. Show them how to clap their blocks together and say "snap." Begin the story. Each time the story reads, "Little Crocodile tried, but all that came out of his mouth was . . . ," wait for the children to chime in with their blocks and say "SNAP!" At the very end, Little Crocodile finally finds the other crocodiles and his mother. On the last page, let the children clap their blocks together each time you point to the word "SNAP!"

FEATURED BOOK

Christelow, Eileen. 1991. *Five Little Monkeys Sitting in a Tree.* New York: Clarion Books.

SUMMARY

Five little monkeys go to the river for a picnic and get into mischief teasing Mr. Crocodile. This counting book is an adaptation of the ever popular finger play and rhyme. Whether you tell this story with puppets, a book storyboard or just from memory as a finger play, it is always a favorite. Ages 2–7

FEATURED BOOK

Jorgensen, Gail. 1989. *Crocodile Beat.* New York: Bradbury Press.

SUMMARY

Mean crocodile is taking a nap in the river so all the animals come out to play. Watch out animals, mean croc is about to wake up! This book is so rhythmic and inviting, it will be a favorite for all time. Every page begs the children to act out the drama in the story. Encourage them to stomp like elephants, chatter like monkeys, and fly like the birds that swoop down to the river. Ages 3–6

ACTIVITY

Pass out the sand blocks. Without giving away the story, show the children the page from the book that says "SNAP!" Talk about how there are not any pictures on the page, but the author is still trying to show us something by using big letters and an exclamation point. Instruct the children to listen and be ready because when they see this page they are going to clap their sand blocks together to make that big "SNAP!" sound. As the leader, be prepared for the group to be a little off the first time. When this happens, simply say, "That was so much fun, let's try that again!" Back up one page, reread it with just as much enthusiasm, cue them up, and turn the page. They will love the chance to participate again. Begin reading the story in a hushed and cautious tone, encouraging the children to imitate the sleeping crocodile. Then, in a lively romp, read about all the animals playing in the river. Take your time as you read, let them fully participate. Let the energy escalate, until the line, " 'Ahhhh!' says croc." Everything should come to a screeching halt as you return to your hushed and cautious tone. If the children are standing up, motion for them to sit back down. Make calming them down a part of the story. You can even whisper something to them like, "Sit down little animals!" Pause for a moment, as if you are listening for danger. When you again have their attention captivated, finish the story.

ADDITIONAL BOOKS TO SHARE

Anholt, Catherine, and Laurence Anholt. 1997. *A Kiss Like This.* New York: Barron's. Little Lion Cub gets lots of kisses from all the animals in the jungle, but Big Golden Lion comes to the rescue when Mean Green Hungry Crocodile tries to give Little Cub a sinister "snippy, snappy crocodile kiss." We recommend this story because it is a favorite in our mommy and me-style classes for toddlers. As you read the story, encourage the caregivers in the group to play along with their own little one. When Little Cub gets a kiss behind his ears, so does baby. When Little Cub gets a kiss on his nose and warm, fat tummy, so does baby. Ages 2–4

Charles, Faustin. 1999. *The Selfish Crocodile.* Waukesha, WI: Little Tiger Press. Crocodile learns a lesson in sharing when a small mouse comes to his aid. Ages 3–7

Chen, Chih-Yuan. 2003. *Guji Guji.* La Jolla, CA: Kane/Miller. This is a story of acceptance and loyalty. A stray crocodile egg rolls, unnoticed, into the nest of a Mother Duck. When the eggs begin to hatch, the baby crocodile is readily accepted into her flock. Ages 3–7

Martin Larranaga, Ana. 1999. *The Big Wide-Mouthed Frog.* Cambridge, MA: Candlewick Press. Wide-mouthed frog asks all the creatures he meets what they like to eat. When he comes up on a crocodile he finds out it is sometimes better to keep your wide mouth shut. Stretch your mouth as wide as you can when you read the speaking parts of the wide-mouthed frog. You may feel ridiculous, but this is sure to tickle the funny bone of your audience. When the frog tries to conceal his identity to the wide-mouthed, frog-eating crocodile, say the lines with your lips held tightly together. Expect uproarious laughter from this book. Ages 2–7

Paye, Won-Ldy, and Margaret H. Lippert. 2003. *Mrs. Chicken and the Hungry Crocodile.* New York: Henry Holt. Clever Mrs. Chicken saves herself from being Crocodile's dinner by convincing Crocodile they are sisters. See if she can convince your audience with this surprising tale. Ages 3–7

Peters, Andrew. 2003. *Monkey's Clever Tale.* Auburn, ME: Child's Play. Ameerah Monkey tricks Crocodile into helping her cross the river in exchange for a big pot of Monkey Tail Soup. This story is slightly longer in length than most of the books we recommend, but the vivid pictures and suspenseful plot are sure to capture the attention of kindergarten and early grade-school children. Ages 4–8

Sierra, Judy. 2004. *What Time Is It, Mr. Crocodile?* New York: Harcourt. The five little monkeys and the mean, hungry crocodile finally call a truce in this humorous account of their age old battle of wits. There are many opportunities for audience participation infused in the structure of this text. One simple way to involve children in the story is to encourage them to chime in on the repeating line, "What time is it, Mr. Crocodile?" Our favorite method  is to use a toy or actual clock with movable hands as a prop for this story. Ellison die-cuts offer a clock with moveable hands. On each turn of the page, the clock turns forward one hour. Each time you change the time on the clock to correlate with the story, hold the prop up to cue the children to ask, "What time is it, Mr. Crocodile?" Then, have your audience call out what time it is indeed. When we have additional staff to assist, we use a crocodile puppet that pops his head up to answer the children's question. This really impresses the children. If you have access to them, a final game we play with this book uses the bells. Ring your bell before you turn the appropriate page, and let the children ring with you, to play the part of an alarm clock. When you put your bell down, ask the children to call out the repeating line. This book is meant to be acted out. Ages 4–8

Willis, Jeanne. 2000. *The Boy Who Lost His Belly Button.* New York: DK Publishing. This story naturally appeals to children; they just can't resist the hilarity of the subject matter-belly buttons! Can you lose your belly button? The young boy in this story did; and his journey to retrieve it led him through the jungle and right up to a sneering crocodile. Would you do what he did next? Ages 3–7

MUSIC AND MOVEMENT WITH SAND BLOCKS

Sing Along: "Do You Wanna Be a Crocodile?"

Sung to the Tune: "Boom, Boom Ain't It Great to be Crazy!"

SNAP! SNAP! Do you wanna be a crocodile?
SNAP! SNAP! Do you wanna be a crocodile?

Long and lean and ALL KINDS OF MEAN!
SNAP! SNAP! Do you wanna be a crocodile?
SNAP! SNAP! Do you wanna be a crocodile?
SNAP! SNAP! Do you wanna be a crocodile?
Bumpy and brown with a BIG HUNGRY FROWN!
SNAP! SNAP! Do you wanna be a crocodile?
SNAP! SNAP! Do you wanna be a crocodile?
He'll start a BIG fight, just to grab a little BITE!
SNAP! SNAP! Do you wanna be a crocodile?
SNAP! SNAP! Do you wanna be a crocodile?
SNAP! SNAP! Do you wanna be a crocodile?
I think I'll just be me, happy as can be!
SNAP! SNAP! I DON'T WANNA BE A CROCODILE!
I just wanna wear my GREAT—BIG SMILE!

Directions

Pass out the sand blocks and play song #17 from the accompanying *The Sound of Storytime* CD. Children can use the sand blocks to "snap" together, or they can simply put their palms together with their fingers stretched out to make the snap of the crocodile. Make sure you use a strong, growly voice when singing the phrase "ALL KINDS OF MEAN," and again with the words "BIG HUNGRY FROWN." Use the same voice during the next verse with the words "BIG" and "BITE!" This song is so easy to learn that even the youngest child in storytime will love it!

ADDITIONAL SONGS TO SHARE

Feldman, Jean R. *Dr. Jean & Friends.* Progressive Music, 1998. Compact Disk. DJ-DO2. Play song #2, "Monkeys and the Alligator." This is the perfect version of this traditional song to sing along with the children. It is slow enough the children can sing and do the movement gestures as well. Sing along and count down with the children from "five little monkeys swinging from the tree teasing Mr. Alligator," to a humorous surprise ending that the children are sure to love.

STORYBOARD

Crocodile Pile

Supplies Needed

Ellison die-cut crocodiles, one in each color—yellow, red, blue, green, white, purple, and brown—seven

Tape or self-adhesive material to attach the crocodiles onto the storyboard

Directions

Stack seven crocodiles in assorted colors on the storyboard. Begin the chant and remove a crocodile, one at a time, until every crocodile is removed from the stack. When you are finished, recount to see how many crocodiles were in the pile. Go back through the crocodiles, this time pointing to one at a time, while asking the children to tell you the colors of the crocodiles.

Seven lazy crocodiles stacked in a pile. Let's call one down to play for a while!
Yellow crocodile on top of the pile, come on down and play for a while!
Six lazy crocodiles stacked in a pile. Let's call one down to play for a while!
Red crocodile on top of the pile, come on down and play for a while!
Five lazy crocodiles stacked in a pile. Let's call one down to play for a while!
Blue crocodile on top of the pile, come on down and play for a while!
Four lazy crocodiles stacked in a pile. Let's call one down to play for a while!
Green crocodile on top of the pile, come on down and play for a while!
Three lazy crocodiles stacked in a pile. Let's call one down to play for a while!
White crocodile on top of the pile, come on down and play for a while!
Two lazy crocodiles stacked in a pile. Let's call one down to play for a while!
Purple crocodile on top of the pile, come on down and play for a while!
One lazy crocodile left in the pile. Let's call him down to play for a while!

Brown crocodile on top of the pile, come on down and play for a while!
Now there's no more crocodiles left on the pile!

MAKE AND TAKE

Supplies Needed per Child

Construction paper, 9" × 12" in size, assorted colors, one

Ellison die-cut crocodiles, one in each color—yellow, red, blue, green, white, purple, and brown—seven total

Glue stick

Washable markers or crayons

Directions

Reinforce the storyboard activity by letting the children create a crocodile pile craft. Have them turn their paper vertically, and stack and glue one crocodile on top of another, until all seven crocs are glued in place. If the children are old enough to write, they can print the colors of each crocodile onto its body and number them. This is a very simple craft that each child should be able to complete by themselves.

MAKE AND TAKE 2

Monkey's Teasing Crocodile Picture

Supplies Needed per Child

Construction paper, 12" × 18" in size, one blue sheet and one tan sheet

Construction paper, 12" × 18" in size, tan, one sheet torn into three horizontal strips (One sheet is enough for three children)

Construction paper, 9" × 12" in size, brown, or large brown sack, one

Ellison die-cut monkey(s) #2, five

Ellison die-cut crocodile, one

Glue stick

Washable markers or crayons

Directions

Tear the tan 12" × 18" sheets of construction paper, horizontally, into three strips. Glue one piece of the tan construction paper horizontally onto the bottom of the blue sheet of paper. The tan-colored strip is to resemble sand on the bottom of the picture. Next, tear the brown construction paper or brown paper sack to resemble a tree and glue it onto the blue sheet. Glue all five monkeys in the branches of the tree and glue the crocodile onto the sand. The children can take their creation home and recite the _Five Little Monkeys_ chant to their families.

LESSON 15

✤

DOGS

CURRICULUM TOPICS

Dogs, Fleas

FEATURED BOOK

Bedford, David. 2001. *Shaggy Dog and the Terrible Itch*. New York: Barron's.

SUMMARY

Shaggy Dog has a terrible itch. She asks different friends to scratch her back, but every time, the itch comes back! Ages 3–7

ACTIVITY

Pass out the sand blocks. Each time the story reads, "the itch came back," allow time for the children to rub their sand blocks together symbolizing the sound of Shaggy Dog's incessant scratching.

FEATURED BOOK

Doyle, Malachy. 2001. *Sleepy Pendoodle*. Cambridge, MA: Candlewick Press.

SUMMARY

A young girl finds a newborn puppy abandoned in an alley. She nurses it to health but wonders when it will open its eyes. An uncle teaches her a little rhyme to help her remember how to care for the puppy. On her way home from her uncle's, the little girl tries to remember the rhyme he taught her. Each time she tries to recite the rhyme to the puppy, she forgets the words. The little girl replaces the lines she does not remember with funny nonsense words. The illustrations in this book are absolutely adorable. The pictures are bright and vivid and can easily be seen by a large group. Ages 3–7

ACTIVITY

Pass out the sand blocks. Each time the text says to "scrubby-scrub your hands," participants rub their sand blocks together.

FEATURED BOOK

Inches, Alison. 2003. *The Big Itch*. New York: Scholastic.

SUMMARY

Clifford has a big itch and can't stop scratching. Ages 3–7

ACTIVITY

Pass out the sand blocks. Every time the story reads, "Clifford scratched against . . . ,"give the children time to rub their sand blocks together to make the sound of Clifford's insatiable scratching.

ADDITIONAL BOOKS TO SHARE

Bailey, Linda. 2003. *Stanley's Party*. New York: Kids Can Press. Have you ever wondered what your dog is up to while you're out of the house? Maybe he has been off to one of Stanley's parties! Find out about the secrets dogs keep, and the ornery things they do while their owners are away. Ages 4–8

Casanova, Mary. 2003. *One-Dog Canoe.* New York: Melanie Kraoupa Books. This Building Block Nominee has our vote too. The playful rhyme and expressive pictures allude to impending comic calamity. Invite your listeners along for the ride by giving them the collective part of the repeating line, "Can I come too?" As you read along, remember to pause in the appropriate places, and cue your audience to say their line. For instance, when the story reads, "Wolf peered from the pines," turn to your audience and ask, "What do you suppose *she* said?" or "What do you suppose *he* wanted?" The children then answer with, "Can I come too?" Another fun way to tell this story is to assign the parts of the dog, beaver, loon, wolf, bear, moose, and frog to the children. Before the program, attach Ellison die-cuts that represent each character onto small craft sticks to make puppets. (Ellison die-cuts-Beagle, Beaver, Duck, Wolf #1, Bear #1, Moose, Frog #2) Pass out the puppets. Give individual children the opportunity to help tell the story by saying the repeating line when it is their assigned character's turn to get in the boat. Ages 3–7

Dunbar, Polly. 2004. *Dog Blue.* Cambridge, MA: Candlewick Press. Bertie's favorite color is blue, and what he wants most of all is a pet blue dog. Bertie spends his days playing with his imaginary blue dog. When a real black and white puppy comes into his life, it seems Bertie's dream has come true except the dog is not blue. Read this story to find out what Bertie's clever solution is. Ages 3–7

Graham, Bob. 2001. *"Let's Get a Pup!" said Kate.* Cambridge, MA: Candlewick Press. A family decides to get a pet puppy from the animal shelter. While visiting the shelter they choose a puppy but have a hard time leaving behind a lonely, older dog. Back at home the family falls in love with their new puppy, but they just can't seem to forget the lonely dog from the shelter. This touching story is complete with hip characters, great pictures, and a happy ending. Ages 3–7

LaRochelle, David. 2004. *The Best Pet of All.* New York: Dutton Children's Books. When his mother refuses to allow him a pet dog, the boy asks if he can have a dragon. You might think his mother would certainly not allow a dragon if she would not allow a dog but surprisingly, mother agrees to the dragon. A modern fairy tale embellished with irresistibly, imaginative illustrations. Any child who has ever wished for a pet will delight in this amusing account of a boy's quest for a dog. Ages 3–7

Yang, James. 2004. *Joey and Jet.* New York: Atheneum Books for Young Readers. As a boy and his dog play fetch, the author subtly weaves the introduction of prepositions and positional words into their adventures. After reading this story, demonstrate and review positional words. As in the story, One-Dog Canoe, use the storyboard. Place a picture of a dog and a ball on the board. (Ellison die-cuts—beagle, small baseball) Encourage the children to approach the storyboard one at a time. Each child takes a turn by choosing how they want to move the ball in relationship to the dog and demonstrating the action on the board. Examples might be: around, behind, below, above, on, or over the dog. Direct the children observing from the group to call out what positional word is being demonstrated. Ages 3–7

Ziefert, Harriet. 1998. *I Swapped My Dog.* Boston: Houghton Mifflin. A fickle farmer makes a series of trades, bartering for a better pet. Disillusioned with each exchange, he ends up making one final swap for the dog he had in the beginning of the story. Reunited with his long lost pal, the story wraps up in a nice happy ending. Entertaining and merry, this quick read aloud is adorned with crisp illustrations. Use the storyboard to make this story interactive. Prepare storyboard pieces of the nine animals mentioned in the story, using Ellison die-cuts. Pass out the eight animals, a horse #1, donkey, goat, sheep, cow, pig #2, hen, and cat #3 made from paper or felt. Place the picture of the dog on the board. As you read the story, have the children play along by swapping the animal on the board for the animal in their hand. Ages 3–7

MUSIC AND MOVEMENT WITH SAND BLOCKS

Sing Along: "Shaggy Dog"

Sung to the Tune: "Old MacDonald Had a Farm"

Shaggy dog she had an itch and didn't know what to do!
All day long she yelped and howled and rolled all over too.
With a scritch scratch here, and a scritch scratch there,
Here a scritch there a scratch, everywhere a scritch scratch!
Shaggy dog she had an itch and didn't know what to do!
Farmer Brown came home that night but didn't know what to do!
He called his wife to help him out, so she brought home shampoo.
With a scrub-a-dub here, and a scrub-a-dub there,
Here a scrub there a scrub, doggy's in the bathtub!
Farmer Brown scrubbed Shaggy dog, now guess who's itching too?

Directions

Play song #18 from the accompanying *The Sound of Storytime* CD. Each time Shaggy dog "scritch scratches," or Farmer Brown "scrub-a-dubs," ask the children to join in by rubbing their sand blocks together. Begin by playing the song on the CD and demonstrating the instrument part as the children watch and listen. Next, pass out the instruments, repeat the song, and encourage the children to play along. This song is very easy to learn, and the children really enjoy it.

ADDITIONAL SONGS TO SHARE

Atkinson, Lisa. *The Elephant in Aisle Four and Other Whimsical Animal Songs.* 2000. Compact Disk. GW1061. Play song #3, *Puppy Kisses,* when children are entering storytime or during craft time.

JUST FOR FUN

Dog Bone Stack

Supplies Needed

Dog treats shaped like bones, one per child

Directions

Give each child a dog bone and ask them to form a single line. Have the children take turns stacking each bone on top of the other until it topples over. When it topples over, repeat the activity until each child has had a couple of turns. At the end of the activity allow the children that have dogs at home, or have friends and relatives with dogs, to take some treats to share with their pet.

STORYBOARD

Shaggy Dog's Day Out

Supplies Needed

Ellison die-cuts—mutt, cow, small butterfly, frog #2, horse #1, colt, hen, duck, pig #2—one of each

Ellison die-cut small bone, two identical

Tape or self-adhesive material to attach items onto the storyboard

Directions

Read through the entire story paying special attention to the ending and the lines each animal says. Practice trying to change your voice a bit when the animals talk back to Shaggy, during the story and again at the end of the story. This makes the presentation more exciting and interesting for the very young and sometimes restless listeners. The story takes you on a walk with Shaggy dog. The object of the story is Shaggy loses her favorite bone and has to return to find it. As you read the following story to the children add the animals onto the storyboard as they are introduced. Have the additional dog bone taped to the back of one of the animals so none of the children are aware. As Shaggy heads home, gently slip the bone out of her mouth and set it aside, trying not to draw any attention. As you direct the children to help you find Shaggy's lost bone, suggest a few of the animals that don't have the bone, making the "hunt" last longer. Lift each animal until the bone appears.

One warm sunny day, Shaggy dog decided to go for a walk. She always carried her favorite bone. She loved this bone so much, and took it everywhere she went. She even slept with it! As Shaggy was on her walk, she saw a cow having a lunch of green grass in the field. Shaggy walked a little farther and saw a bright butterfly flying in the air. Shaggy followed the butterfly a little while, and thought of what it would be like to have wings and fly. The butterfly flew over a pond, and so Shaggy stopped at the pond edge, and watched a green frog hop in and out of the water as if he was playing some kind of game all alone. The longer Shaggy watched the frog, the sleepier she got. Shaggy decided this might be a nice place to lay down and take a little nap. So Shaggy napped, and napped, and napped! When Shaggy woke up, she decided she had better head home before her family started getting worried. On the way home, she saw a horse and her little colt in the pasture. She stopped and watched them play together for a while. Then she remembered she was supposed to be heading back home. She kept walking and only stopped a few more times. She stopped once to watch a duck, another time to greet a chicken, and again to say hello to a pig. Shaggy noticed the sun wasn't as bright as it had been, and she knew that could only mean one thing. Now, it was really time to get home! Shaggy started running toward home, and then all of the sudden she realized she didn't have her bone anymore! Where was the bone? That was Shaggy's favorite bone! She could never go home without her favorite bone! There was only one thing Shaggy could do, she had to go back and find it!

Shaggy then stops and asks each animal described above (*leader and children will chant all the following lines together*)

> "Have you seen my bone?"

Each animal will say:

> "A bone, a bone, an old dog bone? Whatever would I do with a bone!"

It is better to chant the animal's reply each time. Continue asking:

> "Have you seen my bone?"

And answering:

> "A bone, a bone, an old dog bone? Whatever would I do with a bone!"

The story ends when you find the bone behind one of the animals. The children will love chanting back and forth and pretending to be all these animals. Most of all, they love the element of surprise!

STORYBOARD 2

Supplies Needed

Tallman, Susie. *Children's Songs*. Rock Me Baby Records, 2004. Compact Disk. RMBR 91005-2.

Play song #4, "BINGO," to become familiar with this traditional tune. Pass out the sand blocks. Sing the song either a cappella or with the CD. As you sing through the five verses, substitute a letter with a clap. Children clap sand blocks together. When all the letters are gone, children clap through the entire name during the last verse of the song. This easy exercise reinforces letter recognition.

MAKE AND TAKE

Textured Dogs

Supplies Needed

Ellison die-cut mutts or beagles, cut out of index paper stock, two each

Sand, five to eight cups

Plastic container with lid, or large #3 coffee can with lid

Glue, liquid type

Foam paintbrushes, small

Directions

Using small plastic containers or coffee cans, add about one cup of sand per container. Allow the children to choose one or two Ellison die-cut dogs. Ask them to apply glue to both sides of their dogs. They will need to use the foam paintbrush to coat both sides evenly. With assistance, have the child drop their paper dog, one at a time, into the container with sand. After tightly securing the lid onto the container, let the child shake the container. Remove the sand-coated paper dog from the container and allow it to dry a few minutes. If time allows, it is easier to do one side at a time. This allows one side to dry before painting the other side. This would be a good "make and take" activity to make half at the beginning of storytime and half at the end. The children will love feeling the texture of the itchy scratchy dogs. These textured dogs will help them remember the story so they can share with others.

LESSON 16

✦

FLIES AND FROGS

CURRICULUM TOPICS

Flies, Frogs

FEATURED BOOK

Jorgensen, Gail. 1995. *Gotcha!* New York: Scholastic.

SUMMARY

A beastly fly disrupts Bertha Bear's birthday celebration. Ages 3–7

ACTIVITY

Introduce the children to the cover of the book. Discuss where you find the author, illustrator, and title. Encourage the group to sound out the title of the story. Discuss the exclamation point at the end of the word. Explain that it indicates emphasis. Ask the children to guess what the bear is doing in the picture on the front page. Pass out the sand blocks. Explain that each time you come to the title word "GOTCHA!" they can clap their blocks together for emphasis, just like the exclamation point!

FEATURED BOOK

Lillegard, Dee. 1994. *Frog's Lunch.* New York: Scholastic.

SUMMARY

Frog sits on a lily pad patiently waiting for his lunch. Ages 2–7

ACTIVITY

After sharing this short story with your group, pass out the sand blocks. Reread the story. This time, let the participants clap their blocks together on the word "snap."

FEATURED BOOK

Sloat, Teri. 2001. *The Thing That Bothered Farmer Brown.* New York: Orchard Books.

SUMMARY

Farmer Brown and his farm animals are ready for a good night's sleep when they are rudely interrupted by a pesky mosquito. Not only does the mosquito interrupt the household, but he also causes all kinds of trouble in the barnyard. This is a hilarious story that the children are sure to enjoy. Ages 3–7

ACTIVITY

Pass out the sand blocks. Every time Farmer Brown swats at the mosquito, children clap their sand blocks together.

ADDITIONAL BOOKS TO SHARE

Adams, Pam. 2000. *There Was an Old Lady Who Swallowed a Fly.* Auburn, ME: Child's Play. There are numerous versions of this time-honored favorite. Any version can be read or sung; choose the style you like best. We recommend this particular adaptation because it comes in a teacher's big book edition and displays bright, vivid pictures. Children go crazy for this story and do not mind a bit when the main character dies in the end. If dark humor makes you or the mothers who attend your sessions uneasy, change the last rhyme of the story from "she died, of course" to "I'm kidding, of course!" Ages 4–8

Arnold, Tedd. 1993. *Green Wilma.* New York: Dial Books for Young Readers. Wilma wakes up one morning and discovers she has turned green! To make matters worse, she begins croaking and craving flies. Read this book to find out what happens next, when Wilma's parents send her off to school that day. Tedd Arnold is also the author of the ever-popular series of books *Parts, More Parts* and *Even More Parts.* Ages 3–7

Aylesworth, Jim. 1992. *Old Black Fly.* New York: Henry Holt. Whether you read, chant, or sing this story, children are sure to join in the chorus, "Shoo fly! Shoo fly! Shooo," and delight in the wild and frenzied pursuit of a pesky fly. The illustrator, Steven Gammell, ingeniously uses spattered and colorful paint to portray the tracks a fly makes as he buzzes through this rhyming, alphabet book. Extend this story through art by giving the children the opportunity to further explore Gammell's techniques. Children will love creating their own salad spinner art project or squirt bottle painting in the same fashion as Gammell's inspiring pictures. Ages 3–7

Brown, Ruth. 1985. *The Big Sneeze.* New York: Mulberry Books. While the farmer naps on a haystack, a little black fly lands on his nose. The fly tickles the farmer's nose, stirring up an enormous sneeze that starts a chain of events that create mayhem all over the farm. Ages 2–7

Cohen, Caron Lee. 1996. *Where's the Fly?* New York: Greenwillow Books. The pictures in this book illustrate the concept of spatial relationships by proposing increasingly distance viewpoints. The story begins from the close-up perspective of a tiny fly on a dog's nose and ends with a view from outer space. The text leads the listener through the series, encouraging them to consider each relationship and, in the process, conjure up a few spatially related ideas of their own. The twist in the story is the impact it makes in the end, when everything comes full circle. This book begs the children to interact, discuss, and grow. Ages 2–7

Emmett, Jonathan. 2003. *Through the Heart of the Jungle.* Wilton, CT: Tiger Tales. A pesky fly buzzes through the jungle causing quite a commotion. This book is written much in the same style and rhythm as the traditional story, *This Is the House That Jack Built.* Involve your audience in the telling of the story by adding an action for each animal introduced in the tale. The story progressively introduces a new animal with each turn of the page. As your list of animals gets longer, so does the series of actions you repeat. Make the elephant's trunk by extending your arm from your nose. Enact the snake by weaving your hand in front of your body. Be sure to then pause at the comma and say, "hiss!" Create the bird with the bright orange beak by tapping your thumb and fore fingers together, the American Sign Language for bird. Achieve the monkey by curling your arms up at your sides. Be sure to pause at the comma, and let the kids add the sound effects—OHH! OHH! AAAH! AAAH! Make the bear's claws by holding your hands like claws by your face. Create the crocodile by holding your arms together at the elbows and clapping them together. Pause at the comma to say "SNAP!" Form the toad with the googly eyes by putting your hands to your face like you are holding binoculars. When the text says, "that gulped down the spider," pause at the comma to make a big gulping sound. Then, finally, end the verse with the sound "BUZZ!" Everyone is sure to have a rollicking good time. Ages 3–7

Oppenheim, Joanne. 1986. *You Can't Catch Me!* Boston: Houghton Mifflin. The story of a mischievous fly that taunts every creature it meets. Told in irresistible verse, this story has all of the same fun elements as the famous story of the gingerbread man. Even better, you don't have to wait for the holidays to read it! Complete with a taunting repeating line, "No matter how hard you try, try, try, you can't catch me!" and a surprise ending. Encourage your listeners to say with you the part of the fly as you read. Another option for incorporating participation is to pass out storyboard pictures that represent the eight animals fly encounters in the story and the numbers one through eight on index cards. (Ellison die-cuts- cow, goat, horse #1, fox, bear #1, pig #2, lamb #1, turtle #1B) Pause each time you introduce a new character, and allow time for students to bring their corresponding picture to the board. Encourage students to place their picture anywhere on the board. After reading the story, test their memory by collectively deciding what order the animals appeared in the tale. (If the children have already put the animals on the board in the order they appear, simply scramble them up.) Ask the child holding the number one to place his or her piece on the board, and begin the number line from left to right. Decide, as a group, which animal was the first animal to be encountered by the fly. Move the picture of the animal to correspond with the designated number. Next, call for the child holding the second number to place his or her piece on the board. Again, decide what animal was the second animal to be encountered by the fly. Continue with this process until all eight animals have been assigned a number. Flip through the book and check to see if you are right! Ages 3–7

Peters, Lisa Westberg. 1994. *When the Fly Flew In.* New York: Dial Books for Young Readers. Who likes to clean their room? How neat would it be if, while you were out, your pets picked up your messy toys and dirty socks? That is just what happens when a fly flew into this child's room, unaware. As a dog, cat, hamster, and parakeet try to snare a misguided fly, they inadvertently polish the floor and dust the cobwebs from the room. Ages 3–7

Trapani, Iza. 2000. *Shoo Fly!* Watertown, MA: Whispering Coyote. An irritating and persistent fly is determined to annoy a little mouse. Anyone who has encountered such a pest, whether it be an insect or the likes of a little brother or sister, can relate to the exhausting efforts of this forlorn mouse. Read or sing the verses. A melody is provided in the back of the book. Ages 3–7

MUSIC AND MOVEMENT WITH SAND BLOCKS

Sing Along: "Ole Pesky Fly"

Sung to the Tune: "Hot Time in the Old Town Tonight"

Ole pesky fly, you best leave me alone!
I'm tired of chasing you around my home!
I'm warning you, the next time I won't miss!
Are you ready to hear a sound like this? SWAT! SWAT! SWAT!
Ole pesky fly, now did you hear that sound?
I promise you, I'm not just kidding 'round!
Keep on a buzzing—round and round my ear,
and I mean it, a SWATTING is near! SWAT! SWAT! SWAT!
Ole pesky fly, why do you tease me so?
Just leave me alone, and I will let you go!
No more chasing or swatting in the air.
Wait a minute—What's that over there! SWAT! SWAT! SWAT! GOTCHA!

Directions

Pass out the sand blocks and play song #18 from the accompanying *The Sound of Storytime* CD. Instead of the traditional sound of the sand blocks rubbing together, another successful way to use the sand blocks is to hit them together making a loud, cracking sound. When singing this song, every time the "SWAT! SWAT! SWAT!" is sung, encourage the children to hit their sand blocks together to make the swatting sound. You may practice this a few times before you begin the song. At the end of the song after the three swats are made, have the children shout out "GOTCHA!"

MOVEMENT CHANT

Ole Pesky Fly Returns

Ole pesky fly was happy and free, until he started bothering me.
He buzzed around my head, and he buzzed around my toes!
He buzzed around my knees, but he didn't get my NOSE!

Directions

Have each child stand and use their pointer finger in a free flying motion as if their finger was a fly. As you repeat the chant, let the children use their free flying finger to buzz around and touch their head, toes, and knees. Just before you get to the nose, pause and allow the children to make a giant clap in the air directly in front of their noses as if they were catching the pesky ole fly.

ADDITIONAL SONGS TO SHARE

Cedarmont Kids Singers. *Toddler Action Songs*. October Sound and Mattinee Studio, 2002. Compact Disk. 84418-0137-2. Play song #5, "Baby Bumblebee." Lead the children through the hand gestures of this familiar tune.

Reid-Naiman, Kathy. *Tickles and Tunes*. Merriweather Records, 1997. Compact Disk. M9701.

Play song #29, "Criss Cross Applesauce." Every child needs an adult to play along. Follow the directions of each word in this chant:

Criss-cross, *(Make an X on child's back)*
Applesauce, *(Tap each shoulder)*
Spiders crawling up your back, *(Crawl fingers up back)*
Crawling here, *(Tickle one shoulder)*
Crawling there, *(Tickle other shoulder)*
Spiders crawling through your hair, *(Tickle hair)*
Cool breeze, *(Blow on neck)*
Tight squeeze, *(Give a hug)*
And now you've got the shivers! *(Tickle all over)*

Peter, Paul, and Mary. *Peter, Paul & Mommy, too*. Warner Brothers, 1993. Compact Disk. 9 45216-2. Play song #7, "I Know an Old Lady Who Swallowed a Fly," and host a musical puppet show. Set up a puppet stage and have two main puppet characters lead the song. When the song mentions the different animals she swallows, have those animals pop up and look around, or do something silly and hide back away. The song mentions a fly, spider, bird, cat, dog, goat, cow, and a horse, but you do not need to have every character to make this work. If you have a "lady" puppet, put a scarf over her head to make her look old. Bring the lady puppet back out at the end, and take a bow.

JUST FOR FUN

Fly Flew Fast, Faster, Fastest Tongue Twister

Freddy Fly flew fast from France.
Freddy Fly flew faster from France.
Freddy Fly flew fastest from France.

Directions

Have the children start out very slowly repeating this tongue twister. Each time you repeat the verses, go a little faster progressing to a ridiculous fury of F's. The children really have fun trying to increase their speed. You can also have the children pretend they are flying and let them fly fast, faster, and fastest. Pretend flying works very well with small groups. With larger groups, children tend to be a little too rambunctious for the movement portion of the activity.

STORYBOARD

Granny's Flying Pies

Supplies Needed

Ellison die-cut pies, five
Ellison die-cut fly (optional)
Straw (optional)
Tape or self-adhesive material to attach the pies onto the storyboard

Directions

Attach the Ellison die-cut fly to the end of the straw with tape. This can be used as the fly buzzing by each time it is spoken. Pass out the sand blocks and have the children make the buzzing noise by rubbing their sand blocks together, each time you say "a fly flew by . . . ," as you are presenting the storyboard. Start out with five pies attached to the board. As you read the story, remove a pie each time one gets eaten. Read the following story:

Granny baked five pies one day she was too tired to bake anymore.
A fly flew by and ate one pie, then there were four! *(Remove one pie)*

The next day Granny counted four, she was confused as she could be!
A fly flew by and ate one pie, then there were three! *(Remove one pie)*
Now Granny was unhappy, and didn't know what to do.
A fly flew by and ate one pie, then there were two! *(Remove one pie)*
Two pies are all that Granny had left to take to her Grandson.
A fly flew by and ate one pie, then there was one!
"One pie!" Granny said, "Is all I have to take to my Grandson!"
"Forget about that! I baked FIVE pies! Now, I'm going to eat **this** one!" *(Remove last pie)*

MAKE AND TAKE

Thumbprint Flies

Supplies Needed per Child

8½" × 11" sheet of plain paper, one

Stamp pads, black, one or two per craft table

Washable fine-point markers in black, one or two per craft table

Moistened paper towels or wipes for thumbprint clean up

Directions

Let children make several thumbprints on their paper, and then have them add eyes, wings, and legs with their markers. They can draw a picture, or just have lots of unique thumbprint flies buzzing around the paper. Make one ahead of time so you can show an example to the children of how they might look. Feel free to use other colors of ink pads or markers, if you have them available. This makes for some very colorful masterpieces! A book that we have used for great thumbprint ideas is: Emberley, Ed. 1977. *Ed Emberley's Great Thumbprint Drawing Book.* Boston: Little, Brown.

LESSON 17

✤

LICE

CURRICULUM TOPICS
Head Lice, Hair, Bugs, Healthy Habits

FEATURED BOOK
Moss, Miriam. 2001. *Scritch Scratch*. New York: Orchard Books.

SUMMARY
The teacher, of all people, gets head lice. Before long, the whole class is scritch scratching. This story addresses its subject matter with humor and sensitivity. The author weaves factual information into the plot in a way that truly complements rather than detracts from the story. Ages 4–8

ACTIVITY
Pass out the sand blocks. The phrase "scritch scratch" repeats throughout the story. Children rub their sand blocks together twice, each time they hear these words. When the text reads, "Scritch, scratch went Polly," change the wording around to say, "Polly went . . . scritch scratch." Making this slight adjustment cues the children their part is coming, and gives them the opportunity to fully participate.

ADDITIONAL BOOKS TO SHARE
Caffey, Donna. 1998. *Yikes-Lice!* Morton Grove, IL: Albert Whitman. A rhyming read-aloud story pared with the factual information that kids need to know about head lice. Ages 4–8

Cole, Babette. 2003. *The Hairy Book*. London: Random House Children's Books. Children love the gross and outrageous humor in this book. The illustrations show great details without being distracting or busy, and the pictures can be seen from a distance. The kids in your audience will roar with laughter; their mothers will cringe! Ages 4–8

Crabtree, Sally, and Roberta Mathieson. 2001. *My Sister's Hair*. New York: Random House. Big brother wonders what his bald baby sister's hair might be like when it grows in. He tries the wild and crazy hairstyles he concocts on his baby sister's head. Ages 4–8

Hayes, Cheri. 2001. *There's a Louse in My House*. New York: JayJo Books. In fretful and frenzied rhyme, this story tells of one family's account with a louse in their house. A quiz about lice and prevention tips are provided in the back of the book. Ages 4–8

Krosoczka, Jarrett. 2002. *Baghead*. New York: Alfred A. Knopf. Josh wakes up on a Wednesday morning, and decides to wear a bag on his head. He wears it through breakfast, he wears it at soccer, but why? Kids will relate to Josh's predicament when he reveals that he cut his own hair. The pictures and text are in good harmony. The crisp illustrations can be seen from a distance, making this a great read-aloud story. Ages 4–8

Lerner, Harriet, and Susan Goldhor. 2001. *Franny B. Kranny, There's a Bird in Your Hair!* New York: HarperCollins. Despite the opinions of others, Franny loves her wild and curly red hair. Franny is not pleased when her mother insists she go to the beauty shop and have her hair put up for the family reunion. On the way home from the hairdresser, Franny's misfortune turns when, by chance, a little bird lands in her nest of a hairdo. Franny goes to great lengths not to scare the bird away before the family reunion. Much to the horror of her mother and sister, Franny proudly flaunts her new "birdy" hair style for all the relatives. Ages 4–8

Munsch, Robert. 1996. *Stephanie's Ponytail*. New York: Firefly Books. No matter how Stephanie wears her hair, the next day at school, everyone copies her. Desperate to be unique, she finally announces that she is going to shave her head bald! Read this book to find out what surprising twist takes place at school the next day. We have seen this story acted out as a preschool play at one of the daycares in our town. It is a delightful and humorous lesson about dealing with classmates, being an individual, and having self-confidence. Ages 4–8

Ware, Cheryl. 2003. *Roberta Price Has Head Lice!* Beaufort, SC: Rockwell Reading. Roberta, the school bully, takes hats and toys from the other kids. Roberta's orneriness catches up to her when she gets head lice from the items she took from others. The text in this story is well balanced with large, clear pictures, and is very appropriate in length for a good read aloud. Ages 4–8

Wilcox, Leah. 2003. *Falling For Rapunzel.* New York: G. P. Putnam's Sons. This book puts a comic spin on the traditional tale and is sure to conjure lots of giggles and grins. Each time Prince Charming calls for Rapunzel to let down her hair, she repeatedly misunderstands what he is trying to say. Told in unpredictable and clever rhyme, your listeners will never guess what Rapunzel will throw out her tower window next. Bright illustrations compliment straightforward and uncomplicated text. Ages 4–8

MUSIC AND MOVEMENT WITH SAND BLOCKS

Sing Along: "A Hairy Problem"

Sung to the Tune: "La Cucaracha"

I got a problem, a HAIRY problem, and I don't know what to do.
I got a problem, a LOUSY problem, I think I'd rather have the flu!
I scritchy scratchy, and scratchy scritchy, all the day and all the night.
I scritchy scratchy, and scratchy scritchy, I just know this can't be right!
I got a problem, a HAIRY problem, and it's really BUGGING me.
I got a problem, a LOUSY problem, take a look and you will see!
I scritchy scratchy, and scratchy scritchy, all the day and all the night.
I scritchy scratchy, and scratchy scritchy, I just know this can't be right!
I'll fix your problem, your HAIRY problem, this is what you'll need to do.
Follow directions, all the directions, and I'll be back to check on you!
DON'T scritchy scratchy, or scratchy scritchy, not even just a little bit.
DON'T scritchy scratchy, or scratchy scritchy, let's not disturb that little NIT!
Soooo how's your problem? You're HAIRY problem?
They'll be gone, now don't you fret!
So how's your problem? You're LOUSY problem?
Can you tell a difference yet?
NO scritchy scratchy, or scratchy scritchy, no more BUGGING day and night!
NO scritchy scratchy, or scratchy scritchy, I just know that this feels right!

Directions

Pass out the sand blocks and play song #20 from the accompanying *The Sound of Storytime* CD. Throughout the song, ask the children to rub their sand blocks together when they hear the words "scritchy scratchy" and "scratchy scritchy." The chorus is a favorite as it allows the children plenty of opportunity to use their sand blocks. The catchy tune also invites the children to enjoy a little freestyle dancing.

ADDITIONAL SONGS TO SHARE

Scelsa, Greg, and Steve Millang. *Kids in Motion.* Young HeartMusic, 1987. Compact Disk. YM 008–CD. Play song #4, *The Freeze*, and lead the kids to dance along. Freeze in place when the music intermittently stops.

STORYBOARD

If I Were a Bug

Supplies Needed

Ellison die-cut bugs—small ant, beetle, grasshopper, spider—one per child, in a variety of colors

 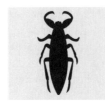  

Washable marker

Tape or adhesive material to attach items onto the storyboard

Directions

In advance, using a marker, print the names of each participating child on a bug. Fold a piece of tape in a circle and place on the back of each bug, then add them onto the storyboard. Before you begin the storyboard activity, share with the children places bugs might live. You may start by reviewing the book *Scritch Scratch* and talk about how some types of bugs actually live on human hair and some, like fleas, like to live on animals. Proceed by sharing some bugs that live in water, trees, soil, or on plants. Feel free to share as little or as much as you have time. Explain some bugs often like to live in our houses, like flies and spiders, while other bugs prefer to live on fruits and vegetables and other types of food. Next, begin a discussion of places you might like to live if you were a bug. You might be silly and say, "If I were a bug, I would live on PIZZA!" The children would join in with silly places they would like to make their homes if they were bugs. Explain to the children you are going to chant a little verse and when their name is called, they may come to the board and remove the bug that has their name on it. Have them share with the class where they would like to live if they were a bug. After the child has shared his or her thoughts, have them stick their bug on their shirt and sit back down. Continue to chant the verse asking the children to join with you, until all of the bugs are removed from the storyboard. This activity allows the children to use their imagination and share their thoughts with others. By having their names on each bug, there is an opportunity for name recognition as well. If some of the children are too timid to speak in front of others, encourage them to whisper their answer to you and then you can help to share their voice. If they do not want to participate in getting up and taking their name from the board, do not force them. Give their name to them after the activity and try to share with them privately where they would like to live if they were a bug. Some children are more reluctant than others to share in a group setting. Hopefully, as time goes by, you will notice a change in the reluctant child.

Chant the following verse changing the child's name each time:

Bugs live here and bugs live there! If [child's name] was a bug, he'd live [where]?

MAKE AND TAKE

This Is My Hair

Supplies Needed per Child

Construction paper, a minimum of 9" × 12" size, either primary red or blue

Paper circles, 5" size or larger in yellow

Washable markers or crayons, black

Construction paper, black scraps

Yarn, assorted colors

Curling ribbon, assorted colors, precurled

Glue stick

Safety scissors

Directions

Begin this art project by reading the following story: Parr, Todd. 1999. *This Is My Hair*. New York: Little, Brown. Write or photocopy the phrase, "This is my hair _____" on the red and blue sheets of paper. Leave a space for the children to insert their own thoughts. First, children choose a red or blue paper to work upon. Second, each child will glue down a yellow circle to make a face. Third, direct the children to glue on yarn and curling ribbon to create their hair. Use the black construction paper and markers to also create hair and facial features as desired. This project really inspires children to concoct some amazing ideas. Be sure to go around the room and write down what they say about their picture. The practice of writing their words down makes a wonderful keepsake and becomes a window into a child's personality. It also creates a concrete connection between the child and meaningful print.

LESSON 18

TEETH

CURRICULUM TOPICS

Teeth, Healthy Habits

FEATURED BOOK

Manning, Mick. 1999. *Wash, Scrub, Brush!* Morton Grove, IL: Albert Whitman.

SUMMARY

All the children in this story have been invited to a party, but first they must get cleaned up. This clever book parallels some outrageous and fascinating facts about the hygiene habits of animals and what children need to know about their own personal hygiene. Ages 3–7

ACTIVITY

Pass out the sand blocks before reading the story. Explain to the children they get to play their instruments three times each time they hear the words "wash, scrub, brush." Encourage the group to rhythmically chant the words and play along with you.

FEATURED BOOK

McGuire, Leslie. 1993. *Brush Your Teeth.* New York: Reader's Digest Children's Books.

SUMMARY

Five toothy animals simply demonstrate how to brush your teeth. Ages 2–7

ACTIVITY

Pass out the sand blocks before the story. Encourage the children to make the sound of the animals brushing their teeth by rubbing the sand blocks together. The children have the opportunity to play their instruments throughout the story every time you read the repeating line "shouldn't you?" Before you begin reading, give the children a chance to try their instruments and practice the sound. Establish the rule that everyone plays together when the leader plays and everyone puts down their instrument when the leader puts down his or her instrument.

FEATURED BOOK

Vrombaut, An. 2003. *Clarabella's Teeth.* New York: Clarion Books.

SUMMARY

Brushing her many crocodile teeth keeps Clarabella so busy that she misses out on all the fun activities her friends are doing. Ultimately her friends solve her problem, and surprise Clarabella with a crocodile-size toothbrush. Ages 3–7

ACTIVITY

Pass out the sand blocks before the story. Talk about the sound the sand blocks make when you rub them together. Give the children a brief opportunity to suggest what things make that sound. During the discussion, suggest the sound of brushing your teeth. Introduce the book and invite the children to make the sound of Clarabella brushing every time the story reads "she brushes."

ADDITIONAL BOOKS TO SHARE

Carson, Jo. 1990. *Pulling My Leg*. New York: Orchard Books. Uncle Tom is on the job when his niece's first tooth becomes loose at a big family gathering. He calls for his pliers, his hammer, and a few other assorted tools. As he teases his young niece, she decides she would be better off bravely extracting the tooth herself. Ages 3–7

Ehrlich, Fred. 2002. *Does a Lion Brush?* Brooklyn, NY: Blue Apple Books. This story uses humor and far-out comparisons to teach children about their teeth and how to take care of them. Ages 2–7

Faulkner, Keith. 2002. *The Mixed-Up Tooth Fairy*. New York: Scholastic. The Tooth Fairy discovers a tooth, but doesn't know to whom it belongs. Look through the die-cut holes in the toothy mouths of the creatures on these pages to help the fairy figure out who's missing the tooth. Each turn of the page sneaks in fun facts about how different animals use their teeth. Ages 3–7

Hobbie, Holly. 2003. *Toot and Puddle: Charming Opal*. New York: Little, Brown. Opal's first loose tooth comes out while spending time away from home at a cousin's house. Will the Tooth Fairy know where to find her tooth if she is not in her own bed? Ages 4–7

Luppens, Michel. 1996. *What Do the Fairies Do with All Those Teeth?* New York: Firefly Books. Have you ever wondered what the Tooth Fairy does with the baby teeth she collects? Does she also visit the animals when they lose their first tooth? The original ideas in this book are sure to spur imaginative discussions at your book talks. Ages 3–7

Lynch, Wayne. 2003. *Whose Teeth Are These?* Milwaukee, WI: Gareth Stevens. The large, color photos of this non-fiction book are attractive and captivating. Wild animals sometimes use their teeth in very different and unusual ways from the way people do. Each page of this book poses a riddle, asking the listeners to guess what animal is being described by how the animal uses its teeth. Ages 4–8

Middleton, Charlotte. 2000. *Tabitha's Terrifically Tough Tooth*. New York: Phyllis Fogelman Books. Tabitha uses every imaginative strategy she can think of to make her loose tooth come out. The illustrations in this book are bright and clear. The text is in good balance with the pictures and appropriate in length for the age group for which it is written. Ages 3–7

Olson, Mary W. 2000. *Nice Try, Tooth Fairy*. New York: Simon & Schuster Books for Young Readers. This clever story is written as a series of notes left under a pillow for the Tooth Fairy. When Emma's grandfather comes for a visit, she wants to show him the tooth she recently lost. The dilemma is that Emma already gave her tooth to the Tooth Fairy. Emma subsequently leaves a note under her pillow asking to borrow the tooth for just one day. The Tooth Fairy returns a tooth, but is sure it isn't Emma's. Over the next few nights, the Tooth Fairy revisits Emma's room, as well as some other surprisingly unexpected guests. Ages 3–7

Sideri, Simona. 2003. *Let's Look at Mouths*. North Mankato, MN: Smart Apple Media. Through colorful illustrations and simple text, this story introduces many different ways that animals and people use their mouths. Ages 3–7

Whybrow, Ian. 2001. *Harry and the Dinosaurs Say "Raahh!"* New York: Random House. The characters from one of our all-time favorite books, *Harry and the Bucketful of Dinosaurs*, are back in this nervous account of a visit to the dentist. These stories will spur on the imagination in any child as if the book itself was a playmate. Ages 3–7

MUSIC AND MOVEMENT WITH SAND BLOCKS

Sing Along: "I Love to Brush!"

Sung to the Tune: "Aba Daba Honeymoon"

I brush, brush, brush, brush, brush, brush, brush in the morning and the night!
I brush, brush, brush, brush, brush, brush, brush in the morning and the night!
I LOVE TO BRUSH!
I brush in the front and I brush in the back,
I brush up and down and after a snack,
I love, love, love to brush, brush, brush my teeeeeeeeth!
I brush, brush, brush, brush, brush, brush, brush in the morning and the night!
I brush, brush, brush, brush, brush, brush, brush in the morning and the night!
I LOVE TO BRUSH!
Healthy teeth are best they say, but I would brush them anyway,
Cause I love, love, love to brush, brush, brush my teeeeeeeeth!
I brush, brush, brush, brush, brush, brush, brush in the morning and the night!
I brush, brush, brush, brush, brush, brush, brush in the morning and the night!

I LOVE TO BRUSH!
Just grab your toothbrush, you'll agree, that brushing's fun for you and me!
Together we will brush, brush, brush our teeeeeeeeth!

Directions

Pass out the sand blocks and play song #21 from the accompanying *The Sound of Storytime* CD. Each time the word "brush" is sung, the children will join in and rub their sand blocks together, making a brushing sound. Lead the children by asking them to watch you first. Then, let them practice rubbing their sand blocks back and forth in unison so everyone sounds like they are brushing their teeth using the same strokes. Make sure to shout, "I LOVE TO BRUSH!" at the end of each verse. The children will become progressively louder as they learn and take ownership of this lively song!

ADDITIONAL SONGS TO SHARE

Twenty-Five Toddler Songs. Straightway Music, 2003. Compact Disk. 7243 5 82858 2 SWD 82858. Play song #20, "Brush Your Teeth." Pass out the sand blocks. Instruct the children to play their sand blocks on the repeating instrumental interludes.

STORYBOARD

What Do We Need to Brush Our Teeth?

Supplies Needed

Ellison die-cuts—toothbrush and tooth, toothpaste—one each

Ten additional Ellison die-cut items that have nothing to do with brushing teeth, e.g., a crocodile, heart #1B, sun #1C, clouds, beagle, feather, toy boat, or cat #3

Dental floss, ⅛" piece (this will lay on the storyboard with no adhesive)

Tape or self-adhesive material to attach items onto the storyboard

Directions

The object of this storyboard is to ask the children what items they need to brush their teeth. Start out with a blank board and explain to the children that you are going to place items on the board we use when brushing our teeth. Ask them to help you decide whether they would need or not need the item shown to brush their teeth. Add a few silly items first, then add the toothpaste. Add a few more silly items that have nothing to do with teeth or brushing, then add the toothbrush. Continue until you have placed all the items onto the storyboard. Explain to them how simple it is to brush their teeth, and just a few items are all that are really needed. As you are adding the items that do not belong, talk about each one and allow the children to tell you what they are and something about them. The more animated you, the instructor, are when placing the silly items on the board, the more fun the children will have with this storyboard activity.

MAKE AND TAKE

Tooth Necklace

Supplies Needed per Child

Ellison die-cut teeth, ten

Drinking straw, plastic, one (pre-cut)

Dental floss, approximately 12" to 18" long, one each

Safety scissors

Hole punch, one per craft table

Directions

Premeasure and cut the appropriate length of dental floss for each child to string around their neck, adding extra length for each. Precut the plastic straws into ½" to ¾" pieces. Punch one or two holes in each tooth. Have the children use the dental floss and string one tooth, followed by a piece of drinking straw, followed by another tooth. Continue the process until they have made a tooth necklace. This is a very simple craft. The children will need very little help putting it together. You may need to assist with stringing the straws and teeth for the younger ones, but encourage them to try as this will help develop their fine motor skills. Take advantage of this lesson and craft to help promote dental hygiene. (Some dentists have very large toothbrushes and toothpaste props. You might try to borrow these items from your local dentist office.)

PART IV

SHAKERS

LESSON 19

BONES

CURRICULUM TOPICS

Bones, Dinosaurs, Halloween, Skeletons, Dance

FEATURED BOOK

Heidbreder, Robert. 2004. *Drumheller Dinosaur Dance.* New York: Kids Can Press.

SUMMARY

In this original rhyming story, dinosaurs in the town of Drumheller in Alberta, Canada, are buried deep into the earth. But when night falls, those Drumheller dinos assemble those dusty, dry bones and rise up and roar! "Boomity-boom/ rattely-clack/ thumpity-thump/ whickety-whack!" They make such a terrible noise, grown-ups think there is a terrible storm going on. Sleep is disturbed for miles around, because those Drumheller dinosaurs are partying loud and long! But when the dark night gives way to the day, all the dinos creep back to their beds, unsnap their tired bones, and go to sleep. The rhyming text makes the story easy to read aloud and offers many opportunities for interaction. The illustrations add personality to the skeletal dinosaur figures. The copyright page offers a few brief facts about the ancient dinosaur bones from Alberta, Canada. Sing the song "Shim-Sham-Shoo" also found in this same chapter, under dinosaurs to complement the story! The children are sure to love the book and enjoy shaking up the place, just like the Drumheller dinosaurs did, in this book. Ages 3–7

ACTIVITY

Pass out two shakers for each child. On the repeating words, "Boomity-Boom Ratttely-Clack Thumpity-Thump Whickety-Whack," children tap their two shakers together in rhythm.

FEATURED BOOK

Nikola-Lisa, W. 1997. *Shake dem Halloween Bones.* Boston: Houghton Mifflin.

SUMMARY

There's a hip-hop Halloween ball in the quiet city tonight, and guess who is invited? Fairy tale characters, but none like you have ever seen before. You will witness "Li'l Red," (Little Red Riding Hood) "shake her ridin' hood." Remember Tom Thumb? Not this Tom Thumb; he is "Li'l Tom" now, and "for a tiny little guy, he can shake it on home." This book is packed with fairy tale characters illustrated in a spectacularly modern style that is all its own. The rapping, shaking, and stomping at this Halloween hip-hop ball will capture all ages. The rhythmic text can be rapped, chanted, or sang. This is a favorite with our storytime groups. It is sure to become a favorite with yours! Ages 3–8

ACTIVITY

Pass out the shakers. Children shake their instruments on the repeating chorus.

ADDITIONAL BOOKS TO SHARE

Capucilli, Alyssa. 1998. *Inside a House That Is Haunted.* New York: Scholastic. In this cumulative rhyming story, a knock on the door of a haunted house causes quite a stir for the spiders, bats, ghosts, and all of the other creatures living inside. With each page turn, another funny reaction from the knock on the door is waiting to happen. This is a rebus read-along story that the children will find to be quite entertaining. Encourage the audience to identify the pictures on each line. Let the children help you read and act out the story. Ages 3–7

Costello, David. 2004. *Here They Come!* New York: Farrar, Straus and Giroux. Green goblins gather in the woods for their annual Halloween party. As they watch the guests arrive, the young goblins are in for a ghastly treat. Warlocks, ghosts, hobgoblins hobnobbing, and the thing that goes bump in the night, to name a few, are arriving. The creatures are enjoying the Halloween party. It is in full swing when the great ghost storyteller delivers a shivering tale. The young goblins have seen and heard so much this Halloween night they cannot imagine any more surprises. Suspense builds until the biggest scare of the evening presents itself; a group of human trick-or-treaters in their costumes parade through the forest. This is an adorable book with enchanting illustrations. In the book there is a four-page wordless spread full of suspense. It is a perfect build-up for the trick-or-treaters to arrive. Although it may seem too scary to read to a young child, this book clearly creates an alternating sense of safety, scariness, and comfort. Your young group of little goblins will love this story! Ages 3–8

Cuyler, Margery. 2002. *Skeleton Hiccups*. New York: Margaret K. McElderry Books. A friendly ghost tries everything he knows to help Skeleton get rid of his hiccups. These endearing characters do not have a scary bone in their body. As you read, the children love making the sound effects of Skeleton's hiccups. Ages 3–7

Druce, Arden. 2001. *Halloween Night*. Flagstaff, AZ: Rising Moon. Traditional Halloween characters are introduced through riddles. Each character revealed says the repeating line, "I Can." Have the children repeat the line with each riddle and turn the page for the Halloween character reveal. This is a skillfully written, nonthreatening Halloween story that is the perfect complement to any Halloween storytime. Ages 2–7

Horn, Emily. 2002. *Excuse Me . . . Are You a Witch?* Watertown, MA: Charlesbridge. Herbert is a lonely black cat who lives on the streets. He visits the public library on really cold days to stay warm and snuggle with a good book. Herbert discovers a book about witches and discovers what they looked like. He also discovers that they loved black cats. There is nothing to do but to find a witch to love and take him home. Many insulting and frightening adventures later, Herbert makes his way back into the public library and finds a group of witch-schoolgirls and their witch-teacher enjoying a visit to their local library. They fall in love with Herbert and take him to live in their witch-school. Ages 3–7

Lane, Adam. 2004. *Monsters Party All Night Long*. San Francisco, CA: Chronicle Books. Count Drac is lonely and bored because he has no friends. He is sure his scary but famous name has something to do with his dilemma. Count decides to throw a party to make new friends, so he invites everyone! Creatures from around the world creep their way to Count Drac's party. From disco to hip-hop to an "All-Fish Band," dance moves are countless on the floor and the monsters party all night long. "Horror d' oeuvres" are served, the tower bell rings in the midnight hour, and the party hits its peak! Count Drac has a monstrously good time and learns a great lesson. All his great wealth and fame enjoys from his name is no fun unless it can be shared with friends. A background of black on each page make the colorful three dimensional illustrations stand out even more. Bold lime green text is the perfect color to add with the dark pages. The children will love this wickedly wacky tale. Ages 3–7

Mitton, Tony. 2003. *Spooky Hour*. New York: Orchard Books. In this frightfully friendly, nonthreatening Halloween adventure, a dog and a cat journey to a party in a castle. As they track through the dark forest, they meet a variety of midnight spooks. Eleven witches, ten floaty ghosts, and nine skeletons make their presence known. They continue making their way through the count down forest until they meet two witchy twins at the castle door. The twins greet them and invite them in for one gigantic pumpkin pie. After eating every tiny crumb of the pie, all the creatures join in some scary party fun. Illustrations and text are a reader's dream! Bold, large text and bright, action-packed pictures. Another must read for a spooktacular fun time! Ages 2–7

Postgate, Daniel. 1999. *The Hairy Toe*. Cambridge, MA: Candlewick Press. In this traditional tale an old woman sets out to pick beans and finds a hairy toe. She takes it home and that night she hears a voice crying, "Where's my Hair-r-ry To-o-oe? Who's got my Hair-r-ry To-o-oe?" The old woman shrinks down under her covers, but the voice gets nearer as the wind howled. The owner is coming back to claim the Hairy Toe and who will it be? This is a spine-chiller as the children will love the build-up to the reveal on the last page. Make sure to read this book with emphasis on the mystery voice asking for his Hairy Toe. Practice this book several times before presenting so you are ready to give it the thrill it deserves. Ages 4–8

Wahl, Jan. 2004. *Knock! Knock!* New York: Henry Holt. A long time ago in Scotland a young witch named Ella La Grimble sits alone at her spinning wheel. She spins and wishes for company, then hears a knock at the door. A pair of big feet walk in and stand before the fire. There is another knock at the door. Along come a pair of teeny-weeny legs that sit right down on the great big feet. Knock after knock at the door, uniquely sized body parts appear. Each time another body part appears Witch Ella sits and spins thinking they are not much company. Finally, a pumpkin-sized head rolls in to complete the body. Witch Ella is scared but asks him a series of questions. The answers make her very nervous. She finally musters up enough nerve to ask him why he has come. He replies, "For YOU, witch, for you . . . ," as she is cornered against a window. As the story ends, the giant finishes his sentence, ". . . to keep you company!" This thrilling and chilling book will hold the children's attention through the end. Each time there is a knock at the door, prompt the children to say and pantomime,

"Knock! Knock!" Cue the children by rearranging the repeating sentence to say, "When at the door—Knock! Knock!" Pause to give them time to say and play their part. Ages 3–8

Yates, Philip. 2003. *Ten Little Mummies: An Egyptian Counting Book.* New York: Viking. Ten little mummies are bored and tired of being stuffed in one room. They decide to go outside and play. In this hilarious countdown book, one by one, each mummy is removed, one disaster after another. In the end, only one tearful mummy is left to go back in the tomb. When he opens the tomb door, a huge surprise is waiting inside. As you turn the pages in the book, have the children follow along and help count down the mummies. It is fun to stop on a few pages through the story and individually count each mummy on the page. Ages 2–7

MUSIC AND MOVEMENT WITH SHAKERS

Sing Along: "Them Old Brittle Bones"

Sung to the Tune: "The Old Grey Mare"

Them old brittle bones, they still got some shakin' left!
Still got some shakin' left! Still got some shakin' left!
Them old brittle bones, they still got some shakin' left,
So I'm gonna shake them bones!
Them old brittle bones, they still got some tremblin' left!
Still got some tremblin' left! Still got some tremblin' left!
Them old brittle bones, they still got some tremblin' left,
So I'm gonna tremble them bones!
Them old brittle bones, they still got some rattlin' left!
Still got some rattlin' left! Still got some rattlin' left!
Them old brittle bones, they still got some rattlin' left,
So I'm gonna rattle them bones!

Directions

Pass out the shakers and play song #22 from the accompanying *The Sound of Storytime* CD. Encourage the children to rattle their shakers throughout the entire song. Have them start by shaking them lightly, so as not to drown out the song. At the end of each verse—". . . so I'm gonna shake, tremble, rattle them bones!"—give them permission to shake loudly!

ADDITIONAL SONGS TO SHARE

Gang, Goanna. *Kids Dance and Play*, Vol. 2. Soundhouse, 2002. Compact Disk. CRG 191032. Play song #3, "Monster Mash," as children are entering storytime and during craft time for some spooky atmosphere.

Wiggles. *Yummy Yummy! Wiggles.* Lyrick Studios, 1999. Compact Disk. 9206. Play song #2, "Shaky Shaky." Pass out the shakers; play and sing along. This is also a great song to use with a parachute, if one is available.

STORYBOARD

Place the Head on the Skeleton

Supplies Needed

Bandana or strip of material to be used for blindfolds, two

Skeleton, paper or cardboard

Tape

Directions

Purchase a paper or cardboard skeleton at your local discount store and remove the head. Prior to the activity, attach the body of the skeleton to the storyboard. Apply tape to the head of the skeleton. Remember to change the tape periodically, between children. Ask the children to approach the storyboard one at a time. Place the blindfold securely on the child and turn them around a couple of times. Give them the skeleton's head, point them in the direction of the storyboard. Tell them to attach the skeleton's head where they think it belongs. After the child has added the head onto the storyboard, remove the blindfold and let them look where they placed the head. To keep the activity flowing swiftly, enlist the help of an assistant or a parent to help with blindfolding the children.

MAKE AND TAKE

Boney Macaroni

Supplies Needed per Child

Construction paper, 12" × 18" in size, black, one each

Dried pasta, assorted (e.g., elbow, spiral, spaghetti, flat noodles, penne)

Glue, liquid

Directions

Prior to the activity, create a skeleton out of pasta so the children will have a visual idea of what they will be making. Give each child a sheet of construction paper and let them glue the dried pasta in the shape of a skeleton. Collect some books with pictures of skeletons in them so the children will have something to look at while they build their skeleton. This is a great project for the imagination. Make sure you leave extra time for the skeletons to dry. If pasta is not available, an alternative medium could be packing foam popcorn pieces.

LESSON 20

DINOSAURS

CURRICULUM TOPICS

Dinosaurs, Dance

FEATURED BOOK

Mitton, Tony. 2002. *Dinosaurumpus.* New York: Orchard Books.

SUMMARY

Dinosaurs gather at the swamp for some dinosaur style singing and dancing. Ages 3–7

ACTIVITY

Pass out the shakers. Everyone participates by shaking their instruments on the repeating lines, "Shake, shake, shudder . . . near the sludgy old swamp. The dinosaurs are coming. Get ready to romp." There is plenty of opportunity to play along and join in the dino fun, because the phrase is repeated on almost every page.

ADDITIONAL BOOKS TO SHARE

Baker, Liza. 2003. *Dinosaur Days.* New York: HarperFestival. When Harold can't sleep, he uses his purple crayon to conjure up a make-believe world of dinosaur adventures. Children relish in the suspenseful predicaments of this tale and marvel at Harold's clever solutions. Create intrigue by reading the story in a cautious tone. The sense of adventure, coupled with bright illustrations, will hold the attention of your listeners. Ages 3–7

Emmett, Jonathan. 2001. *Dinosaurs After Dark.* New York: Golden Books. One sleepless night, Bobby hears a sound outside his window. He discovers the sound is coming from an enormous dinosaur sneaking around his street. Bobby joins the dinosaur for a nighttime adventure through the city. The illustrations in this imaginative story are bright, bold, and perfect for reading aloud to groups. Ages 3–7

Grambling, Lois G. 2000. *Can I Have a Tyrannosaurus Rex, Dad? Can I? Please!?* Mahwah, NJ: BridgeWater Books. An inventive boy tries to convince his father that a Tyrannosaurus would make the perfect pet. The boy proposes scenarios where the gigantic creature would be advantageous. Every child can relate to the pleadings of the imaginative character in this story. For lots of added fun, encourage your audience to interject the repeating line, "PLEASE?" Ages 4–8

Hartmann, Wendy. 2000. *The Dinosaurs Are Back and It's All Your Fault Edward!* New York: Aladdin Paperbacks. At bedtime, an older brother teases that a treasured rock found from the day's adventures isn't really a rock, but a dinosaur egg. The boy embellishes his tale and tries to frighten his brother. When he falls asleep and has a bad dream, he is haunted by his own scary story. Illustrations and text make this book a little difficult for reading aloud to a large group. However, the book is very appealing to children, and we recommend it for a book talk. Dinosaurs are a favorite topic of preschool and early grade school children. Be sure to display plenty of Dinosaur books for check out and additional reading at home. Ages 3–7

Hennessy, B. G. 1990. *The Dinosaur Who Lived in My Backyard.* New York: Puffin Books. A boy daydreams about what his backyard must have been like when the dinosaurs of long ago lived on the very same land. The story discretely weaves science information into the plot, and makes comparisons to familiar objects from a child's daily life. Too often, authors use humor that is over the heads of the child audience for which the book is intended. This story refreshingly relates the wit and humor directly to the children on their level. This story inspires creative thinking and delivers lots of grins. Ages 3–8

Martin, Rodney. 1980. *There's a Dinosaur in the Park!* Milwaukee, WI: Gareth Stevens. While playing in the park, a boy spies a dinosaur lurking about. He bravely approaches the fierce creature and tosses an old soda can right into his mouth. The boy cautiously touches the dinosaur's spikes and even climbs onto his tail! This story encapsulates the rapture of a child's pretend play when the ending reveals, to the unsuspecting reader, a surprising twist. Uncluttered and lucid illustrations harmonize well with the straightforward text making this tale a perfect read-aloud choice. Ages 3–7

McCarty, Peter. 2004. *T Is for Terrible.* New York: Henry Holt. Tyrannosaurus Rex tries to explain his conduct and defend his predator nature. This story reveals the perspective of the fierce carnivore with compassion and delicacy. The author brilliantly blends nonfiction information into the fiction storyline without distracting from the story. The result truly creates a unique synergy. This short read-aloud is packed with punch! Ages 3–8

Milbourne, Anna. 2004. *The Dinosaur.* Tulsa, OK: EDC Publishing. For curious little dinosaur lovers, this story explains the existence of dinosaurs in very simple terms and brilliantly colorful illustrations. Ages 3–7

Most, Bernard. 1999. *Catch Me If You Can!* San Diego, CA: Harcourt Brace. All the other dinosaurs are afraid of the biggest dinosaur around, except for one little dinosaur. She yells, "Catch me if you can!" to the biggest dinosaur. She isn't afraid of his great big claws, great big teeth, or anything about the biggest dinosaur. As it turns out, the biggest dinosaur is her Grandpa, and they are only playing. Prompt the children to shout out the repeating line, "Catch me if you can!" in a little dinosaur voice. Ages 2–7

Shields, Carol Diggory. 2002. *Saturday Night at the Dinosaur Stomp.* Cambridge, MA: Candlewick Press. Word spreads throughout the dinosaur community of a prehistoric party not to be missed. Dinosaurs gather from far and wide to join in the fun of a Saturday night romp. This rhyming story reads like a big band jazz tune. We like to sing or chant the story while keeping the beat on a single shaker. Gently shake the instrument to your side throughout the story. When the story reads, "the ground was rocking—it started to shake," shake the shakers more vigorously. Use the shakers on emphasis lines like, "Boomalacka, boomalacka! Whack! Whack! Whack!" This book is sure to mesmerize your group, so be sure to practice all those dinosaur names ahead of time. Ages 3–7

Strickland, Paul. 1997. *Ten Terrible Dinosaurs.* New York: Dutton Children's Books. Ten dinosaur friends play games together throughout this counting rhyme. With each turn of the page, one dinosaur is eliminated from the fun. There are numerous simple ways to make this book interactive and fun. Before the children arrive for story hour, clearly number ten sheets of 8½" × 11" paper. Begin your presentation by showing the children the bold face type on the last page of the book. Ask them to sound out the word they see (ROAR!). Tell your listeners to pay close attention during the story, because when they see this page they will get to shout out their best dinosaur roar! Enlist the aid of ten volunteers that would like to play the part of the dinosaurs. Stand your assistants in a line across the story telling area. From left to right and counting down from ten to one, give each volunteer their assigned number to hold up. One child sits down each time a dinosaur is subtracted in the story. Pause after each phrase to give the audience time to call out the appropriate number answer. The activity concludes with everybody interjecting one loud collective roar! Children will beg to act out the story again and again. Ages 3–7

Whybrow, Ian. 1999. *Harry and the Bucketful of Dinosaurs.* New York: Random House. When a boy finds a box of toy dinosaurs in his grandma's attic, he repairs and washes them. The boy hauls his bucket of dinosaurs everywhere, even to the library, where he learns from a book the name of each dinosaur. When Harry tells the dinosaurs their names, they come to life. The boy and his dinosaur pals adventure everywhere until one day the bucket of playmates is accidentally left behind. Not even a new video makes Harry feel better. Read this story to find out if Harry finds his dinosaurs. If ever there were adults that could truly remember what child's play is like, it is the team that created this book. This story is literally a demonstration for how to play with toys. By reminding us of moments from our own childhood, this book is sure to help adults better relate to the way the children in their life think. For those children who are too involved in television and are deprived of imaginative play, this book can be the catalyst that inspires creative play habits and research trips to the library! Ages 3–7

Yolen, Jane. 2000. *How Do Dinosaurs Say Goodnight?* New York: Blue Sky Press. Children and their parents will delight in the all too familiar antics of these dinosaur children as they avoid bedtime. The text is just the right length, and the illustrations are uniquely vivid for reading out loud to a large group. However, interesting details are also disguised on each page, so make sure everyone checks out a copy to take home for bedtime reading. Can you find the names of the dinosaurs on each page tonight? Ages 2–7

MUSIC AND MOVEMENT WITH SHAKERS

Sing Along: Shim-Sham-Shoo

Sung to the Tune: "Skip to My Lou"

I know a secret about dinosaurs! I know why there aren't anymore!
Because they fell right through the floor, dancing the shim-sham-shoo!

Shoo, shoo, shim-sham-shoo! Shoo, shoo, shim-sham-shoo!
Shoo, shoo, shim-sham-shoo! Dancing the shim-sham-shoo!
They'd shim-sham-shoo with their heads held high,
and shim-sham-shoo with their arms to the sky!
They'd shim-sham-shoo, shakin' their thighs, dancing the shim-sham-shoo!
Shoo, shoo, shim-sham-shoo! Shoo, shoo, shim-sham-shoo!
Shoo, shoo, shim-sham-shoo! Dancing the shim-sham-shoo!
One day they all gathered round, started to shim-sham,
but felt the ground begin to make an awful sound,
while dancing the shim-sham-shoo!
Shoo, shoo, shim-sham-shoo! Shoo, shoo, shim-sham-shoo!
Shoo, shoo, shim-sham-shoo! Dancing the shim-sham-shoo!
I guess you know what happened then? All the dinosaurs fell right in!
But every dino left with a grin, dancing the shim-sham-shoo!
Shoo, shoo, shim-sham-shoo! Shoo, shoo, shim-sham-shoo!
Shoo, shoo, shim-sham-shoo! Dancing the shim-sham-shoo!
Now when you hear a rumbling sound,
while all is quiet and you're laying around.
It might be the dino's underground, still dancing the shim-sham-shoo!
Shoo, shoo, shim-sham-shoo! Shoo, shoo, shim-sham-shoo!
Shoo, shoo, shim-sham-shoo! Dancing the shim-sham-shoo!
Shoo, shoo, shim-sham-shoo! Shoo, shoo, shim-sham-shoo!
Shoo, shoo, shim-sham-shoo! Dancing the shim-sham-shoo!

Directions

Pass out the shakers and play song #23 from the accompanying *The Sound of Storytime* CD. This song is packed with opportunity to use the shakers. Throughout each chorus have the children shake their shakers keeping to the rhythm of the "shim-sham-shoo." As the children get familiar with this song, have them stand up and dance the "shim-sham-shoo," by following along with the song. Lead them in holding their heads high, putting their arms to the sky, and shaking their thighs. Dinosaurs are always a hit, and this song will soon be a storytime favorite!

ADDITIONAL SONGS TO SHARE

Palmer, Hap. *Rhythms on Parade.* Hap-Pal Music Inc., 1995. Compact Disk. HP102E AC633. Play song #18, "Slow and Fast." Pass out the shakers and play along.

Most Amazing Dinosaur Songs. Dragonfly Studio, 2004. Compact Disk. R2 78987. All the songs on this CD are tons of fun. Consider playing along to song #8, "Going on a Dino Hunt" or song #12, "Hokey Pokeysaurus."

STORYBOARD

Dinosaur Match Game

Supplies Needed

Ellison die-cut dinosaurs, set #1, four of each dinosaur for eight pairs of different colored dinosaurs (16 total) (e.g., two red brontosaurus, two blue brontosaurus, two green pterodactyl, two yellow pterodactyl, two black stegosaurus, two orange stegosaurus, two purple tyrannosaurus, and two pink tyrannosaurus)

4" × 6" white index cards, 16 total

Glue stick

Tape or self-adhesive material to attach the index cards onto the storyboard

Felt-tip marker

Directions

Glue one dinosaur onto each index card on the same side the dinosaur is attached. Use the marker to write the name of each dinosaur onto the bottom of the card. Use tape or self-adhesive material on both sides of the index cards so they can be turned over as needed. Begin with all the cards on the board with the blank side showing. Ask the children to help you match up the dinosaurs by color and type. Let the children take turns approaching the storyboard and turning two cards over until they have a color match. As they choose the correct two cards, give the child a chance to announce the name of that particular dinosaur. If they are unsure, help them. Leave the matched dinosaurs showing and continue the game until all the cards are turned over and matched. Repeat the activity until each child has had a turn or two matching a pair of dinosaurs.

MAKE AND TAKE

Dinosaur Match Card Game

Supplies Needed per Child

Ellison die-cut dinosaurs, set #1, two sets of four dinosaurs, per child, totaling eight dinosaurs (use the same colors as in the Dinosaur Match Game Storyboard)

4" × 6" index cards, eight per child

Glue stick

Washable markers, one or two per craft table (optional)

Directions

Let each child make their own set of Dinosaur Match Game cards. Have the children glue one dinosaur onto each card, for a total of eight dinosaurs. If time permits, let them write the names of the dinosaurs by having the dinosaur identification cards from the storyboard activity available to copy. Explain to the children they can play the dinosaur match game with their friends and family at home.

MAKE AND TAKE 2

Supplies Needed per Child

Construction paper, 9" × 12", assorted colors

Ellison die-cut Dinosaur Set #1—brontosaurus, pterodactyl, stegosaurus, and tyrannosaurus—one set

Glue stick

Washable felt-tip markers, one or two per craft table

Several easy to read books that identify types of dinosaurs

Directions

Have each child glue the set of four dinosaurs onto the construction paper. Provide children with library books about dinosaurs. Encourage the children to discover the names of their paper dinosaurs, just like Harry did in the story *Harry and the Bucketful of Dinosaurs*. Accompanying caregivers or teacher's aids can help the children identify the dinosaurs and assist them with writing the names onto their paper. As the leader, be sure the appropriate information is provided in the books you have gathered. The objective is to make connections with meaningful print.

LESSON 21

RAIN

CURRICULUM TOPICS

Ants, Mushrooms, Rain, Sunshine, Water Cycle

FEATURED BOOK

Ginsburg, Mirra. 1974. *Mushroom in the Rain*. New York: Aladdin Paperbacks.

SUMMARY

A tiny ant looks for shelter from the rain and finds a tiny mushroom just barely big enough for the single small creature to fit under. As the rain continues, a butterfly pleads for shelter so the ant moves over and the two can barely fit under the tiny mushroom. The story progresses as a mouse, a bird, and a rabbit also seek shelter under the tiny mushroom. Each time, the animals squeeze under. Miraculously, the mushroom seems to be able to protect them all from the rain. When the rain stops, the animals come out from under the mushroom and the ant cannot understand how everyone could fit under that tiny mushroom. Finally, with some teasing from an arrogant frog, they realize that the rain caused the mushroom to grow. Ages 3–7

ACTIVITY

Ask the children to generate ideas about where animals might go when it rains. Explain to your audience that you are going to read a story about a rainstorm and they are going to play the sound of the rain with their shaker instruments. Each time the story repeats the line, "The rain came down harder and harder," the children are to raise their shakers over their heads and slowly shake them downward, toward their laps, like raindrops falling from the sky. When their hands reach their lap, they are to lay their instruments down until the next opportunity. Make a note to yourself that the author omits this repeating line after both sparrow and rabbit squeeze under the mushroom. As the leader, simply remember to repeat the words to prompt the children to play their part for a total of five times throughout the story.

FEATURED BOOK

Liu, Jae Soo. 2002. *Yellow Umbrella*. La Jolla, CA: Kane/Miller.

SUMMARY

A yellow umbrella begins this unique wordless book. Turn the page and two umbrellas, one yellow and one blue appear on the wordless page. With each turning page, another brightly colored umbrella appears adding to the count. Many times we look at a wordless picture book and have no idea how we can use it at storytime. Remarkably, this wordless picture book can be used in numerous ways. As you turn through the pages, discuss the abstract pictures. Ask questions like, "I wonder who is under that umbrella?" or "Where do you suppose they are going in the rain?" The intriguing and mysterious umbrellas travel over a bridge, through a courtyard, down the stairs, and as they do, more and more umbrellas join the procession. A CD accompanies the book, which includes background music, and the words and music to a song are printed on the back page of the book. Ages 3–7

ACTIVITY

Pass out the shakers. For this activity, children will make the sound of the rain with their shakers by joining in a rain chorus one at a time. The number of children playing their shakers corresponds to the number of umbrellas added with each turn of the page. At the beginning, the soft sound of just one child's instrument is symbolic of a light sprinkling rain. As more children join with their instruments, the gentle rainfall transforms into a downpour. Discuss this symbolism with the children. If you have a tambourine, add a little thunder and lightning of your own at the end!

You can come up with a repeating line like, "And the rain came down all around, all around till the rain made puddles on the ground." The children will play their instruments and chant theses words with you as you turn each page. Adding the repeating line helps to make a beginning and an end to the instrument's part. This prevents the first child getting tired of playing before the last children have their turn to play along. When it comes to selecting the children to one at a time to join the rain chorus, you have a couple choices. If you know the names of the children in your group, you can simply pass out the shakers and randomly call on children one at a time to stand up and join the activity. If you do not know the children's names, you can invite children to join the procession one at a time by individually handing out the shakers as you tell the story.

FEATURED BOOK

Shannon, David. 2000. *The Rain Came Down*. New York: Blue Sky Press.

SUMMARY

The town is in chaos following an unexpected downpour. Ages 3–7

ACTIVITY

Pass out the shakers. Direct the children to play their shakers and chant on the repeating line, "And still, the rain came down."

ADDITIONAL BOOKS TO SHARE

Appelt, Kathi. 2001. *Rain Dance*. New York: HarperFestival. A very easy to read counting book that depicts the way different animals react to the rain. One froggie hops, two spiders skitter, three chickens flitter, and so forth. The pages are very well illustrated with nice, large pictures on each page, making it easy for the children to join in and count as you point. This book is simple and quick enough to read twice. Challenge the children to read it back to you the second time. Ages 2–6

Bruce, Lisa. 2000. *Fran's Flower*. New York: HarperCollins. Young Fran finds a pot with a tiny sprout poking through the dirt. Determined to help the plant thrive, she feeds it all her favorite things-cookies, pizza, and ice cream. When the plant does not grow even a bit, Fran gets frustrated and throws the pot outside into the elements. Of course, the wind, rain, and sunshine reach the plant and much to Fran's surprise a flower blooms. As you read, ask the children if they think food like pizza will help a plant to grow. When the plant is outside, ask the children to interact by making the sound of the wind. Encourage them to mimic you as you pantomime the sprinkling rain with your fingers. To act out the part of the sun, hold your arms over your head in a circle. At the end of the story, ask the children what things helped the plant to grow. Ages 2–7

Gorbachev, Valeri. 2002. *One Rainy Day*. New York: Philomel Books. Goat and pig are great friends. As goat is sitting on his porch reading the newspaper, pig comes by dripping wet. Goat asks pig why he is so wet. The pig explains that he went out to pick some flowers in the meadow and it began to rain. Pig hid under a tree to stay dry and along came one small, but very fast, mouse. Then along came two porcupines and three buffalo and four leopards and five lions, and the count continues to ten. The goat is captivated by pig's story, but still can't understand why pig is so wet, because the tree was big enough to keep all of the animals dry. Pig finally explains to goat the reason why he got so wet. There is a very funny ending to pig's story that will make the children giggle. Ages 3–7

Kurtz, Jane. 2002. *Rain Romp: Stomping Away a Grouchy Day*. New York: Greenwillow Books. Two cheerful parents attempt to wake up their little darling daughter on a rainy day. She tells them she does not feel shiny and the sky agrees with her. The happier and cheerier her parents are, the more she snarls and frowns. She is sure the rain will agree with her. She gets mad at her parents and storms out of her house with her wild wolverine attitude. She begins to stomp in the rain. As her parents gaze at her from a window, they are angry. The more they watch her stomp the more enjoyment they have watching the activity. They have an idea! They will join her! All three dance, whoosh, stomp, and play in the rain. Just as the grouchy little girl begins to smile and change her mood, the rainstorm begins to break up. The family goes inside and enjoys the day together with games and giggling. They decided they are indeed an all-weather loving family. Ask the children how they would stomp away a grouchy day. Ask them how many stomps it takes to stomp away a grouchy day. Let each child stomp their grouchy day away as everyone counts their stomps. This is a good way to wear down a little excess energy. Go on a grouchy day stomping stampede. Ages 3–7

Lewison, Wendy Cheyette. 2004. *Raindrop, Plop!* New York: Penguin Group. In this beautifully illustrated counting story, a little girl and her dog head out to play in the ever so gently raining outdoors. She begins to count the drops of rain in a simple rhyming chant until the rain becomes unbearable. They go back into their house. The little girl finds another "wet" way to entertain herself by taking a bubble bath and counting her ten tiny little toes as her faithful companion watches. After the bath, she continues to count. She gets dressed counting the buttons on her jacket, and enjoys hot chocolate while counting the marshmallows floating on top. She counts her pretzels as she munches them. They gaze through their window while counting squirrels and birds outside in the rain. She soon notices the rain has stopped and the counting ends. She heads outside to play in the warm sunshine. Have the children think of ways they would entertain themselves on a rainy day; count them. Ages 3–7

Morton-Shaw, Christine. 2004. *Itzy Bitzy House.* New York: Barrons Educational Series. A poor little mouse is caught in the rain by an itzy bitzy house down a twisty turny lane. He wishes he had some way to get dry, but feels all alone and that no one wants him. Mouse hears a noise and runs and hides as a wet cat comes down the twisty turny lane. Cat is also looking for a place to dry out, but suddenly hears a noise and runs for cover. Next comes a drippy droppy droopy roly poly puppy who is feeling all alone and is frightened by a goat and also runs and hides. A loud clap of lightning scares all the animals as they cuddle together under a tree near the itzy bitzy house. They hear a creak at the door, and a wrinkly crinkly man comes out and promises to dry them and love them. The animals live happily ever after, cozy and dozy in their itzy bitzy house. This is a precious little story, cleverly and skillfully written. It is sure to touch the hearts of the children. Ages 2–7

Schaefer, Lola M. 2001. *This Is the Rain.* New York: Greenwillow Books. We all need water to live, and this well-written picture book breaks down and explains in simple text the water cycle. It explains how the sun creates vapor from the ocean, water falls from the clouds as rain, and it finally makes its way to the ocean. An interesting rhyming story about water and a little science lesson all in one. Have the children think of everything they use water for. Ages 4–8

MOVEMENT CHANT

It's Raining Opposites

Discuss the different sounds rain makes. Ask the children to imagine the way rain sounds on a roof, a window, on the grass, and while riding in a car. Pass out the shakers. Allow the children to practice making the sound of rain by asking them to let you hear what it might sound like when it is raining hard. Then ask them what it sounds like when it is showering softly. The following activity plays like any traditional "freeze game." Tell the audience you are going to ask them to shake their shakers to the sound of the rain you are describing. By having your participants stand up to play, you will be allowing a time to stretch. Between each direction allow the children plenty of time to shake their shakers. Recite this verse through once, then repeat the game, this time randomly throw in the direction "Raindrops *STOP!*"

> Raindrops *fast*
> Raindrops *slow*
> Raindrops *hard*
> Raindrops *soft*
> Raindrops *loud*
> Raindrops *quiet*

End by saying, "Raindrops *STOP!*"

MUSIC AND MOVEMENT WITH SHAKERS

"Rainy Day Blues"

Sung to the Tune: "Jimmy Crack Corn"

Let's shake those rainy blues away,
Let's shake those rainy blues away,
Let's shake those rainy blues away,
Let's shake, shake, shake, shake, shake!
Let's shake those blues right out of our head, *(Nod head while shaking near head)*
Let's shake those blues right out of our head,
Let's shake those blues right out of our head,
Let's shake, shake, shake, shake, shake!
Let's shake those blues right out of our arms, *(Shake arms while shaking)*
Let's shake those blues right out of our arms,
Let's shake those blues right out of our arms,

Let's shake, shake, shake, shake, shake!
Let's shake those blues right out of our thighs, *(Tap shakers onto thighs)*
Let's shake those blues right out of our thighs,
Let's shake those blues right out of our thighs,
Let's shake, shake, shake, shake, shake!
Let's shake those blues right out of our knees, *(Tap shakers onto knees)*
Let's shake those blues right out of our knees,
Let's shake those blues right out of our knees,
Let's shake, shake, shake, shake, shake!
Let's shake those blues right out of our feet, *(Tap shakers onto feet)*
Let's shake those blues right out of our feet,
Let's shake those blues right out of our feet,
Let's shake, shake, shake, shake, shake!
Let's shake that rain back into those clouds, *(With arms held high, shake shakers)*
Let's shake that rain back into those clouds,
Let's shake that rain back into those clouds,
Let's shake, shake, shake, shake, shake!

Directions

Pass out the shakers and prepare to chant #24 from the accompanying *The Sound of Storytime* CD. Before you begin, ask the children to identify the body parts they will be chanting and shaking about. Tell the children to follow your lead in this exciting movement activity.

Sing Along: "Rain Freeze"

Sung to the tune of: "London Bridge"

Directions

Sing this song a cappella and have the children stand up and shake out their wiggles. Have the children shake their shakers to the word rain and come to an abrupt stop, freezing their shakers at the word "stop." Children love freeze play activities.

Rain, rain, rain, rain, rain, rain, STOP!
Rain, rain, STOP! Rain, rain, STOP!
Rain, rain, rain, rain, rain, rain, STOP!
Rain, rain, STOP!
(Repeat as time allows)

ADDITIONAL SONGS TO SHARE

Disney's Silly Songs. Walt Disney Records, 1988. Compact Disk. 60819–7. Play song #10, "It Ain't Gonna Rain No More" while the children are entering storytime and during craft time.

STORYBOARD

Growing with the Rain

Supplies Needed

Ellison die-cuts, sunflower, tree, fish #2, toddler, umbrella, hammer, T-shirt, toy boat, one each (select any available Ellison die-cuts that need rain, and some that don't)

Tape or use a self-adhesive material to attach items onto the storyboard

Directions

The object of this storyboard is to discuss how rain makes things grow. This list of Ellison die-cuts can be modified and is an example of items you could use. The first four listed need rain to help them grow, and the remaining four do not need rain for growth. Start out with a blank storyboard, and as you repeat the verse, add an item to the board for discussion. The following chant works well to teach children the importance of rain, as well as having a silly and entertaining interaction.

> Rain comes down from clouds you know,
> But does it help a *sunflower* grow?

Continue repeating the verse, choosing different items to add to the storyboard until all items have been discussed.

MAKE AND TAKE

Mushroom in the Rain Picture

Supplies Needed per Child

Construction paper, 12" × 18" in size, light blue or white, one sheet

Ellison die-cuts—small ant, small butterfly, mouse, bird #3, rabbit #1, fox—one each

Washable markers, blue and brown

Glue stick

Directions

Create a sample picture prior to the presentation. Have it available for the children to see and understand the finished product before they begin. Use the construction paper horizontally for this project. Take the brown marker and have children draw a small mushroom just a little below the center of the paper. Then using the small mushroom as a guide, ask the children to draw around the mushroom making it much bigger in size. Lightly color the outer mushroom. Glue all the rest of the die-cuts under the mushroom. Take the blue marker and make rain drops on the page. This activity will reinforce the feature story, *Mushroom in the Rain.* It will demonstrate to the children how the animals hid under the mushroom as it grew bigger.

LESSON 22

SILLINESS

CURRICULUM TOPICS
Silliness

FEATURED BOOK
Raffi. 1987. *Shake My Sillies Out*. New York: Crown Publishers.

SUMMARY
Night falls in the woods near a campground, but some of the animals in the woods are not ready to sleep. They have to shake their sillies out before they can rest. At the nearby campground the children join in clapping their crazies out as well. Soon the animals and children join together in an outrageous evening of pure silliness and fun. Ages 2–7

ACTIVITY
Pass out the shakers. Encourage the children to act out the story by shaking their instruments, clapping their hands, and jumping as this silly story is read. Another way to present this activity is to read the storybook version to quiet listeners and then play the recorded version of the song, which you can request from a local library. Pass out shakers after the story, and encourage children to play their instruments and dance to the music.

ADDITIONAL BOOKS TO SHARE
Arnold, Tedd. 1997. *Parts*. New York: Dial Books for Young Readers. A five-year-old child combs his hair and loses a few hairs. He begins to worry about what is happening. Could he be going bald? Later, he lifts up his shirt and a little piece of fuzz is sticking out of his belly button. He begins to wonder if his stuffing is coming out. The straw that breaks the camel's back is when the youngster feels a loose tooth in his mouth. His imagination takes over and he decides that little by little his body is going to fall apart. The book has hilarious illustrations of this bug-eyed boy showing things like his arm and head falling off when he coughs. Finally mom and dad intervene with their "Parenting for Beginners" book in hand, and explain to the little boy that he is normal. The combination of humor and the "gross factor" is sure to keep the children asking you to read this book over and over again. Ages 3–7

Barrett, Judi. 1970. *Animals Should Definitely Not Wear Clothing*. New York: Atheneum. This story proposes all the silly predicaments animals would experience if they wore clothes. The bold text and pictures conjures lots of silly giggles and has made this great read-aloud a classic. Ages 2–7

Cole, Babette. 1989. *The Silly Book*. New York: Doubleday. In this quirky book, you will observe lots of silly things people do. The author delivers humor, bold rhyming text, and notable illustrations. Ages 2–7

Faulkner, Keith. 2001. *Super Silly Riddles!* New York: Mondo. This is a fun and silly riddle book to read to young children. Large illustrations fill each page along with a one-line riddle printed in large text. Ask the children the riddle, then lift the flap to read the answer. All children love to giggle and laugh and this book will do the trick. Age-appropriate riddles make this book the perfect storytime accompaniment. Ages 3–7

Grindley, Sally. 2001. *Silly Goose and Dizzy Duck Hunt for a Rainbow*. New York: DK Publishing. Silly Goose is bored with her dull brown nest, so she and her friend, Dizzy Duck, set out to find some pretty and colorful things to put in it. They run into Clever Fox and, being the silly poultry they are, ask him for help. He suggests they dig a hole and catch a rainbow. They both think this is a grand idea, not realizing that Clever Fox has grand ideas of his own. Just in the nick of time, Grizzly Bear spoils the fox's plan. The ending of the story is just as silly and funny as the rest of the book. Ages 2–7

Hoberman, Mary Ann. 1997. *The Seven Silly Eaters.* New York: Harcourt. Mrs. Peters has a son named Peter, and he is a picky eater. He likes milk, but it must be served warm. Not hot, not cold, but warm. Mrs. Peters does not mind, she is patient and kind, and would do anything she could to take care of her darling son, Peter. Before Peter turns two, another baby is born and her name is Lucy. She hates milk, both hot and cold, and warm was worst of all. Lucy likes pink lemonade but not from a can. Oh no, she wants it homemade. Mrs. Peters does not mind, she would do anything for her two youngsters. She smiles and giggles softly to herself at her silly pair of eaters. A year passed and a new baby is born. Little Jack Peters is his name, and all he will eat is applesauce. So Mrs. Peters peels apple after apple, making applesauce for another picky little eater. Year after year, baby after baby is born until there are seven children in the Peters family. All the children are terribly picky eaters and Mrs. Peters grows tired to the bone. The children grow and grow and so do their appetites with each passing day. Poor, tired Mrs. Peters goes to bed worn out night after night. The children know their mother is to have a birthday, so in the morning they all sneak out of bed while their weary mother sleeps and decide to surprise her with a birthday breakfast in bed! The cooking is a disaster. They clean up the mess and pour the ingredients in a pot and hide it in the oven. They creep back up to bed so they will not be found out. The next morning Mother Peters wakes up and makes her way down to the kitchen and smells quite a smell. She sniffs her way to the oven door where she finds the perfect pink plump cake! Their mother dances with glee as she is so overwhelmed that the children would make her a birthday cake. The cake is so good. It is made only with the ingredients that the picky children will eat. They take turns making the cake for every meal from that day forward. This book is a bit long, but is very fun to read to a group of children. Ages 3–7

Mathews, Judith, and Fay Robinson. 1994. *Nathaniel Willy, Scared Silly.* New York: Aladdin Paperbacks. Nathaniel Willy and his Gramma live in a creaky, old house in the country. Every night Gramma tucks Nathaniel Willy in and gives him a big kiss on the chin. She says, "Goodnight—eyes shut tight!", then she closes the door. One bitter cold night when Gramma closes the door, it makes a terrible noise and scares Nathaniel Willy. Gramma tells Nathaniel Willy not to be silly and offers him a cat to sleep with. He thinks it would be a good idea to sleep with a cat, so Gramma treks out into the cold night and retrieves the cat from the shed and plops it on Nathaniel Willy's bed. She repeats her nightly ritual, and as the door closes, Nathaniel Willy becomes scared again. Gramma goes back outside and brings him another animal to comfort him, but each time the door closes, Nathaniel Willy cries out! This silliness continues, animal after animal, trip after trip, door closing after door closing! The bed finally becomes so full of farm animals that it breaks! Gramma is at her wits end, so she goes away and comes back with the old wise woman who lives down the road. Sure enough, the old wise woman solves the problem. The door is squeaky, and so she oils it. Gramma feels very silly for the whole mess. She slings out all the animals, repairs Nathaniel Willy's bed, and one last time puts him to bed. The outrageous silliness of this cumulative tale, along with its humorous repetition, will keep the children interested and tickled. Ages 3–7

Tafuri, Nancy. 2001. *Silly Little Goose!* New York: Scholastic Press. One windy morning, Goose sets out to make a nest. The farmer is busy driving his tractor when all of the sudden the wind catches his hat and whirls it in the air. Goose is looking for someplace nice and warm to make her nest. Each time she settles into where she feels is the perfect place, she soon finds out that it is already occupied. Every time the other farm animals discover she is in their bed, the animals cry out, "Silly Little Goose!" Goose continues her search, but keeps finding herself in the same predicament time after time. Finally she finds the farmer's hat turned upside down in the grass and decides it is warm, soft, quiet, and cozy enough for her to make a nest. Silly Little Goose lays her eggs in the hat and keeps them warm until they hatch. This is an easy-to-read, predictable little story that is perfect for a young group of children. There is opportunity for the children to make different animals sounds and to repeat the words "Silly Little Goose!" several times throughout the story. The illustrations are large and colorful and easy on the eyes. Ages 2–7

Wood, Audrey. 1992. *Silly Sally.* New York: Harcourt Brace Jovanovich. Silly Sally is a red-headed girl with corkscrew curls. She goes to town walking backwards, upside down. She wears a fancy ruffled dress and pantaloons underneath to add to her silliness. She meets animals along the way and invites them to join in her silly method of getting to town. This is a rib-tickling, rhyming, cumulative, and nonsensical story that is brightly illustrated, making it a perfect storytime read-aloud. Ages 2–7

MUSIC AND MOVEMENT WITH SHAKERS

Sing Along: "Shaky Break"

Sung to the tune of: "Ta-Ra-Ra-Boom-Der-E"

Directions

Pass out the shakers and prepare to sing or chant this song a cappella. Invite the children to shake their shakers to the rhythm of the chant. Insert each child's name in the verse until all the children have had their name called and taken a turn. The children will love standing and shaking their shakers till their little hearts' content. Another way to use this song/chant is to ask the children to remain seated until their name is called. At that time, they may stand up, right where they are, getting to be the center of attention for a moment. Ask them to be seated after the verse so that the next child can stand up when they hear their name.

> I'm [child's name] shaky shake!
> I love to shaky shake, my little shaky shake, until my shaky breaks!

When all the children's names are sung, end the song with this verse:

> It's time to put away our shaky shakes today!
> They'll come back out and play, another silly day!

This is a lively song that all the children love and do a great job following the directions, in anticipation of hearing their name called. They especially feel important when it's their turn and they get to stand up and shake their shaky shake! This is a great activity for even the reluctant children in the group.

ADDITIONAL SONGS TO SHARE

Scelsa, Greg, and Steve Millang. *We All Live Together,* Vol. 5. Silverlake Sound, 1994. Compact Disk. YM-014-CD. Play song # 8, "Get Up and Go." Pass out the shakers and play along to the words of the song. There is a long pause between verses. You can stop the CD after this first shaker activity or continue through other creative dance movements. This song is also fun to use with a parachute. Children shake the parachute through the chorus of the first verse. Parents or leaders can hold the parachute overhead on the following verses as the children play and follow directions under the parachute.

Palmer, Hap. *Rhythms on Parade.* Hap-Pal Music Inc., 1995. Compact Disk. HP102E AC633. Play song #12, "Bean Bag Shake." Pass out the shaker instruments and play along to this "freeze dance" style song. The title is the only part of the song that refers to bean bags, so this song lends itself just as well to shaker instruments.

JUST FOR FUN

Silly Tongue Twister

Say something silly so somebody smiles!

Directions

Talk to the children about why we call sentences tongue twisters. Start the sentence slowly, picking up speed each time the line is repeated. Continue until you hear a silly slur of S's. This is always a hit!

STORYBOARD

Seven SILLY Sunflowers

Supplies Needed

Construction paper, 12" × 18" in size, white or light color

Rubber stamp pads with several colors of ink. Stamp pads can be purchased with several bright colors in each ink pad, or Ellison die-cut sunflowers, seven, may be substituted.

Washable markers in assorted bright colors

Scissors

Tape to attach flowers to storyboard

Directions

Press your thumb into a colored stamp pad and then press it down onto the construction paper. Draw flower petals around the thumbprint. When it looks like a flower, draw a silly face over the center thumbprint with a bright colored, washable marker. Continue this process until you have made seven large sunflowers. Remember, these are silly sunflowers, so they can have silly faces, silly colors, and silly looks. Cut out each flower and attach it with tape to the storyboard. Place all seven silly sunflowers on the board prior to the story and prepare the children for a very silly story. As you recite the story below, remove a sunflower one at a time as indicated.

Seven silly sunflowers were planted on a hill.
They were planted on the hill by a silly man named Bill!
Bill watered them and watched them grow, and when they were ready,
He picked all seven sunflowers for his wife named Betty!
Betty loved the sunflowers but they started acting silly,
So she gave one away to her neighbor named Lily! *(Remove one sunflower)*
Six silly sunflowers turning cartwheels end to end,
Betty snatched one up and mailed it to her friend! *(Remove one sunflower)*
Five silly sunflowers were acting their wildest,
So she grabbed another one and took it to her stylist! *(Remove one sunflower)*
Four silly sunflowers were eating bread and butter,
Betty snatched one up and gave it to her mother! *(Remove one sunflower)*
Three silly sunflowers giving their petals a shakin',
She took one to the grocery store and traded it for bacon! *(Remove one sunflower)*
Two silly sunflowers still messing around,
So she took one to the circus and gave it to a clown! *(Remove one sunflower)*
One silly sunflower, quietly reading a book,
Betty decided to keep it and taught it how to cook!

MAKE AND TAKE

Seven SILLY Sunflowers

Supplies Needed per Child

Construction paper, 12" × 18" in size, white or light color, one each

Rubber stamp pads with several colors of ink. Stamp pads can be purchased with several bright colors in each ink pad.

Washable markers in assorted bright colors, several per craft table

Moist paper towels or wipes for thumb cleaning

Directions

Let the children make the silly sunflowers just like you prepared for the storyboard activity. Do not cut them out. Have the children place their thumb into a stamp pad and press it down onto the paper. Show them how to draw a flower around it. If they are sharing stamp pads, the flower petals can be drawn first, and the thumbprint could go into the center after the petals are drawn. Have them draw silly faces on the sunflowers. Ask the children to draw seven silly sunflowers with seven silly faces on the paper. Have a sample prepared in advance so the children can have a visual aid of the end result of the picture. Write the words "Seven Silly Sunflowers" on the top or bottom of the sample picture and encourage the older children to copy the letters.

LESSON 23

SNAKES

CURRICULUM TOPICS

Character Values, Obedience, Snakes

FEATURED BOOK

Arnosky, Jim. 2000. *Rattlesnake Dance.* New York: Putnam.

SUMMARY

A rattlesnake slithers into a cave and shakes and wriggles in a rattlesnake dance of pure bliss, while other hissing snakes join in the underground ball. Ages 3–7

ACTIVITY

Ask the children to leave their shakers lying next to them until you give them the sign to pick them up and start shaking. Let them shake "their little hearts out" during this story. You can also ask them to stare straight ahead with their eyes opened wide, and have them sway back and forth like the rattlesnakes do in this tale.

FEATURED BOOK

Moroney, Lynn. 2003. *Baby Rattlesnake.* San Francisco: Children's Book Press. Willful Baby Rattlesnake throws tantrums to get his rattle before he is ready. He misuses it and learns a valuable lesson. This is a bilingual English/Spanish book. Ages 3–7

ACTIVITY

Pass out the shakers. When reading this story, ask the children to shake their shakers each time the baby rattlesnake shakes. When the chief's daughter smashes the baby rattlesnake's shaker, have the children stomp their feet and pretend to grind it into the floor just like she would have. Ask the children to lay the shakers down beside them for the remainder of the story.

ADDITIONAL BOOKS TO SHARE

Brenner, Emily. 2004. *On the First Day of Grade School.* New York: HarperCollins. In this spin-off of "The Twelve Days of Christmas," a first-grade teacher is loved by her students so much that they bring her gifts. They just so happen to bring her a wide and wild variety of animals. The first day of first grade she is given a python—one that will not squeeze her to death, of course. She continues receiving an interesting menagerie of animals, ranging from rats to bees to burping goats. On the twelfth day, she receives twelve zookeepers to help reign in the "gifts." This book can be sung or read to the children. Either way, they will love this outrageously silly book. Ages 3–7

Burns, Rose Marie. 2004. *Slithery Jake.* New York: HarperCollins. A humorous story in rhyme about the hysteria that ensues when a new pet snake turns up missing from his cage. With just the right combination of shivers and slapstick comedy, this read-aloud book makes the coziest household objects suddenly a source of delicious, slithery fun. Ages 3–7

Cox, Phil Roxbee. 2004. *Give That Back, Jack! A Cautionary Tale.* London, England: Usborne. Jack is a very bad boy. He was bad even as a baby! Jack always takes things from people that do not belong to him and will not give them back. When Jack starts school he takes pencils, toys, drinks, lunches, and even money. The children shout, "Give that back, Jack!" One day Jack's class goes on a field trip to the zoo. Jack continues to be bad and grabs a banana from the gorilla's cage, steals a fish from the penguin pool, and takes a ball from a sleeping lion's paws. The children shout, "Give that back, Jack!" Jack simply will not learn his lesson. Then he makes his way into the reptile house. He spots Mac Python quietly sleeping and decides to take him home for a pet. This is a thrilling read-aloud with a wickedly funny twist on the last page. Have the children help you shout "Give that back Jack!" every time Jack takes something that does not belong to him! Ages 3–7

Gray, Libba Moore. 1994. *Small Green Snake.* New York: Orchard Books. With a zip and a zag, and a wiggle and a wag, Small Green Snake thinks he is invincible. Mama warns him to stop wandering so far away or he will be captured and put in a glass jelly jar. He ends up falling prey to that glass jelly jar and a curious cat as well. Add some fun! Display a glass jar with a fake snake inside as you read this tongue-twisting story. Ages 3–8

Grossman, Bill. 1998. *My Little Sister Ate One Hair.* New York: Crown Publishers. A little sister eats all kind of nasty, creepy crawly things. On this gross counting book's menu is one hare, two snakes, three ants, and four shrews, just to name a few. She continues to eat gross things all the way to ten. The tenth item to eat is ten peas, which make her sick! And oh, what a mess! This book is disgustingly funny, and the kids will giggle themselves silly with the wild illustrations in this gross tale. Ages 3–8

Johnson, Angela. 1993. *The Girl Who Wore Snakes.* New York: Orchard Books. When the man from the zoo visits Ali's school, he brings a caravan of animals. It is the colorful snake that catches Ali's eye. The man allows her to wear one all day, which makes her want more. Soon she is wearing many snakes, to the dismay of many. Not until she visits her aunt does she find out there is a fellow snake lover in the family. Ages 3–7

Kudrna, C. Imbior. 1986. *To Bathe a Boa.* Minneapolis, MN: Carolrhoda Books. A boa has no greater wrath than when he does not want to take a bath! In this rollicking verse story, the bathroom becomes a battleground between a clean-conscious youngster and his elusive reptile. Last line: "I should have known that I'd get wet, for every time I bathe my pet, this very thing is what I see . . . My boa ends up scrubbing ME!" Ages 3–7

Polisar, Barry Louis. 1993. *The Snake Who Was Afraid of People.* Silver Spring, MD: Rainbow Morning Music. This is a story of a snake named Leo whose fear of people is confirmed when a child holds him captive in a jar. He narrowly escapes, but not before a series of humorous mishaps keeps Leo squirming for his life. Ages 3–7

Strete, Craig. 2004. *The Rattlesnake Who Went to School.* New York: G. P. Putnam's Sons. Crowboy is going to school for his first time. He is very unhappy about it and decides that he will become a mean old rattlesnake so he will not have to go to school or be nice that day. He starts his morning by wrapping himself around the kitchen chair just like a snake would, but his family ignores him. In spite of his idea, Crowboy's mother still makes him go to school. On the bus ride to school, he is a very naughty rattlesnake. All day long Crowboy misbehaves in school, just like a mean old rattlesnake would. Everyone is still nice to him, and one little girl in particular seems very interested in Crowboy. No matter how naughty he is, or how much he tries to frighten the class, it does not work. The next day during lunch, the little girl finds Crowboy and gives him a special rattlesnake snack. From then on, they become friends and bonded in a very unique and special way. Ages 4–8

MUSIC AND MOVEMENT WITH SHAKERS

Sing Along: "Snakey Tail"

Sung to the Tune: "Row, Row, Row Your Boat"

Shake, shake, your snakey tail, shake it very hard!
Shake that tail wherever you want, but please, not in my yard!
Shake, shake, your snakey tail, shake it very hard!
Shake that tail wherever you want, but please, not in my yard!
Shake, shake, your snakey tail, shake it very hard!
Shake that tail wherever you want, but please, not in my yard!

Directions

Pass out the shakers and play song #25 from the accompanying *The Sound of Storytime* CD. Let the children sing and shake throughout the song. Repeat this song several times, or if you have adult assistance, sing it in a round!

ADDITIONAL SONGS TO SHARE

Silverstein, Shel. *Where the Sidewalk Ends.* Sony Music Entertainment, 1992. Compact Disk. If you prefer not to sing, play this spoken version of *Boa Constrictor* from the CD and act out the directions below.

Chenille Sisters. *1-2-3 for Kids.* Red House Records, 1989. Compact Disk. RHR CD 33. Play song #5, "I'm Being Swallowed by a Boa Constrictor" for a singing version of this traditional favorite. Act out the directions below.

Supplies Needed

One or more sleeping bags or a spiral tunnel large enough for a child to fit into

Directions

If you have more than one sleeping bag or tunnel to work with, you can have several children participating in this activity at the same time. You, the leader, step into the sleeping bag and leave it down, bunched around your feet. As you chant the story of the boa constrictor swallowing you up, slowly pull the sleeping bag or tunnel up to each body part being highlighted in the rhyme. Pause for a moment at the toe, knee, middle, and neck, and then pull it over your head using a mumbling tone as it goes over your head. Next, let each child who would like to participate slip into the sleeping bag or tunnel and help them pull it up, stopping at the correct intervals. You can chant this rhyme or sing along with the CD. It is much more enjoyable if the children see how it is done by you sharing first. This allows them to see that it is really a fun activity, and that they need not worry about a scary or troublesome ending.

Stewart, Georgiana Liccione. *Motor Skill Activity Fun.* Long Branch, New Jersey. Kimbo Educational, 2002. Recorded at Mastertune Studios, New York City. Play "Sneaky Snake" by Georgiana Liccione Stewart.

Directions

This activity is a series of hand and arm stretches that develop strength and control in the fingers. It is a repetitive, sequenced exercise series that follows a story line and allows children to exercise and pantomime. The more spontaneous, dramatic, and uninhibited you are in leading this activity, the more the children will get out of it. This CD comes with an easy-to-follow booklet and gives illustrations of the activity. Set to exciting music, the children are sure to love the rhythm and movement.

STORYBOARD

Five Brave Rattlesnakes

Supplies Needed

Ellison die-cut snake #1, five

Ellison die-cut sun #1C, one

Tape or self adhesive material to attach items onto storyboard

Directions

Prior to the activity, add all five snakes and the sun to the storyboard. Pass out the shakers and let the children shake their shakers throughout the verses. Ask them to help you make the noise the rattlesnake hears when he gets scared. Each time a rattlesnake slithers away, remove a snake.

Five brave rattlesnakes soaking up the sun,
Heard a *footstep* and away slithered one! *(Remove one snake)*
Four brave rattlesnakes soaking up the sun,
Heard a *big snore* and away slithered one! *(Remove one snake)*
Three brave rattlesnakes soaking up the sun,
Heard a *loud clap* and away slithered one! *(Remove one snake)*
Two brave rattlesnakes soaking up the sun,
Heard a *big sneeze* and away slithered one! *(Remove one snake)*
One brave rattlesnake soaking up the sun,
Heard his mama calling, so he had to run! *(Remove last snake)*
No more rattlesnakes! They thought they were so brave!
But where are they now? Hiding in a cave!

MAKE AND TAKE

Snake Bracelet

Supplies Needed per Child

Heavy paper or card stock. (Trace six snakes per 9" × 12" sheet of card stock.)

Snake, one each

Crayons or markers in assorted colors

Scissors

Tape

Directions

Print the pattern of a snake onto card stock. The snake needs to be approximately 5" or 6" in length. Precut the snakes and let each child color their snake with crayons or markers and finish by helping tape the snakes around each child's wrist.

LESSON 24

❧❧❧

TRAINS

CURRICULUM TOPIC

Trains

FEATURED BOOK

Lewis, Kevin. 1999. *Chugga-Chugga Choo-Choo*. New York: Hyperion Books for Children.

SUMMARY

In a sleeping little boy's bedroom, a child's train set comes alive at night. Toys around the room gather to help load and unload the freight, empty boxcars, and greet a passing train. From night to morning, the whistle blowing train makes its journey. The rhyming text is well written and does a great job of taking the reader or listener for an imaginary train ride. Children are bound to love the bold shapes and 3-D look of the images on each page. There are plenty of busy toys to view on each page. Be sure to turn the pages slowly so the children can take it all in. A clever, creative, and calming story full of imagination that is sure to be a hit at storytime. Ages 2–7

ACTIVITY

Children chant the repeating line "Chugga-chugga choo-choo" as they shake their shaker instruments. Everyone sings out together the sound of the train's whistle, "whooo-whooo!"

FEATURED BOOK

Wormell, Christopher. 2001. *Puff-Puff, Chugga-Chugga*. New York: Margaret K. McElderry Books.

SUMMARY

It all starts when the train conductor thinks, "I have a funny feeling today will be a busy one." Three extremely large animals, Mrs. Walrus, Mr. Bear, and Mrs. Elephant, one by one wait for a train ride, with shopping bags in hand, to buy food in town. At each stop, the conductor gets out and greets the large animal and thinks to himself the animal will not fit in the train car. But much to his surprise, each animal does fit in. With all of them riding together, the conductor doesn't think the train can pull the animals, but it does. After much shopping, the animals reboard the train car, precariously balancing their packages. Again, the conductor is afraid the train won't be able to carry such a load. But it does, until a bee crawls up Mrs. Elephant's trunk and causes her to sneeze. The train cars erupt and food is scattered everywhere. The animals call for their family and friends to come and have a picnic. They all eat and eat. The conductor is not amused because the train cars are turned over and off the track. The animals set the train back on the track, but then the conductor is afraid all the animals will need a ride home. Much to his surprise and joy, all the animals are too tired from their picnic. The conductor happily makes it back home with his train empty. This is a cute story and a fun one to build on. The illustrations are darling and the text is easy to read. Ages 2–7

ACTIVITY

Pass out the shakers. Ask the children to shake their instruments in rhythm and chant the repeating words, "Puff-puff, chugga-chugga, puff-puff, chugga-chugga." After the third time in the story that the line repeats "but she did," encourage the children to chime in and say these words for you by pausing and asking them to deduce what they think will happen.

ADDITIONAL BOOKS TO SHARE

Crebbin, June. 1995. *The Train Ride.* Cambridge, MA: Candlewick Press. A mother and her energetic and inquisitive child travel by train to get to a relative's house. The child looks out the train window as it is chugging down the track, anticipating the view. They ride through a farming community where the child has the opportunity to see a tractor, sheep, and a gaggle of geese. As they near their destination, the child spies a hot air balloon in the sky. In the end, a welcoming grandma is waiting at the train station for mother and child with open arms. Large, bold text and soft, pleasant illustrations make this book an easy and enjoyable book to share. Encourage children to chime in on the repeating line, "What shall I see?" Ages 2–7

Crews, Donald. 1992. *Freight Train.* New York: Mulberry Books. In this Caldecott Honor book a colorful freight train journeys through tunnels by cities and over trestles. The train starts out by moving slowly but continues to progress in speed, zooming across the pages in a remarkable blur of color, speed, and sound. Ages 3–8

Galef, David. 1996. *Tracks.* New York: Morrow Junior Books. A nearsighted railroad worker named Albert is given the job of laying railway tracks from one town to another. Albert, with map in hand, simply points his finger and the crew lays down the track. Anywhere Albert points the track is laid. One day, as he is bending over, Albert's glasses fall off his face. They hit a rock and crack into several pieces. Albert has no time to worry about broken glasses, so he puts them right back on and points at a pond. One of the crew asks Albert if he is sure he wants to lay the track across the pond, but Albert says yes. After the breaking of Albert's eyeglasses, the track starts making some strange turns. If the crew asks questions, Albert replies, "Don't ask questions!" He is in a hurry to get this job done and does not realize that his eyesight is such a problem. In the end, the new railroad line is opened and the townspeople are invited to ride the train along with Albert. They take a wild, hilarious ride from one town to the other. Albert realizes what he has done and is very nervous for the ride to end. The mayor gets off the train and congratulates and thanks Albert for giving him the most exciting ride he has ever taken. This book is illustrated by the one and only Tedd Arnold, whose cartoon-like drawings are always top notch. The children are sure to giggle their way through the journey with Albert, the near-sighted railroad worker. Make sure to show the children the map on the title page where the tracks are to be laid between the two towns. Point out that it is a straight line from one town to the other. Ages 3–7

Gurney, John Steven. 2002. *Dinosaur Train.* New York: HarperCollins. Jesse's favorite play things are dinosaurs and trains. One magical night, just before bed, Jesse is summoned by a dinosaur at his bedroom window and invited to ride along on the "dinosaur train." Ages 3–7

Piper, Watty. 1994. *The Little Engine That Could.* New York: Platt & Munk. When the other engines refuse, the Little Blue Engine tries to pull a stranded train of toys and food over a steep mountain. Using a positive attitude and self-encouragement, the train is successful! Let the children help you chant the words "I think I can! I think I can!" each time they appear in the text. Ages 2–7

Sturges, Philemon. 2001. *I Love Trains.* New York: HarperCollins. Through bright pictures and simple text, this story describes the different types of train cars and their purpose. Ages 2–7

Ziefert, Harriet. 2000. *Train Song.* New York: Orchard Books. Young train enthusiasts will love this story as a freight train with many cars passes by. A little boy stands on a nearby hill, with his toy train in hand, watching each train car intently. He counts a car of cows, and another car of ducks, geese, roosters, and hens. He spies one car piled high with logs and another with three big hogs. As he listens to the freight train sing a noisy song, he spots a shiny tank car and wonders what is inside. He watches and listens to the train sound her whistle and run through a tunnel, go over a bridge, and pass a station, clickety-clacking along the way. The sights and sounds of a freight train are described in simple text that grabs the attention of young listeners and keep them excited for each turn of the page. Colorful double-page illustrations make the book even more desirable. Be sure and point out that the train conductor looks just like the little boy watching the train on the nearby hill. Ages 2–7

MUSIC AND MOVEMENT WITH SHAKERS

Sing Along: "Hurry Back Train!"

Sung to the Tune: "Jingle Bells"

Choo-choo train, choo-choo train, chugging down the track,
Choo-choo train, choo-choo train, won't you hurry back?
Choo-choo train, choo-choo train, your wheels go round and round,
Choo-choo train, choo-choo train, come back and make that sound!
Choo-choo-choo, choo-choo-choo, choo-choo-choo-choo-choo!
Choo-choo-choo, choo-choo-choo, choo-choo-choo-choo-choo!

Choo-choo-choo, choo-choo-choo, choo-choo-choo-choo-choo!
Choo-choo-choo, choo-choo-choo, choo-choo-choo-choo-choo!
Choo-choo train, choo-choo train, where is it that you go?
Choo-choo train, choo-choo train, you know I miss you so!
Choo-choo train, choo-choo train, chugging down the track,
Choo-choo train, choo-choo train, won't you hurry back?

Directions

Pass out the shakers and play song #26 from the accompanying *The Sound of Storytime* CD. Anytime the words "choo-choo" are used in the song, allow the children to shake their shakers. When the second verse begins, ask the children to shake their shakers to the rhythm of the music. When the music ends, ask the children to pretend they are a train and blow their whistle. Make a noise like *wooooo! wooooo!* Because the ever-popular "Jingle Bells" has an easy flowing rhythm, the children will learn this new song quickly.

ADDITIONAL SONGS TO SHARE

Disney's Silly Songs. Walt Disney Records, 1988. Compact Disk. 60819-7. Play song #9, "A Peanut Sat on a Railroad Track," as the children are entering storytime and during craft time.

Gang, Goanna. *Kids Dance and Play*, Vol. 2. Soundhouse, 2002. Compact Disk. CRG 191032. Play song #9, *The Locomotion*. This song gives another opportunity for the children to parade around the room like a train and dance.

STORYBOARD

Counting Trains

Supplies Needed

Ellison die-cut train set, five trains, total (four trains per set in die-cuts)

Tape or adhesive material to attach trains onto the storyboard

Directions

Pass out the shakers to each child. Attach one train to the storyboard to start. Continue to add a train as you read the verses. Let the children count with you each time a train is added. Pause and let them shake their shakers the same amount of times as number of trains. In this activity the children have the opportunity to count up to five and then down from five. Predictable counting is a great way to introduce numbers to young children. Shaking the shakers the same amount of times per line will reinforce this counting activity.

One little train with nothing to do, *(Shake one shake)*
Along came another, then there were *two!* *(Shake two shakes)*
Two little trains as tired as they could be,
Along came another, then there were *three!* *(Shake three shakes)*
Three little trains, still looking for one more,
Along came another, then there were *four!* *(Shake four shakes)*
Four little trains trying to look alive,
Along came another, then there were *five!* *(Shake five shakes)*
Five little trains just sitting on the track,
One checked the clock and said, "I have to get back!"
Four little trains staring at the sky, *(Shake four shakes)*
One blew his whistle and said, "bye, bye!"
Three little trains sitting in a row, *(Shake three shakes)*
One squeaked his wheels and said, "It's time to go!"
Two little trains making lots of smoke, *(Shake two shakes)*
One said, "I'm leaving, the smoke will make me choke!"
One little train, he said, "I can take a hint!" *(Shake one shake)*
So he fired up his engine and away he went!
No little trains left on the track, *(Lay shakers down)*
I hope they stay longer the next time they come back!

MAKE AND TAKE

Candy Chew-Chew Trains

Supplies Needed per Child

Glue gun, cool melt type

One package of hard candy, e.g., LifeSavers, one each

Wrapped hard candy discs, e.g., butterscotch or peppermint candy, four each

Wrapped chocolate drops, e.g., Hershey's Kisses, one each

Directions

This craft works better if you have adults handling the glue guns, even if they are the cool type. Have the adult add the glue where needed and let the children add the candies. Lay the roll of candy down horizontally; add a drop of glue to the four areas where the wheels will be placed. Still keeping the hard candy roll laying horizontally, add a drop of glue to the top of one of the ends of the candy roll and let the children attach the chocolate drop to the top. This is extremely simple and candy crafts are always a hit. The children will be lucky to make it home without tearing into their little chew-chew trains.

MAKE AND TAKE 2

Train Pictures

Supplies Needed per Child

Ellison die-cut train set in assorted colors, 1 set of four train cars per child

Glue stick

Construction Paper, 12" × 18" size, any color, one sheet

Washable markers or colors

Directions

Children draw a train track and other appropriate scenery on their paper and attach the paper train set with glue. Make one ahead of time with simple landscape such as clouds, smoke from the engine, grass, sun, and railroad signs to give the children a visual idea of what they would like to add to their picture. (This is a perfect opportunity to have a display of train books with colorful illustrations for the children to view just before the Make and Take.)

PART V

TAMBOURINES

LESSON 25

꧁❀꧂

ABC's AND 123's

CURRICULUM TOPICS

Alphabet, Numbers, Monkeys

FEATURED BOOK

Archambault, John. 2004. *Boom Chicka Rock*. New York: Philomel Books.

SUMMARY

While the cat is asleep, twelve mice party and rock around the clock in this concept book about numbers and time. Ages 3–7

ACTIVITY

Children tap and shake their tambourines to the beat of the repeating words, "Boom Chicka Rock, Chicka Rock, Chicka Boom!" Practice playing and chanting the words before the story by asking the children to echo you. Strike the tambourine on the words "boom" or "rock," and shake the tambourine on the word "chicka."

FEATURED BOOK

Martin, Bill, Jr., and John Archambault. 1989. *Chicka Chicka Boom Boom*. New York: Scholastic.

SUMMARY

Capital and lowercase alphabet letters race to the top of a coconut tree in this classic alphabet concept book. Ages 3–7

ACTIVITY

Children chant the repeating line "chicka chicka boom boom" with you as they shake their tambourines on the words "chicka chicka" and strike their tambourines on the words "boom boom." If you do not have tambourines, children can stand up and flap their arms like a chicken on the words "chicka chicka" and pat their legs or stomp their feet on the words "boom boom." Both ways are fun to play.

ADDITIONAL BOOKS TO SHARE

Aylesworth, Jim. 2003. *Naughty Little Monkeys*. New York: Dutton Children's Books. Mom thinks her little monkeys are absolutely angelic—all twenty six of them. When she leaves them home alone, they can't resist naughty monkey tricks. From A to Z, monkeys try every naughty antic in the book. With rhyming text and repeating lines kids can chant, this one is worth a look! It is rare to find a concept book that is as entertaining as it is didactic. Hilarious illustrations depict the monkeys and their misadventures with irresistible kid-like characteristics. This book is so fun to read. Don't feel like you need to interrupt the flow of the verse to point out the alphabet letters. After the story, flip back through a few pages. Point to a letter on the page and ask the children to tell you what it is. Give your listeners the opportunity to test their skills by asking them to tell you what items on the page start with that letter. Ages 3–8

Fleming, Denise. 2002. *Alphabet Under Construction*. New York: Henry Holt. Mouse gets out his tools and constructs all the letters of the alphabet from different materials and mediums. The last page of the book is a picture of a work schedule on a calendar. This book has twenty-six craft ideas of its own. Whether you meet with participants once a week at the library or every day in a classroom, make your own alphabet work calendar. What a great way to introduce the multiple concepts of time, numbers, days, weeks, months, years, and alphabet letters. Make a different letter each time you meet. Provide large Ellison die-cut alphabet sets (letters) the children can decorate.

Give the children an opportunity to experience all kinds of sensory exploration. Glue buttons on the letter B, cotton balls on the letter C, google eyes on the letter E, and yarn on the letter Y. Punch holes in the letter L, Q, or S and have the children "lace," "quilt" or "sew" their letters with yarn. Paint the P, make the D from dough, and tile the T. The ideas are endless. What an easy, entertaining, educational, and economical way to incorporate art throughout the whole year! The four E's! Ages 3–7

Lionni, Leo. 1996. *The Alphabet Tree*. New York: Alfred A. Knopf. A bug teaches the letters on the alphabet tree to form words. Next, a caterpillar teaches the words to form sentences that say something important. This book abounds with inspirational art ideas. Show the children how to make their own alphabet tree by tearing a tree trunk from brown paper and stamping or tearing green leaves to make branches. Give the children safety scissors and old magazines and allow them to tear and cut letters from meaningful print. Paste the letters on the tree. Alternatively, children can make a caterpillar from simple paper circles. Use old magazines and have the children find letters to glue on each circle to form an important word or message. Provide a list of meaningful words like peace, love, harmony, diversity, happy, or share. Encourage the children to brainstorm ideas of their own, too. They can come up with some really beautiful thoughts. Write down each child's chosen word for them and then let them go on a letter scavenger hunt with their safety scissors and the magazines. Children, especially younger ones, may want to make their name, which is a pretty important word too! These inspirational caterpillars make a wonderful "Ideas Give Us Wings" bulletin board. Ages 3–7

Mockford, Caroline. 2003. *Cleo's Alphabet Book*. Cambridge, MA: Barefoot Books. Twenty-six riddles comprise this refreshingly unique approach to the traditional alphabet book. The word puzzles are right on the target audience's developmental level. The riddles are just difficult enough to provoke a second thought, but simple enough for children to solve by themselves, triumphantly gaining self-confidence. Ages 2–7

Seeger, Laura Vaccaro. 2003. *The Hidden Alphabet*. Brookfield, CT: Roaring Book Press. Each page of this alphabet concept book contains a picture in a black frame. The objects in the pictures are in alphabetical order, from A to Z; lift the frames and you will see the pictures transform to corresponding alphabet letters almost magically. Make alphabet letters for the storyboard by printing large letters from your computer or by cutting out the alphabet from felt or construction paper. If the pieces are to be made from paper, laminate and place tape on the backs of them. Pass out the twenty-six letters of the alphabet, at least one to each participant. As you read through the alphabet book, children will bring up the appropriate letter and place it in alphabetical order on the board. Ages 3–7

MUSIC AND MOVEMENT WITH TAMBOURINES

Sing Along: "The Alphabet Tree"

Sung to the Tune: "The Alphabet Song"

A B C D E F G—Monkey's climbing up the coconut tree?
H I J K L M N O P—Monkey's eating coconuts, lets go see!
Q R S T U V—Monkey's looking down and smiling at me!
W X Y and Z—Monkey's throwing coconuts—HE HIT MY KNEE!
Now we've sang our ABC's, lets RUN from the monkey in the coconut tree!

Directions

Pass out the tambourines and play song #27 from the accompanying *The Sound of Storytime* CD. This is a silly song that the children will warm right up to. Sing through the song and ask the children tap their tambourines to the beat of the alphabet letters, stopping between verses of letters. Another way to enjoy the song is have the children pretend to be the monkey while you pretend to be the crowd. The children can act out climbing up the coconut tree and pretend to crack a coconut open and eat it. Have them pretend they are high in a tree, with their heads lowered and their hand placed above the brow, gazing down at the crowd. Tell the children to continue looking down with a great big mischievous grin. For the grand finale, have the children pretend to throw coconuts at you! You, the leader, grab your knees pretending to be injured! The more you practice this song and the actions, the more animated, amusing, and entertaining this song becomes. As the children get familiar with both parts, reverse the activity and have the children become the crowd and you be the monkey.

ADDITIONAL SONGS TO SHARE

Scelsa, Greg, and Steve Millang. *We All Live Together*, Vol. 5. Silverlake Sound, 1994. Compact Disk. YM-014-CD. Play song #2, "The Number Game." When the song says, "This is number one," hold up the number on the right hand. When it repeats, "And this is number one," hold up the same number on the left hand. Next, the song says, "we're rollin' one." Roll your hands over each other with the correct number of fingers showing. Verses continue through the number five.

JUST FOR FUN

I Spy an Alphabet

Directions

Pass out the tambourines. Explain to the children that you are going to look around the room for something starting with an A. Chant the verse, then ask the children to raise their hands if they would like to guess what letter it is. When the child guesses correctly, instruct him or her to whisper an item to you that the children will look for next. Whatever the child chooses, use the first letter of the item and chant the verse. It helps to sound out the letter you are going to ask them to look for after chanting the verse. Continue the activity until each child has had a turn.

Ask children to stand up and shake their tambourine to the beat of the chant:

Boom, Chicka, Boom, Chicka, Boom, Boom, Boom!
I spy a letter in this room! *(Don't forget to sound out the letter)*

Repeat, changing letters

STORYBOARD

Letter Tree Recogition

Supplies Needed

Construction paper, 12" × 18" in size, brown, or a large brown paper sack, one

Construction paper, 9" × 12" in size, green, one

Letters of the alphabet cut out of magazines.

(Look for letters large enough to be seen from a distance from the storyboard.) If you have more than twenty-six children, you will need more letters; any letter of the alphabet is fine

Glue stick

Tape or self-adhesive material to attach items onto the storyboard

Directions

Tear the brown construction paper or large brown paper sack into the shape of a tree trunk and add some branches. Tear the green construction paper to the shape of the tree leaves. Glue the leaves and the coconuts to the tree. The pictures of the coconut tree in the featured book, *Chicka Chicka Boom Boom,* by Bill Martin, are a good visual aid. Gently tape all of the letters of the alphabet to the tree. If you have too many to fit, lightly tape the letters around the trunk, on the trunk, or on the ground below the trunk. The tree and letters need to be on the storyboard prior to this activity. Make sure you have left room on the top of the storyboard. This is where the children will be placing their letters they remove from the tree. The object of this activity is to have each child approach the storyboard when they hear their name called and take a letter from the tree. Give them the opportunity to tell you and the other children what letter they chose. Be sensitive to the child who may have forgotten or does not fully know the alphabet. If the child pauses or seems reluctant, help them out. Continue to sing the verse of the song until all the letters have been removed from the alphabet tree.

Sung to the Tune: "Clementine"
Here comes [child's name] to take a letter, to take a letter from the tree!
Place it high up on the storyboard, so that everyone can see!
(Pause the singing and ask the child)
What letter is it? _____

Continue singing a cappella and repeating the verse, singing each child's name, and pausing to ask them what letter they removed until all of the children have participated.

MAKE AND TAKE

Alphabet Coconut Trees

Supplies Needed per Child

Alphabet letters cut from magazines, approximately ten letters each

Construction paper, 12" × 18" in size in any color, one

Construction paper, 9" × 12" in size, brown, or large brown paper sack, enough to tear tree trunks and branches for each child

Construction paper, 9" × 12" in size, green, for tearing leaves

Construction paper scraps, in a variety of colors, for coconuts

Glue stick

Directions

Have each child create an alphabet coconut tree like the one prepared for the storyboard activity. Let them tear the grocery sack to make a long tree trunk and branches. Have them rip the green construction paper to make the tree leaves. Use the multicolored construction paper to tear small circles for colorful coconuts. Have the children glue the tree on the large sheet of construction paper and add the letters onto the coconut tree. They may want to choose letters to spell out their name or something meaningful to them. Encourage them to share their Alphabet Trees with their family and friends and show them what they have learned.

LESSON 26

CLEANING UP

CURRICULUM TOPICS

Chores, Character Values—Helping

FEATURED BOOK

Harper, Lindsay. 2001. *Nora's Room.* New York: HarperCollins.

SUMMARY

"Crash! Bang! Crash! Bang! Boom! Something's going on in Nora's room!" Nora is a young girl whose bedroom is upstairs. Her mother is busy downstairs with her two baby siblings when she hears all kinds of strange and loud noises exuding from Nora's bedroom. The family dog is trying to nap and is disgusted as well with all of the noises coming from Nora's room. Throughout the pages are all kinds of thoughts that mother, the siblings, and the dog are having about what those noises might be. Finally, mother has had enough and, with a baby on each hip, she trudges upstairs to Nora's room to see what all the ruckus is about. When mother asks Nora to explain, she replies, "Oh, nothing." All the noises the family has been hearing seem to represent the toys scattered over Nora's floor. This is a fun and humorous read aloud, and the children will enjoy using their tambourine to make all of the commotion throughout the story. Ages 3–8

ACTIVITY

Children will use their tambourines to chant and play the repeating line, "Crash! Bang! Crash! Bang! Boom!" Then they will quiet their instrument and say only, "Something's going on in Nora's room." Give a brief book talk to introduce the story. Show the children the bold, repeating words printed on the inside front cover of the book. Explain each time you flip back to this inside front-page that they will say their line and play their instrument. Pass out the instruments and teach them the rhythm you want them to play. Give them a chance to practice by letting them echo you a few times. Begin the story. The way the author has written this book, the repeating line only repeats a couple of times. To give the children lots of opportunity to play along with you, flip back to the repeating line on the inside cover after every two-page spread or so.

ADDITIONAL BOOKS TO SHARE

Anderson, Peggy Perry. 2002. *Let's Clean Up.* Boston: Houghton Mifflin. Joe is a young frog with a very messy room. One day his mother decides it is time for Joe's room to be cleaned. She cleans high and low and makes it spotless for Joe. The young frog is so excited by the amount of room he has to play in, and the amount of toys he can play with that; he decides to pull them all out and play with them. Joe's mother returns to find a horribly messy room and she begins to cry. Feeling guilty, Joe promises her he will clean his room by himself. Mom waits and waits and finally Joe comes and takes her back into his clean room. Mother hugs little Joe with pride and joy, until she spots his bedroom window opened. Mother goes to the window with her young son and realizes what Joe had done. "Now what shall we do about the yard?" Joe has thrown all his toys out the window and into the yard so the room will be clean and his mother will be pleased with him. This mischievously sweet story is told in rhyme. Both parents and young listeners alike will relate to the plight of these characters. Although this book is not large in size, the illustrations are big and bold, making it a great storytime read. Ages 2–7

Brown, Margaret Wise. 2002. *Robin's Room.* New York: Hyperion Books for Children. Robin is a really, really bad little boy and was bad even as a baby. He is every parent's worst nightmare! He paints pictures on the doors and windows and plants flowers in the bathtub. He even saws legs off chairs. His parent's are at their wit's end and do not know what to do with him. They finally decide they will give him a room of his own. They give him a nice, big colorful room but he takes one look at the room, stamps his foot, and demands three carpenters. His parent's hire three carpenters and give him everything he asks for to remodel his room. No one is allowed into Robin's room for one week. The parent's can hear all kinds of noises inside and are very curious. The day finally comes when the parent's can see Robin's room. He has made himself quite a room. The parent's are so impressed, they invite all kinds of people to come and see the room. They also enjoy reading in the window seat and hanging out in Robin's room. Robin is not happy with his room being such a spectacle. So he orders everybody out and say they could only visit when his custom-designed clock says they could. He cuts out a space in his clock from four o'clock to suppertime and that is when he can do whatever he wants in his room. Best of all, do it alone! The children will love this story of individual expression. During the construction/remodeling of Robin's bedroom, readers are guided to turn the book upside down and to begin reading the pages backwards to forward. It is a bit confusing, but after reading the book, you'll understand the reason. Ages 3–8

Cummings, Pat. 1994. *Clean Your Room, Harvey Moon!* New York: Aladdin Books. Harvey Moon is a young boy who is settling in for a Saturday morning full of his favorite cartoons. His mother has a different idea! She sends him to his room to clean up his awful mess. Harvey reluctantly goes to his room and begins to clean it up. He discovers all kinds of gross and fuzzy things growing in his room. Harvey continues to work and clean his room, but spends just as much time watching the clock and lamenting about the cartoons he is missing. Just when Harvey thinks he is finally done, he discovers his idea of clean is not the same as his mother's! Ages 3–8

Ericsson, Jennifer A. 2002. *She Did It!* New York: Melanie Kroupa/Farrar, Straus and Giroux. *She Did It!* is a playful story about four sisters who are all different ages and different sizes, but who are all full of orneriness. No matter what goes wrong in the household, when asked, the sisters point their fingers at each other and say, "She did it!" From pillow fights in the morning to an extremely messy and wet bathroom to a chaotic kitchen calamity, the girls are ruthless in their endeavor to continue to blame each other for every mess made. The day continues, as does more and more chaos with every turn of the page. Finally, their mother has had enough and sends them to their room. The four sisters decide to try to redeem themselves by cleaning up their messes. They pull together as a team of fabulous cleaners. Their mom is surprised and overjoyed by their hard work. When she asks the question of who did it this time, she gets a unanimous answer, "We did it!" This rhyming book with lots of noisy words will bring giggles and excitement. The illustrations provide a lot of humorous detail on every page. While prereading this book, look for the humorous detail in the pictures. As you are sharing the story with the children, be sure to take some time at the end of each page to point out the "extras." Encourage and prompt the children to say the repeating line, "She did it!" Ages 3–8

Fearnley, Jan. 2003. *Billy Tibbles Moves Out!* New York: HarperCollins. The Tibbles are a family of furry felines. Billy Tibbles is the big brother and has a younger sister and baby brother. He enjoys being the oldest and really likes not having to share his bedroom with his baby brother. One day everything changes. Billy's parents announce they are going to move baby brother into Billy's room. Billy is so unhappy with the announcement, he decides to move out. He tries the bathtub, but it is too hard. Then he tries the shed, but it has too many spiders! Billy goes back inside just in time for a bedtime story. He and his sister are sitting on their dad's lap, but they are pushing and shoving and wiggling around so much that their dad sends them to bed, but not before he gives them a lecture on sharing. As Billy and his sister go upstairs for bed, they hear some scary noises. The closer they get to Billy's room, the louder the noises became. Their imaginations are running wild as they continue to tiptoe to the door. When they peek inside, there is baby brother making all kinds of noise, jumping up and down on Billy's bed. Billy orders baby brother off his bed, but when brother tells him no, Billy and his little sister decide to join in. They decide that sharing is fun until they break the bed. Mom and dad are hardly amused and end up having to share their bed with all three of the kittens. This story is a good lesson in sharing and teaches the children that there are both good and bad things about sharing. Large text and bright, vivid illustrations make this book an excellent choice to read aloud. There are a number of chances for the children to use the tambourines to make the loud noises while sharing this story. Ages 3–7

Parnell, Robyn. 2005. *My Closet Threw a Party.* New York: Sterling Publishing. A young girl's room is a pigsty and she blames it on her cluttered closet throwing a party with her messy room. Clean clothes and stinky clothes partner together in an unusual dance. In this rhyming text the little girl's room comes to life. The bright and vivid illustrations capture the imagination of young children, as most can relate from their own messy room experiences. A must share for storytime! Ages 3–8

Provencher, Rose-Marie. 2001. *Mouse Cleaning.* New York: Henry Holt. It is spring cleaning time again, but Grandma Twilly can't find the motivation to clean her house. All she wants to do is sit and rock in her rocking chair. As she is sitting and rocking one day, she hears the squeak of a mouse. The one thing Grandma Twilly will not put up with is a mouse. She decides that she will start cleaning and rid herself of that pesky mouse. Day after day she cleans, but she still find signs of the mouse in her house. She scrubs and tidies every drawer and closet but she still finds signs of that mouse. She has a revelation one day as she is sitting and rocking while still worrying about the mouse. Without that mouse in her house, she would have never done her spring cleaning!

Grandma Twilly decides to thank the mouse in a generous way for helping to clean her house. Young children will love hunting for the mouse throughout the story. On each page that the mouse is hiding, the author kindly adds, in parenthesis, a note as to where the mouse is hiding. Ages 2–7

Van Kampen, Vlasta. 2003. *It Couldn't Be Worse!* New York: Annick Press. A poor farmer and his family of six children, a wife, and the grandparents live in a one-room house. It is very crowded. They all quarrel and fight and continue to get in each other's way. The farmer's wife goes to the market one day to buy some fish and asks the wise fishmonger what she should do about their problem. "It couldn't be worse," she tells him. The fishmonger tells her to take a goat into the house and things will get better. The farmer's wife is uneasy and frustrated by the fishmonger's reply, but knows he is very wise and takes his advice. The following day the farmer's wife goes back to the fishmonger and tells him, "Things couldn't be worse!" The fishmonger then advises her to take a sheep into their small house. The family brings the sheep into their tiny one-room house, and the tale continues as they bring in animal after animal to live with them, each time lamenting, "Things couldn't be worse!" In the end, the fishmonger advises the farmer's wife to let all the animals out of their tiny house and things will get better. With all the animals out of the house, there is no quarreling and there is lots of room for everyone! This is an adaption of a classic folktale with predictable but hilarious colored illustrations. Have the children join with you in repeating the line, "Things couldn't be worse!" After the story, ask the children what they think about moving different farm animals into their house. This discussion could end in some funny imaginative interpretations from your young audience. Use the storyboard to involve the children in the telling of the story. Pass out Ellison die-cuts of a goat, sheep, pig #2, rooster, and cow. Pass out Ellison die-cut hens to all the remaining participants. As you tell the story, have the children bring their animal to the board. If you like, you can put a simple outline of a house on the board and add the animals to cover the house. Ages 3–7

MUSIC AND MOVEMENT WITH TAMBOURINES

Sing Along: "My Messy Room!"

Sung to the Tune: "Mary Had a Little Lamb"

I don't want to clean my room, clean my room, clean my room!
I don't want to clean my room, because it's such a mess!
Will you help me pick up toys, pick up toys, pick up toys?
Will you help me pick up toys? Then we'll leave the rest!
Well—maybe we can pick up clothes, pick up clothes, pick up clothes!
Maybe we can pick up clothes! Then we'll leave the rest!
Well—maybe we can make the bed, make the bed, make the bed!
Maybe we can make the bed! Then we'll leave the rest!
Well—Maybe we can sweep the floor, sweep the floor, sweep the floor!
Maybe we can sweep the floor! Then we'll leave the rest!
I can't believe my room is clean! My room is clean! My room is clean!
I can't believe my room is clean! What happened to my MESS?

Directions

Pass out the tambourines and play song #28 from the accompanying *The Sound of Storytime* CD. Ask the children to pretend they are picking items up off the floor, and then pretend they are making the bed and sweeping the floor. Before they realize it, they have cleaned their room, with just a little extra help. Another way to enjoy this song is to let half the children gently tap their tambourine and the other half pretend to pick up toys. When the song is over, ask the children to trade places and repeat the activity.

ADDITIONAL SONGS TO SHARE

Harper, Jessica. *Nora's Room.* 4th Street Recording Studio, 1996. Compact Disk. ALA 2005. Play song #1, "Nora's Room," as children enter storytime and at craft time.

Palmer, Hap. *Rhythms on Parade.* Hap-Pal Music Inc., 1995. Compact Disk. HP102E AC633. Play song #17, "Stuff It in the Closet." Pass out the tambourines. Have the children answer all the questions in the song with the chant, "Stuff it in the closet!" Every time the song repeats, "Now open the door, just once more. . . . CRASH!", ask the children to shake and bang their tambourines.

Piggyback Songs: Singable Poems Set to Favorite Tunes. Kimbo, 1995. Compact Disk. KIM 9141CD. Play song #16, "Time to Pick up the Toys." In this song, a leader sings the verse and a chorus of children echo. Instruct your audience to listen to the first verse and then echo it with the children on the CD. There is a long interlude at the end of the song that gives the children time to pick up toys.

Play movement song #20, "Toes Are Tapping." Get the wiggles out by clapping and tapping along to this simple upbeat song.

Play song #35, "Housework Song." Perform the different household tasks by mimicking the actions in each verse.

STORYBOARD

My Messy/Clean Room

Supplies Needed

Pictures of toys cut out of Christmas catalogs, magazines, and toy store flyers, one per child

Decorated shoe box with lid or hinged wooden box—something made to look like a toy box that will hold the storyboard toys, with a lid that easily slips on and off

Tape or self-adhesive material to attach the toys onto the storyboard

Directions

Have enough pictures of toys available for one per child. Put all the toys on the storyboard. Tell the children they are going to pretend this is a messy room and they need to help clean the room. Call children to the storyboard, one at a time, and ask them to remove one toy from the board and put it in the toy box that you have made available for this lesson. As they approach the storyboard and take a toy, ask them to tell you what they chose and to share something about it, if they like. They may want to share that they own that particular toy, or they chose it because it is their favorite color, or they would like a toy like that. Whatever they share, be positive and enthusiastic. Let them lift the lid off the box, add their item, and put the lid back on or shut the hinged door. This helps them learn to complete a task. Continue to follow through this process until each child has had a turn. When the storyboard is all clean, make a big deal about how clean they made the room. This is a good learning lesson for the children. This activity teaches that with patience, and a little help, one by one we can complete a task and maybe even enjoy it a bit.

MAKE AND TAKE

Messy/Clean Room Door Hangers

Supplies Needed per Child

Ellison die-cut, plain door hanger, assorted colors, one

Washable markers and crayons in assorted colors

Stickers and rubber stamps (optional)

Directions

Let each child decorate their door hangers. On one side, have them write "messy" at the bottom of the door hanger and then draw a messy picture. On the other side have them write "clean" at the bottom of the door hanger and then draw a happy, clean room picture. If you have stickers or rubber stamps available, let the children decorate their hangers. Explain to the children that they will need to hang them on their door knobs and turn them as their room changes from messy to clean.

LESSON 27

❧

FARM LIFE

CURRICULUM TOPICS
Farm Animals

FEATURED BOOK
Ziefert, Harriet. 1995. *Oh What a Noisy Farm.* New York: Tambourine Books.

SUMMARY
When the bull chases the cow, a crashing, banging procession ensues as more and more farmyard animals, including the farmer and his wife, join this cumulative tale. Ages 2–7

ACTIVITY
The farmer's wife cries, "Stop, Stop!" and the farmer bangs a pot, "Crash, Bang!" When the goat joins the story, on about the fourth page, a repeating list of actions begins to accumulate. Pass out the tambourines before the story. Children will cry out, "Stop, Stop!" and then strike their tambourines on the words, "Crash, Bang!" each time the list repeats. Another way to play along is to divide the group in half. You can divide them down the middle or by boys and girls. One group plays the part of the farmer's wife and calls out "Stop, Stop!" and the other group plays the part of the farmer on their tambourines.

ADDITIONAL BOOKS TO SHARE
Bateman, Teresa. 2004. *April Foolishness*. Morton Grove, IL: Albert Whitman. The day the grandkids come out to the farm for a visit, Grandpa's farm animals raise a ruckus. The grandkids keep pleading with Grandpa to come outside and check on the loosed animals, but for some reason Grandpa just continues to ignore the kid's emphatic warnings. When Grandpa reveals to Grandma that the kids are trying to play an April Fools' prank on him, everyone is in on the comedy and roars with laughter. Grandma in turn reveals to Grandpa that April Fools' Day is tomorrow! The joke is on Grandpa after all, and he runs out the door to corral his farm animals. This tale is told in a rollicking rhyme, and your listeners can participate by crying out the repeating line, "Grandpa, oh, Grandpa!" The best April Fools' book we have ever seen! Ages 2–7

Bateman, Teresa. 2001. *Farm Flu*. Morton Grove, IL: Albert Whitman. When the farm animals come down with the flu, a farmer boy does just what he thinks his mom would do to take care of them. The animals soon get too accustomed to such pampering until the clever boy takes away their television privileges. The quick wit of this child character gives him a heroic quality that children cheer for. The humor is adorable and right on the level of the audience for which it is intended. When the animals repeatedly sneeze in the tale, encourage your listeners to chime in with their wildest "ka-chooo!" You and your listeners will love this Building Block Award Nominee book. Ages 2–7

Bock, Lee. 2003. *Oh, Crumps! Ay, Caramba!* Green Bay, WI: Raven Tree Press. One evening the animals on Farmer Felandro's farm cause one catastrophe after another. As the night drowns on, the heavy-eyed farmer repeatedly drags himself from bed to straighten things out. Encourage the children to chime in on repeating lines like, "Oh, crumps!" and to act out or pantomime the lines where Farmer Felandro puts "his feet into his old, brown work boots, clumpidy clumped down the steps." Participants can stomp their feet on the floor with you to make the "clumpidy clump" sounds. The real humor infused in the story is when each time the sleepy farmer crawls back into bed, he recites the long list of chores he has to do in the morning. The more tired he gets, the sillier the list becomes. He gets so mixed up that he says things like, "climb the cow, mow the fence, milk the hay." Read the list of chores like you are really trying to remember each activity. Act it out by counting on your fingers and scratching your forehead. Add a sleepy yawn here and there, and read this part slowly enough so the children "catch on" to the mixed-up list. Text is printed in both English and Spanish. Ages 4–8

Brown, Ken. 2001. *The Scarecrow's Hat*. Atlanta, GA: Peachtree. Chicken wants scarecrow's hat to make a nest, but she does not have anything scarecrow wants to trade for. The astute little hen hatches a plan and makes a series of barters with the other animals on the farm to get what she needs to trade with scarecrow. Ages 3–8

Cohen, Santiago. 2003. *Fiddle-I-Fee*. Maplewood, NJ: Blue Apple Books. A traditional song of nonsense words and farm animals is told in cumulative verse on large board-book pages. Children can sing the silly words with you as the repeating list gets longer and longer. To extend this story prepare and pass out Ellison die-cuts of a cat #3, hen, horse #1, pig #2, cow, and beagle. As each character in the story is introduced, have the child with the appropriate animal bring it to the board and place it in vertical order as the illustrator does in the story book. Ages 1–6

Cowen-Fletcher, Jane. 2001. *Farmer Will*. Cambridge, MA: Candlewick Press. When young Farmer Will takes his toy farm animals out to play, they stretch out in his life-size imagination. The gang frolics and plays all day, then tucks into bed together to rest. The pastel illustrations will captivate and inspire little ones to pretend play and exercise their own imaginations. Ages 2–6

King, Bob. 1991. *Sitting on the Farm*. New York: Orchard Books. When a series of farm animals wear out their welcome at a picnic, a girl calls on larger and larger animals to come and help. This story has great repeating lines the children love to chant. Encourage them to reply "No siree!" and "Munch! Munch! Munch!" Ages 2–7

Park, Linda Sue. 2004. *Mung-Mung*. Watertown, MA: Charlesbridge. Books that talk about animal sounds are overly abundant, but did you know people who speak different languages use very different words to describe animal sounds? We never knew this until a couple years ago when one of our friends hosted a foreign exchange student who laughed out loud when she found out that we say chickens "cock-a-doodle-doo" instead of "ko, ko, ko." In fact, we all had a chuckle, and your audience will too with this clever little book. Begin this story by reading the author's notes on the last couple of pages. The book reads like a guessing game. Read the new animal sounds and tell the children which country uses each different sound. Ask the children to guess which animal they think the words are describing. Lift the flap to find out. Then let your audience tell you how they say that animal's sound. Extend this story by introducing the children to a big wall map or globe. Point out on the map a few of the countries from the story. Much like a storyboard activity, hang a wall map on a bulletin board. Give each child a small card with a symbol of a fun place like Walt Disney World, Hershey Park in Pennsylvania, or their own hometown. Let them bring their cards up one at a time and help you place their symbol on the correct place on the map. Leave these materials out after your storytime session and encourage the children to continue exploring them. Ages 3–7

Root, Phyllis. 2000. *Kiss the Cow!* Cambridge, MA: Candlewick Press. Annalisa refuses to kiss the family cow in repayment for the sweet milk she gives. Without that kiss, there will be no milk for Mama May's children. Will they all go hungry, or will Annalisa obey her mother. Would you kiss a cow? Ages 3–7

Rostoker-Gruber, Karen. 2004. *Rooster Can't Cock-A-Doodle-Doo*. New York: Dial Books for Young Readers. When rooster wakes up with a sore throat, he cannot cock-a-doodle-doo loud enough to wake the farmer. All the animals pitch in to help wake Farmer Ted and help him get his chores done after his late start on the day. Ages 2–7

Tepper, Danny. 2005. *Look Who's Talking on the Farm*. New York: Random House. Books of farm animals making their traditional farm sounds are abundant, but the illustrations and great big pictures that fold out very simply make this book a unique read-aloud. If you pause after each rhyming verse and hold your hand to your ear like you are listening for something, your participants will understand that you are inviting them to read along with you. Ages 1–6

MUSIC AND MOVEMENT

Sing Along: "Wake Up, Farm!"

Sung to the Tune: "The Farmer in the Dell"

Oh! What a quiet farm!
Oh! What a quiet farm!
It's time to wake the animals on the quiet farm!
The rooster wakes the cow!
The rooster wakes the cow!
Cock-a-doodle, doodley doo!

The rooster wakes the cow!
The cow wakes the pig!
The cow wakes the pig!
Moo, moo, moodlly moo!
The cow wakes the pig!
The pig wakes the duck!
The pig wakes the duck!
Oink, oink, oinkedy oink!
The pig wakes the duck!
The duck wakes the horse!
The duck wakes the horse!
Quack, quack, quackedy quack!
The duck wakes the horse!
The horse wakes the dog!
The horse wakes the dog!
Neigh, neigh, neighly neigh!
The horse wakes the dog!
The dog wakes the cat!
The dog wakes the cat!
Woof, woof, woofedy woof!
The dog wakes the cat!
The cat wakes the farmer!
The cat wakes the farmer!
Meow, meow, meow meow!
The cat wakes the farmer!
The farmer wakes his wife!
The farmer wakes his wife!
Wake, wake, wakedy wake!
The farmer wakes his wife!
The wife wakes the child!
The wife wakes the child!
Kiss, kiss, kissidy kiss!
The wife wakes the child!
The farm is now awake!
The farm is now awake!
Oh! What a noisy farm!
The farm is now awake!

Directions

Play song #29 from the accompanying *The Sound of Storytime* CD. This energetic song is easy for the children to follow and along with, and they will love making the many different animal sounds!

ACTIVITY

Sing Along: "Tambourine Action!"

Sung to the Tune: "When the Saints Go Marching"

Oh! Can you shake—that tambourine?
Can you shake it loud and clear!
Can you shake it high above you—so that everyone can hear!
Oh can you tap—that tambourine?
Can you tap it loud and clear!
Can you tap it on your knees—so that everyone can hear!
Oh can you ring—that tambourine?
Can you ring it loud and clear!
Can you ring it back behind you—so that every one can hear!
Oh can you drum—that tambourine?

Can you drum it loud and clear!
Can you drum it on the ground—so that everyone can hear!
Oh can you hold—that tambourine?
Can you hold it quiet and still?
Can you pull it to your body—so that only you can feel!
Shake, shake, shake, shake!
Shake, shake, shake, shake!
Shake, shake, shake, shake, shake, shake, shake, shake, shake!
Shake, shake, shake, shake, shake, shake, shake, shake, shake!
Shake, shake, shake, shake, shake, shake, shake, shake!

Directions

Pass out the tambourines and play song #30 from the accompanying *The Sound of Storytime* CD. Play and sing along and follow the directions of the song.

ADDITIONAL SONGS TO SHARE

Gang, Goanna. *Kids Dance and Play*, Vol. 2. Soundhouse, 2002. Compact Disk. CRG 191032. Play song #8, *The Chicken Dance*. Lead the children in this popular dance routine. To perform the chicken dance, pinch fingers together to make a chicken's beak, then flap arms like chicken wings, shimmy downward, and finally clap four times. There are four counts to each movement.

Reid-Naiman, Kathy. *Tickles and Tunes.* Merriweather Records. 1997. Compact Disk. M9701. Play song #18, "See the Ponies." Dance along in place or pull out the parachute for some group activity fun. To play along with the parachute, everyone holds on to the outside and walks, trots, and gallops in a circle as the song directs.

STORYBOARD

Wake Up, Farm!

Supplies Needed

Ellison die-cut farm animals—rooster, cow, pig #2, duck, horse #1, mutt, cat #3, one of each

Ellison die-cut farmer, woman, toddler, one of each

Directions

Add a musical element to your storyboard activity! Now that the children have sung the song *Wake Up, Farm!* from the accompanying *Sound of Storytime* CD, have the children sing along as you add the animals to the storyboard. It is important to have them organized and in order so that you can attach them quickly. Let the children make the animal sounds in the song. If you have a small group, give each child a farm animal to bring to the board as the song plays.

Have the children line up in the order of the animals waking up on the farm so that they can attach the animal in the amount of time allowed on the song. Be organized and ready; this storyboard will be fast and fun!

MAKE AND TAKE

Farm Animals in a Fence

Supplies Needed per Child

Ellison die-cut farm animals, assorted—rooster, goat, pig #2, cow, horse #1, mutt, sheep, cat #3, for example, five each

Construction paper, 12" × 18" in size, two sheets, one green and one blue sheet

Craft sticks, small size, approximately 10 to 15 each

Glue stick

Washable markers or crayons

Directions

Prior to the activity, tear green construction paper into two or three horizontal strips. This becomes grass, when glued to the bottom of each blue sheet of construction paper. Instruct the children to glue the grass to the bottom of the blue paper first. Next, have the children glue farm animals on the grass. Let them glue four or five assorted animals each. They may color the farm scene, adding flowers, clouds, sun, trees, barns, or anything they like. The last step is glue the craft sticks on the picture vertically to make a fence. Glue the craft sticks every two inches. If there are extra craft sticks, let the children glue some sticks horizontally, about an inch from the top of each vertical craft sticks. Their favorite part of this farm picture will be building the fence.

LESSON 28

HIPPOS

CURRICULUM TOPICS

Hippopotamus, Jungle Animals, Dancing, Self-Expression

FEATURED BOOK

Wilson, Karma. 2004. *Hilda Must Be Dancing*. New York: Margaret K. McElderry Books.

SUMMARY

Hilda Hippo loved to dance and practiced each and every day. She would twirl, spin, twist, and whirl, and then leap and land on her tippy-toes. She could tango, square dance, flamenco, rumba, samba, and disco dance, to name a few. She loved dancing so much that she told everyone that it was her hobby. There was one problem with Hilda and all her dancing: the jungle animals could not stand it. She shook the whole jungle floor every time she would dance and a tidal wave would fill the lake. Her jungle friends hoped it was just a stage she was going through, but after one loud shaky year, they decided it was not just a phase. The animal friends tried to introduce her to other hobbies they thought Hilda would enjoy, and at the same time give themselves some peace. She tried knitting and singing, but both were disasters. In the end she found a hobby everyone was happy with, including Hilda. She took up water ballet and swam and danced in bliss as the jungle animals lived happily ever after. This is a noisy story told in rhyme that is sure to hold the interest of your young listeners. The vibrant tropical outfits Hilda wears are hilarious. The bold text and images, along with the opportunity to implement instruments at almost every turn of the page, make it a pleasure to read aloud and a great lesson in self-expression. Ages 2–7

ACTIVITY

Pass out the tambourines. Each time the author uses onomatopoeia to describe Hilda's loud bouncy dance, have the children chant, shake, and drum on their tambourines.

ADDITIONAL BOOKS TO SHARE

Faulkner, Keith. 2004. *The Hiccuping Hippo*. New York: Dial Books for Young Readers. Poor Hippo has the horrible hiccups! He tries to get them to stop but they will not go away. Many of his friends offer suggestions to cure the hiccups, but they just keep getting worse. His jungle friends all decide to work together to find the right solution to cure Hippo's horrible hiccups once and for all. They decide to scare Hippo out of his hiccups, and it works. The children will love the surprise ending in this well-constructed pop-up book. The last page has a gigantic pop-up illustration that will make a young audience giggle in anticipation. Make sure to practice those hiccups before reading to your group. The sillier and more uninhibited you can be when presenting this story, the more captivated the group will become. Ages 2–6

Laguna, Sofie. 2002. *Too Loud Lily*. New York: Scholastic Press. Lily Hippo is a little girl who is too loud. No matter what she tries to do, she gets scolded for being too loud. She sings too loudly and wakes up the baby. Her brother accuses her of making more noise than a herd of wild elephants. Even when she tries to do something very quietly, she is still too loud. One day a new teacher named Mrs. Loopiola comes to Lily's school. Mrs. Loopiola teaches music and drama. Because she likes her new teacher so well, Lily decides to be in the school play. When she first starts rehearsing, Lily tries to do everything quietly, but Mrs. Loopiola encourages her to be a little louder. Each rehearsal she is encouraged to be a little louder, and so Lily really loves her teacher. Lily is in charge of crashing cymbals, banging drums, growling, and making all kinds of fierce noises, as well as singing and clapping in the play. On the night of the play, Lily gets very nervous and worries about forgetting her part and, even worse, being too loud! Once again, her teacher encourages Lily to step out and be loud, and Lily does. She does her best ever and is just as loud as she can be—and she is praised for it. Lily finds there is a time and place for her special talent. She is very proud of her debut! Ages 2–6

Matsuoka, Kyoko. 1989. *There's a Hippo in My Bath!* New York: Doubleday. A little boy and his duckie prepare to take a bath. As the little boy begins to wash all over, duckie dives down to the bottom of the tub and quickly exclaims that there is something down there. One by one, a turtle, two penguins, a bubble-blowing seal, a fat hippo, and a water-spouting whale join in the bath. The little boy tries to explain to them this is not the ocean, but they continue to stay and play. Before long the boy is scrubbing down the hippo while the whale is rinsing them off. The door begins to rattle and the little boy hears his mother coming. As she enters, she asks what all the rumpus is about? Much to the little boy's surprise, everyone except duckie is gone. The mother asks the little boy if he had a nice bath, and he replies, "Oh, yes . . . the best!" This is a captivating fantasy read-aloud that intuitively understands and depicts the imagination of meandering little minds. The simple but colorful illustrations awaken the imagination with subtle soft tones. (Note: The male anatomy of the little boy is very simply illustrated and not revealed as offensive, but you will want to view the book and make your own decision before reading to a group of children.) Ages 2–6

Stephens, Helen. 2000. *Ruby and the Noisy Hippo.* New York: Kingfisher. Noisy Hippo is so loud that Ruby does not want him to accompany her to the candy store. When his loudness saves her from a monster, she decides that sometimes it is okay to be noisy. Ages 2–6

Wild, Margaret. 2003. *Kiss Kiss!* New York: Simon & Schuster Books for Young Readers. Baby Hippo wakes up one morning and is in such a hurry to go and play that he forgets to kiss his Mama goodbye. As he makes his way through the jungle he hears, "kiss, kiss!" from all the animal mothers and their babies. Baby Hippo suddenly remembers that he forgot to do something very important. He hurries back to find his mama but it is not so easy. Finally Baby Hippo spots his mama out in the water. "Peekaboo!" says Mama. Baby Hippo reunites and gives his mama the long-awaited kiss, kiss! This is a an adorable and loving story that is a great complement to Mother's Day and Valentine's Day, as well as this lesson. There is a repeating verse throughout most of the story, "And this is what he heard . . ." Prompt the children to repeat the line with you and smack their lips together to make fun kiss, kiss sounds. Ages 2–6

MUSIC AND MOVEMENT WITH TAMBOURINES

Sing Along: "The Hippo Groove"

Sung to the Tune: "Good Night Ladies"

Let's *dance* like a hippo? Let's *dance* like a hippo!
Can you *wiggle* those hips, OH! And *shake* your tambourine!
Let's *twirl* like a hippo? Let's *twirl* like a hippo!
Can you *wiggle* those hips, OH! And *shake* your tambourine!
Dance and twirl and wiggle and shake,
wiggle and shake, wiggle and shake!
Dance and twirl and wiggle and shake,
and shake your tambourine!
Let's *swim* like a hippo! Let's *swim* like a hippo!
Can you *shimmy* those hips, OH! And *shake* your tambourine!
Let's *groove* like a hippo! Let's *groove* like a hippo!
Can you *shimmy* those hips, OH! And *shake* your tambourine!
Swim and groove and shimmy and shake,
shimmy and shake, shimmy and shake!
Swim and groove and shimmy and shake,
and shake your tambourine!

Directions

Pass out the tambourines and play song #31 from the accompanying *The Sound of Storytime* CD. Ask the children to stand up and get ready to do some hippo moves. Let them practice dancing freestyle while shaking their tambourines. Ask them if they can wiggle their hips while still shaking their tambourine. Then ask how many know how to shimmy and shake their hips, and allow them some practice time. Have them twirl around in a circle, with their tambourines held over their heads. Show them how to do the swim by plugging your nose with one hand and shaking your hips back and forth while bending your knees as if you were dipping under the water. Ask them how they would groove like a hippo? Tell them that they can move any way they think a hippo might. Explain to them that when the music starts, they will be making those moves that they were just practicing. With great enthusiasm and animation, you, the leader, can command a dancing experience that the children will not soon forget!

STORYBOARD

H-I-L-D-A

Supplies Needed
Construction paper, 9" × 12" in size, any color, one sheet
Scissors
Marker
Tape or adhesive material to attach letters onto the storyboard

Directions
Use Ellison die-cut Alphabet Letters or write the letters H-I-L-D-A across the construction paper and individually cut them out in block style. Make sure the letters are large enough for all the children to see them even from a distance. For some letter recognition practice, place the letters H-I-L-D-A on the storyboard one at a time. Each time you add a letter, turn to your audience and ask them to call out what the letter is and what sound it makes. Ask the children to sound out the name. Introduce the activity by explaining that most everyone has heard the song that goes, "I know a farmer who had a dog and Bingo was his name-O!" Today we are going to sing new words to the tune of BINGO. Teach the following verse:

There was a hippo who loved to dance,
And Hilda was her name-O!
H-I-L-D-A
H-I-L-D-A
H-I-L-D-A
And Hilda was her name-O!

Sing the verse five more times, each time removing one more letter from the name. Start with the letter H. As you remove letters, clap in place of singing the letters being removed in the verse. Repeat until no letters are left and you clap through the whole chorus.

MAKE AND TAKE

Edible Marshmallow Hippo

Supplies Needed per Child
Marshmallows, large in size, three
Marshmallows, miniature in size, five
Toothpicks, two
Decorative tube of cake frosting, black, one per craft table
Decorative tip that screws on to the tube of frosting
Sandwich bag, one
Moist paper towels or wipes for clean up

Directions
Put in each sandwich bag three large marshmallows, five miniature marshmallows, and two toothpicks. Have one bag available for each child. They can remove their items as needed. When the craft is over, the children may place their edible hippo back in the bag and take it home. Using one toothpick, have children connect two large marshmallows, flat ends together, making the hippo's body. Add the third large marshmallow to one end of the body with the remaining toothpick, but slightly tilt the marshmallow in an upward position to make it look like a head. Squirt a small amount of frosting on the flat end of one side of each of the four miniature marshmallows and attach them to the bottom of the body to make the hippo's squatty little legs. Help the children pinch off or cut a small amount of the last miniature marshmallow to form two ears. Use the tube frosting to attach them. You can also forego the last marshmallow and make ears with the frosting. Screw the small frosting tip to the tube of frosting and help the children make two eyes

below the ears. Add two dots of frosting to the flat end of the marshmallow for the nostrils. Next, make a mouth. Children love edible crafts, and these hippos usually do not make it home before they are eaten. Caution the children about the toothpicks. Remind them to be sure to remove them before biting into their hippos.

MAKE AND TAKE 2

Supplies Needed per Child

Construction paper, 12" × 18" in size, any color, one sheet

Ellison die-cut Hippo, one

Ellison die-cut alphabet letters—H, I, L, D, A

Washable markers in assorted colors

Crayons in assorted colors

Glue stick

Directions

Have the children glue a paper hippo on the construction paper and attach the letters to spell the name Hilda. Using the crayons or washable markers, have the children draw a "dancing" outfit on Hilda. Encourage them to draw other jungle animals on their masterpiece as well. Ask them to take their pictures home and share the song they learned at storytime with their family.

LESSON 29

JUNGLE LIFE

CURRICULUM TOPICS
Jungles, Drums, Jungle Animals

FEATURED BOOK
Lillegard, Dee. 1989. *Sitting in My Box*. New York: Dutton.

SUMMARY
A little boy sits alone in a large cardboard box reading a book about wild animals when someone knocks. One by one, a giraffe, an elephant, a baboon, and other animals knock and join him. The box becomes very crowded, but everyone refuses to leave the box until an uninvited flea, who doesn't knock, pays a visit. Ages 3–7

ACTIVITY
Pass out the tambourines. Have the children lay them on the floor in front of them. Each time an animal knocks on the box, prompt the children to knock three times on their tambourines. Stop a couple of times throughout the story and ask the children to help you count how many animals are now in the box.

FEATURED BOOK
Wundrow, Deanna. 1999. *Jungle Drum*. Brookfield, CT: Millbrook Press.

SUMMARY
The rain forest is filled with the sounds of the echoing jungle drum, dripping water, and the many animals talking. Ages 3–7

ACTIVITY
This activity is completed in three parts: you read the book, lead a discussion, and then reread the book. While reading this story the first time through, you will be modeling how to play the instrument the children will be using later. As you chant the "Ba-da-doom-doom" of the jungle drum, rhythmically tap in the center of a single tambourine. When finished, ask the children where they think the mysterious sound of the drum is coming from. Is it an animal making the sound? Is it the sound of someone marching through the jungle? Is the sound a person beating a drum? Allow the children to be creative and share their ideas. (Note: The Bantu tribes of Central Africa use two-tone drums to communicate with other tribes, like "talking drums." Playing the drums in this way is similar to Morse code but uses Bantu words instead of letters.) Before passing out the tambourines, explain to the children you are going to reread the story. This time the children will help you echo the drum sounds of the responding "tribe." Be sure to tell the children to hold the tambourines tightly to their chest to silence the tambourine until it is their turn to "beat their drum." Before you read the story again, help the children practice softly tapping their drums and chanting the following:

> Presenter: *Ba-da doom!*

Now ask the class to echo you.

> Children: *Ba-da boom!*
> Presenter: *Ba-da doom doom!* Children: *Ba-da doom doom!*

Presenter: *Ba-da doom!* Children: *Ba-da doom!*
Presenter: *Ba-da doom doom!* Children: *Ba-da doom doom!*

Begin the story again and let the children play their part throughout the story.

ADDITIONAL BOOKS TO SHARE

Base, Graeme. 2004. *Jungle Drums.* New York: Harry N. Abrams. Tired of being teased by the bigger warthogs and other jungle animals, little Ngiri, the smallest warthog in Africa, wishes for things to be different. When Old Nyumbu, the Wildebeest, gives Ngiri a set of magic drums, his wish is granted in a most unexpected way. This book is quite long but worth reading. Try reading it to an older group of children. As you show them the delightful pictures, tell the story to a younger audience. The illustrations are like no other, absolutely magnificent in every way. Graeme Base takes it to another level—everything might seem normal in the jungle, but look closely at the pictures; you will see that none of the animals or the other creatures watching from the trees are quite the way they had been before Ngiri made his wishes. Additionally, you will find Old Nyumbu the Wildebeest hidden somewhere on each two-page spread. This is the perfect book to order duplicate copies through your local library. Allow the older children to sit down in small groups and search for Old Nyumbu the Wildebeest along with the other colorful surprises in this unique African tale. Ages 5–8

Guettier, Bénédicte. 2002. *In the Jungle.* La Jolla, CA: Kane/Miller. A die-cut cover opens to form a hole for readers to poke their heads through and take on the identities of a half dozen animals. The presenter could easily memorize this book and turn it toward the children and make silly faces through the hole while reading. It is also fun to pass the book around the circle to allow the children to put their heads in the hole to become the face of the animal. Provide a mirror for the children to see themselves as jungle animals. Ages 2–6

Hewitt, Sally. 2003. *Face to Face Safari.* New York: Harry N. Abrams. This story takes you on a safari in which the reader comes face to face with familiar African animals. There are six huge pop-up pictures of larger-than-life faces of an elephant, lion, giraffe, rhinoceros, hippopotamus, and chimpanzee. This book will become a new favorite as the huge faces will astonish and excite each child. Face the book away from the audience and try reading this book like a riddle. Ages 3–7

Krebs, Laurie. 2004. *We All Went on Safari.* Cambridge, MA: Barefoot. Several Tanzanian children went on safari one day. They embark on an exciting counting adventure through the grasslands of Tanzania! Along the way, the children discover many species of African animals including lions, hippos, warthogs, and monkeys. They learn how to count from one to ten in both English and Swahili. (Note: This book has great illustrations as well as a map of Tanzania and information about the Maasai people and Swahili names.) Ages 3–7

Laird, Elizabeth. 2003. *Beautiful Bananas.* Atlanta, GA: Peachtree. A young African girl named Beatrice sets off through the jungle to take a beautiful bunch of bananas to her grandfather. On the way she runs into one mishap after another. Giraffe accidentally flicks the bananas Beatrice is proudly carrying with his tufty tail, so he replaces them with some flowers. Bees swarm the flowers but give Beatrice some honeycomb instead. Some naughty monkeys spy the honeycomb and snatch it away, but they replace it with mangoes. This predictable process goes on until a sorry elephant makes it all better. This is a sweet story with a happy ending that children are sure to love. The book is full of colorful artwork that is the perfect companion to the large bold text. This is a circular tale from East Africa. Ages 3–7

MUSIC AND MOVEMENT WITH TAMBOURINES

Sing Along: "Jungle Drum Echo"

Sung to the Tune: "Jingle Bells"

Jungle drums, jungle drums!
I hear them loud and clear!
Jungle drums, jungle drums!
Sounding far and near!
Jungle drums, jungle drums!
I can hear them pound! Pound, pound, pound!
Jungle drums, jungle drums!
Now I'll return the sound!
Pound, pound, pound! Pound, pound, pound! *(First group starts)*
Pound, pound, pound, pound, pound! *(First group ends)*
Pound, pound, pound! Pound, pound, pound! *(Second group echoes)*
Pound, pound, pound, pound, pound! Pound! *(Second group ends)*

Pound, pound, pound! Pound, pound pound! *(First group starts)*
Pound, pound, pound, pound, pound! *(First group ends)*
Pound, pound, pound! Pound, pound, pound! *(Second group echoes)*
Pound, pound, pound, pound, pound! *(Second group ends)*

Directions

Divide the children into two equal groups and give them tribe names. Pass out the tambourines and play song #32 from the accompanying *The Sound of Storytime* CD. Ask them to lay their tambourines on the floor directly in front of them and pound them like a drum. Have the children sing along with the song until it is time to pound their drums. Have the first group pound their tambourines through the first two lines, and have the second group echo what they just heard the first group pound out. The tune "Jingle Bells" is one most children are familiar with, so they will catch on to the rhythm quickly. Have the children quiet their tambourines a little more with each line. By the end, they should be making a very faint sound. Repeat the activity so the children have a chance to become acquainted with the tambourines. The more the children are allowed to practice with the tambourines, the more skilled they will become.

MOVEMENT CHANT

Monkey See, Monkey Do!

Supplies Needed

One stuffed, full-bodied monkey (optional)

Directions

The stuffed monkey is fun to use but not necessary. Use the monkey to make the following movements. If you do not have a stuffed monkey available, do the movement yourself and have the children imitate you as you say:

Monkey see, monkey do,
Monkey can *jump*, can you?

Ask the children to jump.

Monkey see, monkey do,
Monkey can *touch his toes*, can you?

Continue repeating this verse and change the movement each time. Additional movements:

Scratch his head

Pat his tummy

Clap his hands

Count to ten

Smile real big

Turn around

Touch his nose

Say, I LOVE BOOKS!

Feel free to make up more movements. This activity is a good way to introduce body parts. You could have the children touch their knees, elbows, head, neck, arms, legs, and more.

ADDITIONAL SONGS TO SHARE

Chenille Sisters. *Teaching Hippopotami to Fly!* CanToo Records, 1996. Compact Disk. CTR CD 01. Play #1, "Deepest Africa." Lead the children by acting out the verses of the song. For example, when the song sings about "teaching hippopotami to fly," put your arms out like an airplane and twirl your body as if flying.

Wiggles. *Yummy Yummy!* Lyrick Studios, 1999. Compact Disk. 9206. Play Song #13, *The Monkey Dance*. Have everybody stand and sing and dance along. Make all the animal gestures sung in the song—scratch like a monkey, put your claws up and roar like a tiger, make an elephant trunk with your arm and trumpet like an elephant. Everybody jumps on the chorus in this wild song.

STORYBOARD

Deep in the Jungle

Supplies Needed

Ellison die-cut jungle animals, twelve different—for example, lion #2, panther, monkey #2, hippo, elephant #1, giraffe #1, zebra, tiger #1, snake #1, crocodile, lizard, rhinoceros (These items can also be cut out of magazines, coloring books, or other types of jungle-related publications)

Tape or adhesive material to attach animals onto the storyboard

Directions

If you have more than twelve children, you can repeat the same animals by doubling or tripling the amount. Have the jungle animals placed on the storyboard. Ask each child to line up and pick a jungle animal from the board and take it to his or her seat. As the children are choosing their animals, you can ask each to identify the animal they are taking. You may also want to assist them by saying, "[child's name] has the [name of the jungle animal]." Tell them that when you call their name, they may come to the storyboard and add their animal to the board and say the name of the animal. When every child has an animal and is seated, teach them the following chant. Repeat the chant as many times as you need to allow each child a turn. The children could use the tambourines, clap their hands, pat their legs, or stomp their feet with this activity as well.

Begin this chant:

> Deep in the jungle where we hear the drums beat,
> What kind of animal would [child's name] like to meet?

Ask the child to place their animal picture on the storyboard and share the name of the animal, then repeat:

> Deep in the jungle where we hear the drums beat,
> What kind of animal would [child's name] like to meet?

Continue repeating chant until every child has had a turn.

MAKE AND TAKE

Jungle Scene

Supplies Needed per Child

Ellison die-cut jungle animals, three each, using the same variety as used in the storyboard activity, or pictures of animals from magazines or coloring books; children can also draw them onto the paper with washable markers or crayons

Construction paper, 12" × 18" in size, any color

Construction paper, assorted scraps, large and small

Glue stick

Washable markers or crayons

Directions

Give each child a sheet of construction paper. This sheet will be used to create a jungle scene. Give them additional scraps of construction paper to tear in strips to make trees, plants, grass, and other vegetation. Have the children glue the torn strips of paper, leaving room to draw the jungle animals onto the paper by using markers or crayons or attaching the animals that have been made available to them through magazines, coloring books, or Ellison die-cuts. Talk about the books that have been read in the lesson and how bright and bold the pictures are in the books. Invite the children to use their imagination and create a bright and bold jungle scene of their own. Children seem to love the tearing and gluing activities best.

MAKE AND TAKE 2

Jungle Play Boxes

Supplies Needed per Child

Plain cardboard boxes, standard size 28" L × 20" W × 25" D one box for every four children

Tablecloth or floor covering, one for each box

Washable markers or crayons, in assorted colors

Directions

Lay the tablecloths or floor covering on the floor and let the children work together (four per box) coloring their boxes in a jungle motif. This activity is so much for the children. They can color on all four sides, on the bottom, and on the top flaps, and they can even crawl inside the boxes to color some more. When finished, let the children play in their jungle boxes. Stack and store them, then pull them out after each storytime until they wear out! What is better to play with than an empty cardboard box? This is a great follow up for the featured story, *Sitting in My Box*.

LESSON 30

❧

TRASH

CURRICULUM TOPICS

Recycling, Trash, Community Helpers, Trucks

FEATURED BOOK

Kirk, Daniel. 1997. *Trash Trucks!* New York: G. P. Putnam's Sons.

SUMMARY

Trash trucks clamor through the city streets doing their dirty work and gobbling up the trash. Ages 3–7

ACTIVITY

Introduce the title on the cover of the book. Point out and discuss how the illustrator used leftover paper labels, newspapers, and other trash to make the picture collages and words in the story. Ask the children to help you read aloud the repeating title words as you come to them during the story. Tell the children to pay special attention to the pictures because they will be making their own "trashy" collages at craft time. Following the story, pass out the tambourines and sing and play song #33, "Boom, Boom, Crash!", from the accompanying *The Sound of Storytime* CD.

ADDITIONAL BOOKS TO SHARE

Beadle, David M. 2004. *The Day the Trash Came Out to Play*. South Pasadena, CA: Ezra's Earth Publishing. Robin carelessly tosses a candy wrapper on the ground. When others see the littered trash, they think it is okay for them to litter too. When the whole neighborhood becomes plagued with garbage, everyone learns the importance of doing their part and the town builds a recycling center. Ages 3–8

Bridges, Sarah. 2005. *I Drive a Garbage Truck*. Minneapolis, MN: Picture Window Books. Children are fascinated by garbage trucks! Share a few fun facts about garbage collection, the occupation, and the equipment with this nonfiction book. Display this book and encourage children to check it out for reading at home. Ages 3–8

Gilkey, Gail. 2003. *No More Garbage*. Barrington, RI: Windy Hill Press. When a rabbit gets its foot injured by getting it caught in a can someone threw on the ground, two sisters come to its rescue. This story pulls at the heart strings of children and really causes them to think about the consequences of their actions. Ages 3–8

Hayes, Sarah. 1986. *This Is the Bear*. Cambridge, MA: Candlewick Press. A boy's beloved teddy bear accidentally falls into the trash can and ends up at the city dump. The boy searches through the trash determined to find his bear. This is a Read and Share series book told in the similar style of *This Is the House That Jack Built*. Discussion ideas and related games are suggested on the back pages of the story. Ages 2–6

Lish, Ted. 2002. *It's Not My Job*. Victorville, CA: Munchweiler Press. Everyone in the family declares that it is not their job to help take out the trash, and the garbage begins to pile up everywhere. When they finally lose the baby in all the mess, they decide something must be done. Can they all work together to clean up? Ages 3–7

McMullan, Kate. 2002. *I Stink!* New York: Joanna Cotler Books. An animated truck describes the dirty work it does and makes no apologies for being stinky and smelly. The story ends asking the children, "Who am I?" When you read this last line, give your listeners the opportunity to say an answer out loud. Ages 3–7

Testa, Fulvio. 2001. *Too Much Garbage*. New York: North-South Books. Two boys decide their city has too much trash and not enough flowers. The story is left open-ended with a thought-provoking challenge. Lead a discussion with your listeners about what they can do to improve their environment. Ages 4–8

Wallace, Nancy Elizabeth. 2003. *Recycle Every Day!* New York: Marshall Cavendish. Minna's class is given an assignment to make a poster about recycling. To help their daughter think of an idea for her poster, her rabbit family spends every day of the week practicing a different form of recycling. Ages 5–8

Ward, Helen. 2001. *The Tin Forest*. New York: Puffin Books. An old man dreams of clearing away all the garbage to make room for a forest full of plants and animals. Overwhelmed by all the trash and metal, he begins to build a forest from the scrap when something magical happens. Fanciful, thought-provoking illustrations inspire imaginative discussion topics. Ages 5–8

Zimmerman, Andrea, and David Clemesha. 1999. *Trashy Town*. New York: HarperCollins. Mr. Gilly, the trash man, drives his truck all over town picking up the garbage. The text is skillfully written, incorporating the repeating word "STOP!" There is a rhyming phrase the children can say and act out with you as well as repeating question the children can call out the answer to on nearly every page. Coupled with delightful illustrations, this story contains the formula for a terrific read-aloud. For some simple added fun, make miniature stop signs from red construction paper and craft sticks before the children arrive for storytime. Use a white-out pen to write the word "STOP" on the signs. Pass one sign out to each child. Ask the children to guess what the word is on their sign. Tell them to hold up their sign each time the word "stop" appears in the story. This activity helps children make connections with meaningful print, and it is a fun way to get the children involved in the story. After the phrases that start with "There are trash cans by the . . ." pause and ask the children to tell you how many trash cans there are at each stop. Ages 3–7

MUSIC AND MOVEMENT WITH TAMBOURINES

Sing Along: "Boom, Boom, Crash!"

Sung to the Tune: "Three Blind Mice"

Boom, Boom, Crash! Boom, Boom, Crash!
They're collecting the trash! They're collecting the trash!
Scoop it up, and squish it down!
Collecting trash wherever it's found!
They're driving all around the town,
Boom, Boom, Crash!

Directions

Pass out the tambourines and play song #33 from the accompanying *The Sound of Storytime* CD. Let the children practice making different sounds with their tambourines by hitting it in different areas. Tell them to hit it on their thighs when they hear "Boom, Boom," and to strike the tambourine with their open hand on the "Crash!" They can pretend to scoop up the trash with the tambourine held upside down while using their other hand as though they are squishing the trash down. Caution the children to pretend to push on the inside of the tambourine, but not to apply pressure on the inside of the drum. They can also pretend their tambourine is a wheel when the song says, "They're driving all around the town." This is another song you should be prepared to repeat a few times because the children will beg to sing it again!

ADDITIONAL SONGS TO SHARE

Feldman, Jean R. *Dr. Jean & Friends*. Progressive Music, 1998. Compact Disk. DJ-DO2. Play song #11, *Tooty Ta*. This song is packed full of very silly movements. The song directs you to put your thumbs out, and as each verse progresses another movement is added. No instruments are required with this song, just a willingness to look silly and have a great time!

Scelsa, Greg, and Steve Millang. *Big Fun*. YoungHeart Music, 1997. Compact Disk. YM-016 CD. Play #3, *In My Backyard*. This is an amusing song with silly lyrics about throwing things in someone else's backyard. Play this song when children are entering storytime or during the craft activity.

STORYBOARD

Supplies Needed

Plastic tubs or trash cans, three

Labels or stickers, three

Marker

Clean, safe containers as described below, one per child

Directions

Instead of the traditional storyboard story, prepare three clean/new trash cans or plastic tubs at the front of the storytime area. Label one trash receptacle for plastic recycling, one for aluminum recycling, and one for paper recycling. Pass out clean, safe containers like plastic butter tubs, yogurt containers, plastic two liter bottles, empty cereal boxes, newspapers, aluminum cans (no sharp edges, use a safety can opener), and sheets of aluminum foil. Each child will need just one of these assorted items. For the activity, have children come to the front, one at a time, and decide which recycling tub the item should go in.

MAKE AND TAKE

Trash Collage

Supplies Needed per Child

Construction paper, 9" × 12" in size, assorted colors

Variety of clean trash items—gum wrappers, cereal boxes, macaroni boxes, newspapers, magazines, product labels, candy wrappers, and other assorted paper items. Five to ten each, depending on size of product

Glue stick

Safety scissors

Directions

Prior to this activity, enlist several staff members, family members, or parents and caregivers of storytime participants to help collect clean trash items like the examples listed above. Let the children make a collage from the trash using the pictures in the featured book *Trash Trucks*. For older children have a letter scavenger hunt from these same items by having them cut out the letters to make the words "trash truck" like the illustrator did for the pictures in the book! Fun!

PART VI

VOCAL CHORDS

LESSON 31

BABIES

CURRICULUM TOPICS
Babies, Emotions and Feelings, Family, Clothing and Dress

FEATURED BOOK
Fleming, Candace. 2004. *Smile, Lily!* New York: Antheneum Books for Young Readers. Baby Lily won't stop crying! The family members take turns trying to stop her from crying. When everyone is exhausted from trying to hush Lily, young brother grabs his chance. He knows *just* what to do! Ages 2–7

ACTIVITY

Supplies Needed per Child

One tissue (optional enrichment)

Open the conversation with the children by asking how many of them have baby brothers or sisters. Ask them what their baby brother or sister likes to do. At this point, one or more of the children will let you know they like to cry. Ask them what their cry sounds like? Ask them if they cry loudly or softly? This is the perfect segway into the activity. There are several ways for the children to interact with this adorable book. Our favorite is to pass out tissues before you begin reading the story. Tell the children this story is about a baby who will not stop crying! Ask them to help you with the sound effects in this delightful story. Each time you read the repeating line, "But Lily keeps on crying," ask them to hold up the tissue to their eye and pretend to cry—"Waa! Waa! Waa!" Right after the crying, there is another opportunity for the children to take part when you repeat the line, "Oh, who knows what to do?" Have the children help you say, "I do!" It is fun for the children to practice once or twice before the story begins. Ask them how they would cry like a baby. Let them practice saying "Waa! Waa! Waa!" in a baby voice and the repeating line, "I do!" You may need to help them get started, but they will soon pick up on the appropriate lines, and their vocals will intensify as you continue reading the story aloud.

ADDITIONAL BOOKS TO SHARE
Beaumont, Karen. 2004. *Baby Danced the Polka.* New York: Dial Books for Young Readers. It is naptime at the farm, but one wide-awake baby has a different plan. Baby wants to dance! This baby dances the cha-cha with a cow, boogie woogies with a goat, polkas with a pig, and dances with many other farm animals. Ages 3–6

Cowell, Cressida. 2003. *What Shall We Do with the Boo-Hoo Baby?* New York: Scholastic Press. Baby will not stop crying in spite of the efforts of a cow, cat, dog, and duck. Each animal tries a new trick to placate baby, but only duck succeeds. Ages 3–6

Fisher, Valorie. 2003. *My Big Sister.* New York: Atheneum Books for Young Readers. This book introduces a loving, big sister from a baby's perspective. The photographs depict the sibling from ground level, with shots that focus on her feet, a toy animal zoo, and expressive kisses and scowls. Ages 3–7

Fleming, Candace. 2004. *This is the Baby.* New York: Farrar, Straus and Giroux. This is an adorable book about a baby who does not like getting dressed. In this battle of wills, page after page, the mother adds another article of clothing on her baby while the baby struggles with her. On every page there is a repeating line the baby says, "No! No! Nooo!" Have the children repeat the line in a baby voice. In this rhyming, cumlative text, the mother finally succeeds in getting the baby completely dressed, but the baby has a surprise for her. The baby removes one layer at a time and is soon "free and undressed," diaper and all! Ages 2–7

French, Simon, and Donna Rawlins. 2002. *Guess the Baby.* New York: Clarion Books. After Sam's baby brother visits his class for Show and Tell, all the children bring their baby pictures to school. The students have fun guessing which picture is whose. After they have guessed each picture, one remains. The children need help guessing whose picture it is. This book acknowledges children's fascination with babies and their curiosity about growing up. As in the story, encourage your participants to bring their baby picture to storytime for show and tell. Invite children to come, one at a time, and place their photo on the storyboard for everyone to see. Bring a baby picture of yourself to share! Ages 3–7

MacLachlan, Patricia. 2004. *Bittle.* New York: Joanna Cotler Books. Nigel the cat and Julia the dog think they will have no use for the new baby in their house. They soon realize the baby is not so bad after all. Ages 3–6

Packard, Mary. 2004. *The New Baby.* New York: Children's Press. Big brother is jealous of his new baby brother until Mommy gives him a hug and the new baby gives him a smile. Ages 3–6

Westcott, Nadine Bernard. 1988. *The Lady with the Alligator Purse.* Boston: Joy Street Books. Miss Lucy's baby, Tiny Tim, is sick and she calls the doctor, the nurse, and the lady with the alligator purse to diagnose Tiny Tim. The doctor and nurse think they know, but it is the lady with the alligator purse who comes up with the correct and hilarious diagnosis and cure. This book is so silly and fun to read. The children love it year after year. Ages 3–7

MUSIC AND MOVEMENT WITH VOCAL CHORDS

Sing Along: "Waa! Waa! Waa!"

Sung to the Tune: "Miss Lucy Had a Baby"

I love my baby sister, she eats and sleeps all day.
But when she isn't happy, this is what she'll say!
Waa! Waa! Waa!
I love my baby sister, she scoots and crawls all day.
But when she isn't happy, this is what she'll say!
Waa! Waa! Waa!
I love my baby sister, she laughs and plays all day.
But when she isn't happy, this is what she'll say!
Waa! Waa! Waa!
I love my baby sister, she walks and talks all day.
But when she isn't happy, this is what she'll say!
I'M GONNA TELL!

Directions

Play song #34 from the accompanying *The Sound of Storytime* CD. In this catchy little song, the baby progresses in age and finally does something besides cry! On the last line, say "IM GONNA TELL!" in an obnoxious, whiny voice, with one hand on your hip and the other pointing out at the audience, just like a bratty sibling might do. It is also fun to pass out tissues with this song and let the children enjoy them as suggested in the activity for the featured book, *Smile, Lily!*, in this lesson.

ADDITIONAL SONG TO SHARE

Cedarmont Kids Singers. *Toddler Action Songs.* October Sound and Mattinee Studio, 2002. Compact Disk. 84418-0137-2. Play song #13, "John Brown's Baby." The CD insert, on the back of the cover art, gives the instructions for leading the simple actions to this song. The verse repeats five times, omitting another key word each time. Children continue to perform the actions even when the words are omitted. Children can use their tissue prop again with this song.

STORYBOARD

Poor Little Baby!

Supplies Needed

Ellison die-cut circles, 3", beige, five

Felt squares in assorted colors—green, yellow, blue, pink, and red—five (construction paper using the same colors will work as well)

Scissors

Washable marker, black

Tape or adhesive material to attach the items onto the storyboard

Directions

Draw a baby's face, (make sure eyes are identical on every face) on each die-cut circle with the black marker. Draw a frown or sad face on each baby except one. Draw a big smile on the remaining baby's face. It is very important that the top half of each baby's face is identical. Cut out the felt squares or colored construction paper to imitate a blanket. This should be large enough in size to cover the baby's face except its eyes and forehead. Attach all five baby faces to the storyboard and cover them with the felt or paper blankets prior to the storyboard activity. This is a guessing game, so the children can't see where the smiling baby is placed. Begin reciting the chant below. When you get ready to lift the colored blanket, let the children choose which color to lift to find the smiling baby.
Chant:

> Poor little baby, are you still sad?
> Let's lift the *(green)* blanket
> And see if you're glad!
> Poor little baby, are you still sad?
> Let's lift the *(yellow)* blanket
> And see if you're glad!
> Poor little baby, are you still sad?
> Let's lift the *(blue)* blanket
> And see if you're glad!
> Poor little baby, are you still sad?
> Let's lift the *(pink)* blanket
> And see if you're glad!
> Poor little baby, are you still sad?
> Let's lift the *(red)* blanket
> And see if you're glad!

Repeat the storyboard activity a couple times so the children can enjoy the guessing game. Don't forget to move the faces and blankets around each time! This activity is a confidence builder! As soon as the children choose the smiling baby, their faces light up with joy and pride. The verse is so simple the children will learn it easily and will soon be chanting it with you.

MAKE AND TAKE

Peek-A-Boo Baby

Supplies Needed per Child

Ellison die-cut circles, 3", in multicultural skin tones, one circle each

6" squares cut from construction paper of assorted colors, one each

Glue stick

Washable markers or crayons in assorted colors

Construction paper, 9" × 12" in size, assorted colors, one each

Directions

Have the children draw a baby's face on the circle and glue it onto the construction paper. Put a narrow line of glue across the top of each square blanket and place them over the lower half of the baby faces, creating their own personal "lift-a-flap" of the peek-a-boo baby.

LESSON 32

GETTING STUCK

CURRICULUM TOPICS

Ducks, Trucks

FEATURED BOOK

Lewis, Kevin, and Daniel Kirk. 2002. *My Truck Is Stuck*! New York: Hyperion Books for Children.

SUMMARY

When a dump truck gets stuck in the mud, progressively larger vehicles try to pull it out. The rhyme, illustrations, and subject matter of this read-aloud widely appeal to its target audience. Ages 2–6

ACTIVITY

Make a cardboard sign, like the sign the dog holds up in the story, with the words, "Help! Please help!" Encourage the children to say these repeating words with you each time you hold up the sign. For some storyboard fun, pass out Ellison die-cut pieces of a red dump truck, green car #1, blue truck, red jeep, yellow school bus #1A, and gray tow truck. When the story repeats, "Does anyone know how to make my stuck truck go?", the child with the appropriate piece adds it to the line-up of vehicles on the storyboard.

FEATURED BOOK

Root, Phyllis. 1998. *One Duck Stuck.* Cambridge, MA: Candlewick Press.

SUMMARY

One duck is stuck in the muck and cries for help. You can count on the animal friends that come from far and near to help free the duck in this action adventure concept book. Ages 3–7

ACTIVITY

As the leader, you play the role of the duck. Explain to the children that they are going to play the part of the animal helpers. Each time you say the repeating line, "Help! Help! Who can help?" ask the children to respond, "We can! We can!" We like to read this book with a simple duck puppet that pops up and cries for help. If you do not have a duck puppet, use one of the paper bag puppets the children will be making at craft time. After the children make their own puppets at the end of the session, you will inevitably see them playing with their puppets just the way you did! You might need to have an easel ready to place the book on as you read and act out this story. Finally, as you read action words like swim, plod, leap, jump, crawl, slide, slither, and whir, demonstrate movements the children can imitate and provide a few seconds for them to act out these actions.

ADDITIONAL BOOKS TO SHARE

Alborough, Jez. 1999. *Duck in the Truck*. New York: HarperCollins. This rollicking rhyme is the tale of one duck's frustrating mishap when his truck gets stuck in the muck. Passers by, frog, sheep, and goat lend their assistance only to find themselves stuck with their own messy problems. Ages 2–6

Beck, Andrea. 2002. *Elliot Gets Stuck*. New York: Kids Can Press. Elliot is so excited to go outside and enjoy the new spring weather, but he can't reach the doorknob to open the door. In his hast, he decides to try and squeeze through the letter slot. It is no surprise when Elliot gets stuck. Can his friends help free him? Ages 3–7

Donaldson, Julia. 2003. *The Snail and the Whale*. New York: Dial Books for Young Readers. A humpback whale helps a tiny snail fulfill its big dream to travel the world. When the whale gets beached on land, snail gets the opportunity to repay the whale's kindness and devises a plan to get help to free the whale. Ages 5–8

Enderle, Dotti. 2004. *The Cotton Candy Catastrophe at the Texas State Fair*. Gretna, LA: Pelican Publishing. Jake arrives at the state fair and heads straight for his all-time favorite treat—cotton candy. As Jake walks away from the counter, cotton candy in hand, the machine gets stuck and Jake unknowingly leaves behind a string of sticky cotton candy that eventually encases the entire fairground. Ages 5–8

Fox, Frank G. 2003. *Jean Laffite and the Big Ol' Whale*. New York: Farrar, Straus and Giroux. An enormous whale gets stuck between the banks of the Mississippi river and stops the flow of the water. The hero of this American tall tale, Jean Laffite, rescues the whale and restores the river. This story is perfect for early grade-school children, providing a rich exposure to history, social studies, and geography. Ages 5–8

Greene, Rhonda Gowler. 2004. *Santa's Stuck*. New York: Dutton Children's Books. When too many Christmas cookies gets Santa stuck in the chimney, his reindeer, the dog, a cat and her kittens, and a clever mouse all struggle to free him. If it is nearing the holidays, be sure to include this merry tale in your repertoire. Children and adults alike find Santa's holiday bungle hysterical. The crafty rhyme rolls off the tongue and the expressive illustrations invoke comedy. Ages 3–7

Palatini, Margie. 2001. *Tub-Boo-Boo*. New York: Simon & Schuster Books for Young Readers. Henry gets his toe stuck in the tub spout, and so does everyone who tries to free him. Children really like this kind of humor. Since this book is a little long, save it for the children on the upper end of the age category. Ages 5–8

Partis, Joanne. 2002. *Stripe's Naughty Sister*. Minneapolis, MN: Carolrhoda Books. Stripe is to help watch his little sister, but she is so naughty! Being a good big brother, Stripe protectively follows his little sister through prickly cactuses, mucky swamps, and down a hole, but what is he to do when she gets herself stuck in a tree? Ages 3–7

Townsend, Una Belle. 2003. *Grady's in the Silo*. Gretna, LA: Pelican Publishing. This story is based on an actual event that occurred on a farm in Yukon, Oklahoma, in 1949. When a cow gets stuck in a silo, people from all over the world send letters suggesting how to get the cow out. How would you try to rescue a cow in a deep, dark hole? Over the years, there have been many fantastic animal rescues in the news. The topic of famous animal rescues makes for great, high-interest, research projects children and adults both marvel at. Encourage the children in your classroom or with whom you work at the library or visit at the local schools to research such an event. On a bulletin board in the library, post the children's reports and artwork about their chosen mishap. Be sure to also make a book display of the recommended reading from this lesson. Both public libraries and schools benefit when they build strong partnerships. The best library bulletin boards we have seen are of local children's artwork the teachers brought in and displayed in the library for the parents and the public to enjoy. Ages 5–8

Wheeler, Lisa. 2004. *Bubble Gum, Bubble Gum*. Boston: Little, Brown. This is a delightful story about a variety of animals getting stuck in a blob of icky-sticky pink bubble gum melting in the middle of the road. They come up with an ingenious way to get away from the sticky mess when they must survive encounters with a big blue honking truck and a burly black bear. The creative use of rhyme and the witty storyline make this picture book a hit every time it is shared. Ages 2–7

MUSIC AND MOVEMENT WITH VOICES

Sing Along: "Have You Ever?"

Sung to the Tune: "Did You Ever See a Lassie"

Have you ever had your foot stuck?
Your foot stuck? Your foot stuck!

Have you ever had your foot stuck, and couldn't get out?
You'd pull this way and that way, and that way and this way!
Have you ever had your foot stuck, and couldn't get out?
Have you ever had your arm stuck?
Your arm stuck? Your arm stuck!
Have you ever had your arm stuck, and couldn't get out?
You'd push this way and that way, and that way and this way!
Have you ever had your arm stuck, and couldn't get out?
Have you ever had your head stuck?
Your head stuck? Your head stuck!
Have you ever had your head stuck, and couldn't get out?
You'd move this way and that way, and that way and this way!
Have you ever had your head stuck, and couldn't get out?
If you ever get stuck! Get stuck? Get stuck!
If you ever get stuck, here's what you do!
HELP! HELP!

Directions

Play song #35 from the accompanying *The Sound of Storytime* CD. Talk to the children and ask them if they have ever been stuck? Maybe they have gotten their sled or tricycle stuck, or been in an automobile during inclement weather and their car was stuck, or their foot caught under something. Give them a few scenarios and they are sure to fill your ear with some exciting tales. Tell them we are going to pretend to be stuck. Ask how it would feel if their foot was stuck? Ask the same for the arm and the head. Remember to keep this conversation upbeat and amusing, as not to frighten the children or have any serious worries about being stuck. As you sing this song, pretend that each body part is truly stuck. Try to pull the foot while keeping it firmly planted on the floor. Grab at the arm, keeping it stiff while trying to push with the free arm. Again at the head, stick it out as if it were stuck in something. Try moving the rest of your body a bit, while keeping the head still. You can also use your arms and hold the head as if you were tugging at it. At the end of the song, let the children shout out, "HELP!"

ACTIVITY

Sing Along: "Stuck, I Am!"

Sung to the Tune: "Row, Row, Row Your Boat"

Stuck, stuck, stuck I am!
I'm stuck as I can be!
I need a push, I need a pull,
Please come and set me free! *(Repeat)*

Directions

Singing this song a cappella in a round without background music works best. Divide the children into three equal groups. Start out by letting everyone sing the short song together until they are familiar with it. Tell the children they are all going to sing, but each group will start at different times. This is called a round. Tell them you will point to their group when they are to start singing, and that they are to continue singing the song until it is over. Explain that it might be difficult to stay with their group while hearing the song being sung at a different time by two other groups. Continue working until they can sing through the song three times to get the full effect. This will certainly help the children to follow specific directions, and it will help them develop their listening skills. Be patient, this could take a few rounds before the children catch on to this concept. If you could enlist adults to lead each group, it will go much smoother.

ADDITIONAL SONG TO SHARE

Birthday Party! Singalong. Little Buddha Studios, 2001. Compact Disk. R2 74261. Play song #5, *The Freeze Dance.*
  This song is self-explanatory. The narrator directs children to hop, tippy toe, turn around, and perform other fun movements. Each time the narrator says "stop," everyone freezes.

STORYBOARD

Five Ducks Stuck

Supplies Needed

Construction paper, 12" × 18" in size, or a large brown paper sack, one sheet

Ellison die-cut ducks, five

Scissors

Tape or adhesive material to attach the ducks onto the storyboard

Directions

Using the scissors and the large brown paper sack or construction paper cut out a shape that resembles a large mud puddle. Be sure it is large enough to hold five ducks. Attach the mud puddle to the storyboard and add the ducks as you read the following lines:

> One duck stuck in the yucky muck,
> Called for another duck to help him get unstuck! *(Add first duck)*
> Two ducks stuck in the yucky muck,
> Called for another duck to help them get unstuck! *(Add second duck)*
> Three ducks stuck in the yucky muck,
> Called for another duck to help them get unstuck! *(Add third duck)*
> Four ducks stuck in the yucky muck,
> Called for another duck to help them get unstuck! *(Add fourth duck)*
> Five ducks stuck in the yucky muck,
> Let's give them a hand and help them get unstuck! *(Add fifth duck)*
> *(Remove each duck, counting them out of the muck . . . one, two, three, four, five.)*

As you are counting the ducks out of the yucky muck one by one, slowly pull each duck out as if it is really hard to do. Count the numbers in a long, expressive "pulling" voice. Make sure to have the children count along with you. This storyboard is easy to put together and easy to use. If time permits, repeat this short and playful activity.

MAKE AND TAKE

Duck Puppet

Supplies Needed per Child

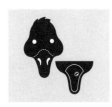

Brown paper sack, lunch size

Ellison die-cut, two-piece paper bag puppet-duck

Glue stick

Washable markers or crayons

Directions

With the paper sack folded flat and the bottom of the sack face up (make sure the open end is closest to you), glue the duck's face to the bottom of the sack. Carefully lift up the bottom flap that you have just glued and glue the bottom portion of the ducks bill under the flap. This makes a really cute paper puppet. The children can use markers or color on the rest of the sack, if they would like. An additional enrichment for the children who can print is to have them write "Help! Help!" on their sack to help remind them of the story, *One Duck Stuck*.

LESSON 33

❧❦❧

LOVE

CURRICULUM TOPICS

Love, Valentine's Day, Mother's Day, Father's Day, Self-Esteem, Family

FEATURED BOOK

Marzollo, Jean. 2000. *I Love You: A Rebus Poem*. New York: Cartwheel Books.

SUMMARY

Through charming and whimsical illustrations, this rhyming love poem is told through words and rebus picture clues. Ages 3–7

ACTIVITY

Introduce the cover of the book by pointing out and reading the title to your audience. Discuss how this story is told with words and rebus pictures. Encourage your listeners to collectively decipher the rebus picture words on the front cover. Explain to the children that when you are reading the words, they are to use the picture clues to guess the rhymes and repeat the phrase, "I love you."

ADDITIONAL BOOKS TO SHARE

Beaumont, Karen. 2004. *I Like Myself!* New York: Harcourt. This is a joyous story about a curly haired African-American girl who is very happy with everything about herself, inside and out. She says, "I'd still like me with fleas or warts, or with a silly snout that snorts." The brilliantly illustrated little girl gushes with character and charm. Make sure to read this book with confidence and a cheerful tone. With added expression from the reader, this story is true love in the purest sense. Ages 2–8

Bedford, David. 2004. *The Way I Love You*. New York: Simon & Schuster Books for Young Readers. A young girl shares all the reasons she loves her best friend and playmate—her puppy. Ages 3–7

Genechten, Guido Van. 2003. *The Cuddle Book*. New York: HarperCollins. How do you suppose a porcupine cuddles? Everybody, even animals, enjoys a good cuddle. It is a mommy's cuddle that is always best. Ages 2–6

George, Lindsay Barrett. 2005. *The Secret*. New York: Greenwillow Books. Do you know how keep a secret? Mr. Snail whispers his romantic secret to Mouse, who passes it to the beetle, who passes it to the turtle, and so on. The secret finally reaches Mrs. Snail and the mystery is revealed. Ages 2–6

Horning, Sandra. 2005. *The Big Hug*. New York: Alfred A. Knopf. Through the mail, Owen sends a great big hug to his granny. The great big hug is handed off from one postal worker to another as it travels across the country spreading cheer from here to there. This story can be easily adapted into a simple puppet show for Valentine's Day. Ages 3–7

Jordan, Deloris, and Roslyn M. Jordan. 2004. *Did I Tell You I Love You Today?* New York: Simon & Schuster Books for Young Readers. To tell her children how special they are to her and how much she loves them, a mother explains all the things she does throughout the day. Bold illustrations sweetly depict this mother's day spent dreaming about the activities her children like to do and the ways she can bring out the best in them. In the author's note, she comments that it is her wish that this story will help children to more clearly *see* all the ways parents show their children love. Ages 3–7

McBratney, Sam. 2004. *You're All My Favorites*. Cambridge, MA: Candlewick Press. The tender story of this bear family and their three, uniquely wonderful bear cubs affectionately explains how all children are their parent's favorites, whether or not they are a girl or boy, big or little, and no matter what they look like. Ages 3–7

McCourt, Lisa. 1997. *I Love You Stinky Face.* Mahwah, NJ: Bridge Water Books. When this inquisitive and imaginative child questions the conditions of his mother's love, Mother conjures a few innovative ideas of her own to reassure her child she will always love him. Ages 3–7

Moss, Miriam. 2004. *Don't Forget I Love You.* New York: Dial Books for Young Readers. Billy piddles through his morning routine playing with his favorite stuffed rabbit. When Billy's slow-poking makes them late for school and Mama's work, she rushes off, accidentally forgetting to say, "I love you." No matter how hurried parents are, they are always thinking of their children. So it is no surprise when Mama quickly returns with Billy's stuffed rabbit in hand. The two exchange comforting words and hugs and restart their days off right. When reading this story, add interest by really role-playing the characters. Each time mom calls out requesting Billy to continue getting ready, put your hand to your mouth as if calling from another room. Repeat this same action each time Billy replies, "In a minute." Ages 3–7

Parr, Todd. 2003. *The Family Book.* New York: Megan Tingley Books. The author of both *The Daddy Book* and *The Mommy Book* continues to demonstrate how these important relationships can be uniquely celebrated in *The Family Book.* Childlike drawings are wonderfully displayed in bold, primary colors that can easily be seen in even the largest storyhour crowds. Ages 3–7

Schertle, Alice. 2004. *1, 2, I Love You.* San Francisco: Chronicle Books. Told in the tradition of 1, 2, Buckle My Shoe, this joyful poem celebrates the playful adventures, love, and affection shared between parent and child. Ages 2–7

Walsh, Melanie. 2002. *My Nose, Your Nose.* Boston: Houghton Mifflin. Although we may seem very different, we all have things in common, too. Learning about diversity helps us to open our hearts to each other. Whether noses turn up or down, they all love the smell of chocolate cake! Help children discover what else they may have in common with others and to embrace their neighbor through this simple, yet poignant, book. Ages 2–7

Willis, Jeanne. 2005. *Never Too Little to Love.* Cambridge, MA: Candlewick Press. Tiny Too-Little really wants a kiss from Topsy Too-Tall, but their enormous size difference makes it seem impossible. Tiny Too-Little devises a plan to stack a mountain of things together to climb up on top of and get his kiss, but he becomes discouraged when the pile topples over. Will Tiny Too-Little ever get kissed? Ages 3–7

MUSIC AND MOVEMENT WITH VOICES

Sing Along: "You & Me"

Sung to the Tune: "Polly Put the Kettle on"
(Adult sings and child guesses last word in each line)
Flowers, they need rain to *grow*!
Cars, they need gas to *go*!
Needles, they need thread to *sew*!
And I need you, you know! *(Adult and child sing this line together)*
(Child sings and adult guesses last word in each line)
Every tic-tac needs a *toe*!
Runny noses need a *blow*!
Grown ups like to say NO NO!
And I need you, you know! *(Adult and child sing this line together)*
(Adult sings and child guesses last word in each line)
All the birds need wings to *fly*!
All the stores need people to *buy*!
All the stars, they need the *sky*!
And we, make you and I! *(Adult and child sing this line together)*
(Child sings and adult guesses last word in each line)
You always say that I must *try*!
You never like it when I *cry*!
When I am bad, you ask me *why*?
And we, make you and I! *(Adult and child sing this line together)*
(Adult sings and child guesses last word in each line)
Every train needs a *track*!
Every sidewalk has a *crack*!
Every big kiss makes a *smack*!
And you, I have your back!

(Child sings and adult guesses last word in each line)
You feed me when I need a *snack*!
When we take a trip, you help me *pack*!
You say listening skills is what I *lack*!
And you, I have your back! *(Adult and child sing this line together)*

Directions

Play song #36 from the accompanying *The Sound of Storytime* CD. This is a sweet song that is fun to learn for adults and children alike. The verses are sung so that an adult sings all but the last word of a the first three lines, and the child guesses the last word of each line, then the adult and child sing the fourth line together. It then switches, and the child sings the next three lines, with the adult guessing the last word in each line, and then the adult and child both sing the fourth line. It continues the same way throughout the entire song. After hearing it all of the way through once, everyone will be ready to sing it again!

JUST FOR FUN

Chocolate Walk

Supplies Needed

Construction paper, 9" × 12" in size in any color, one per child

Washable marker

Masking tape

Chocolate candy (Hershey's Kisses or Hershey's Hug chocolates are favorites for this activity)

CD of above song, "You & Me," still available to use

Numbers on a sheet of paper cut into strips and folded up for drawing (if you have twenty-one children, then you have numbers one through twenty-one cut into strips and folded)

Directions

Prenumber each sheet of construction paper with the marker. Then tape down these numbered sheets on the floor, forming a large circle. (This should be done prior to storytime.) Have each child stand on a number. Have "You & Me," song #36 from the accompanying *Sound of Storytime* CD, ready to play. Explain to the children that when the music starts, they need to begin walking around the circle until the music stops. When the music stops, they need to be standing on a number. Draw out a number. The child standing on the corresponding number on the floor gets to come and get a piece of chocolate candy. Repeat until all the children win. If there is not enough time, make sure every child gets a piece of chocolate at the end of the game.

STORYBOARD

Heart Puzzles

Supplies Needed

Construction paper, 9" × 12" in size in assorted colors

Scissors

Washable markers or crayons in assorted colors

Tape or self-adhesive material to attach heart pieces to storyboard

Large heart-shaped template made out of cardboard, or card stock

Make a large heart-shaped template. Trace around the heart on the assorted colors of construction paper. Make one heart per sheet of construction paper. Use the markers or crayons to color or draw polka dots, hearts, or any other unique shape onto each heart. Make sure each heart is different. Cut out the hearts. Then cut each heart into three pieces. You will need enough pieces to give one piece to each child participating in storytime. If you have twenty-one children attending, then you will need seven unique hearts cut into three pieces each. Explain to the children that each heart is different in color and design. They are to match the hearts together with the ones that look alike in order to make the heart puzzle complete. Give each child one piece of a heart. Let each child come to the board and add their heart piece. Ask the younger children to come to the board first, as they will not have to do anything except add their piece to the storyboard. Wait to apply the tape to the back of each piece as the children come forward to attach their heart puzzle piece. Have the older children come up last to add the last pieces to complete the heart puzzles. If you have a large group at storytime, it is nice to have an additional helper with this activity as the children get so excited for their turn Without help, it is a bit difficult to keep order, apply tape, and help the child at the board all at one time. When you are finished, take time to teach them "I Love You" in American Sign Language. The easiest way to teach this is to have them hold up their hand with all five finger stretched out; now pull down the middle finger and the ring finger, leaving the pointer, pinky, and thumb stretched out. This is the sign for "I Love You!" Let them practice this a few times.

MAKE AND TAKE

Hugs and Kisses Card

Supplies Needed per Child

Card stock paper, 9" × 12" in size, pastel colors, one sheet prefolded in half

Hershey's Kisses and Hershey's Hugs chocolates, one each

Washable markers or crayons

Tape

Glue gun, cool type, (adult use only)

Directions

Prior to the activity, prefold the sheets of card stock paper in half to form cards. Ask the children to write their name on the inside of the card and draw a picture of a heart. You may want to help them draw around their own hand, as something endearing and personal is nice on the inside of the card. After they are finished with the inside of the card, have the children fold the tape and apply it to the bottom of the wrapped Hershey's Kisses and Hershey's Hugs chocolate. Next, have them apply the candy on to the front of the card. Or attach them by using the cool type glue gun. Explain to the children that they are making a card with a hug and a kiss on it, and they will need to give it to someone very special.

LESSON 34

⁕

MICE

CURRICULUM TOPICS

Mice, Cats

FEATURED BOOK

Fearnley, Jan. 2004. *Watch Out!* Cambridge, MA: Candlewick Press.

SUMMARY

Wilf is so busy having fun that he does not pay attention when his mother calls for him to "Watch out, Wilf!" All throughout the story, the book repeats "Crash bang wallop!" and Wilf continues to find himself in one calamity after another. Wilf loves his Mommy and does not want her to be upset. He decides he must settle down and puts his mind and energy into making Mommy a surprise instead. Finally, in an endearing turn of events, Mommy gets so excited when she sees her surprise that, uh oh, "Crash bang wallop!" Ages 3–7

ACTIVITY

Children will repeat the phrase "Watch out, Wilf!" each time the leader cues them to do so. Introduce the book by pointing out the title on the cover of the book. Explain that little Wilf does not listen to his Mommy when she tells him to watch out. Tell the children they are going to get to play the part of Mommy. Each time you read, "Mommy said . . ." turn back to the front cover and point to the title. Give the children time to say their line. To give the children a direct cue, you need to reverse the phrase, from "Watch out, Wilf!' said Mom" to "Mom said . . . Watch out, Wilf!" There is also a line that repeats, "Crash bang wallop!" Pass out the tambourines and let the children make the loud noises with the instruments.

FEATURED BOOK

Geraghty, Paul. 1990. *Look Out, Patrick!* New York: Macmillan Publishing.

SUMMARY

A mouse enjoys a long walk in the woods, totally oblivious to many dangerous situations and narrow escapes. Ages 3–7

ACTIVITY

Read the title of the book to your audience. Point out the picture of the mouse on the cover and introduce your listeners to this character. Patrick does not look at what is going on around him when he takes his walk. Ask the children to help Patrick stay safe by warning him of danger. Explain that every time you say, "Oh no!" the children are to say, "Patrick! Look Out!" After the children say their repeating line, and before you turn the page, ask the children to tell you what the danger to Patrick is in the picture.

FEATURED BOOK

Waite, Judy. 1998. *Mouse, Look Out!* New York: Dutton Children's Books.

SUMMARY

A mouse hides from the cat in an old abandoned house. Ages 3–8

ACTIVITY

Before reading the story aloud, point out and teach the children the repeating rhyme, "Mouse, Look Out! There's A Cat About." Ask the children to shout out the repeating warning each time the story mentions the cat's shadow. Emphasize the word *shadow* to cue the children to chime in. For more fun, tell the story with a black cat puppet. The puppet can be either a paper Ellison die-cut cat #3 on a craft stick or a stuffed commercial puppet. When the children call out, simply sneak the puppets head up from behind the book as you read. If you have access to a puppet stage, have an additional staff member slip the puppet's head up at the appropriate times in the story.

ADDITIONAL BOOKS TO SHARE

Donaldson, Julia. 1999. *The Gruffalo*. New York: Dial Books for Young Readers. Little mouse is on a stroll in the deep dark woods when he comes across a fox who wants to eat him. Mouse invents the gruffalo but gets more than he bargained for! Children of all ages will enjoy this adventurous tale. Ages 3–8

Jeram, Anita. 1995. *Daisy Dare*. Cambridge, MA: Candlewick Press. Daisy Dare is a little dare devil mouse, who will do things that her friends wouldn't dream of doing. Anything Daisy's friends dare her to do, she does. The real adventure starts when Daisy begins to slip the bell off of the sleeping cat's collar. After the story, ask the children if Daisy should have taken all of those dares? Ages 3–7

Lakin, Patricia. 2002. *Clarence the Copy Cat*. New York: Random House Children's Books. Clarence the cat does not like chasing mice and cannot find a place to live that does not expect him to catch mice. Then one day he happens on a kind librarian who takes him in. Clarence likes living at the library. He earns the name "Copy Cat" because he enjoys cat napping on the copy machine. Life could not have been better until the day a mouse shows up in Mr. Spanner's library. Ages 4–8

Larranaga, Ana Martin. 1999. *If You See a Mouse*. New York: Golden Books. In this lift-the-flap board book the children are directed to kiss, sing, tickle, and cuddle when they see certain things. But if they see a mouse, they are directed to scream! This is a sweet book that even the youngest children will enjoy. Ages 2–6

MacDonald, Alan. 2002. *Scaredy Mouse*. Wilton, CT: Tiger Tales. Big sister, Nibbles, takes scaredy mouse, Squeak, on an adventure past the sleeping cat to the kitchen for a bite of chocolate cake. Squeak thinks he sees the cat in every shadow along the way and repeatedly cries out, "It's the cat! It's the cat!" Encourage your listeners to repeat these words with you. Ages 3–7

MacDonald, Margaret Read. 2001. *Mabela the Clever*. Morton Grove, IL: Albert Whitman & Company. Read this fabulous African folktale about a mouse that heeds her father's good advice and avoids being tricked by the cat. The father passes on the wise ideals of this tale to the children you share with. Be sure to read the author's note about the interesting history of this story. MacDonald also includes a fun, group game idea and a little marching tune you can play and sing. Ages 3–8

McFarland, Lyn Rossiter. 2005. *Mouse Went Out to Get a Snack*. New York: Farrar, Straus and Giroux. Mouse is hungry for a little snack. He creeps into the kitchen, trying to be careful not to wake the cat, and discovers a huge spread of food on the kitchen table. The next trick is to get as much food back to his home without waking the cat. This is a funny read-aloud with whimsical illustrations. Ages 2–7

Robbins, Maria Polushkin. 2005. *Mother, Mother I Want Another*. New York: Alfred A. Knopf. Mrs. Mouse gives baby mouse a kiss goodnight when baby mouse cries, "I want another, Mother!" Mrs. Mouse thinks baby wants another mother, when all he really wants is another kiss! Mother mouse runs out looking for other animal mothers to help put her son to bed. The illustrations are adorable and large enough to be a perfect complement to storytime. Ages 2–7

Ryan, Pam Munoz. 2001. *Mice and Beans*. New York: Scholastic Inc. This Spanish-speaking grandma loves to cook for her family, and what better reason to plan a party than her granddaughter's seventh birthday? Even though Grandma's house is tiny, she believes, "When there's room in the heart, there's room in the house, except for a mouse." So each day she makes birthday celebration plans, and then sets a trap to keep the mice away. Before the story, invite the children to help tell the tale by clapping their hands together and saying the repeating word "SNAP" every time Grandma sets another mouse trap. As the leader, you will demonstrate this action the first time it appears in the story. Every time thereafter, read the repeating words, "When it was set and ready tooooo . . ." Then pause long enough for the children to interject "SNAP!" In the end, Grandma decides that there may be room in her house for a few helpful mice after all. Take a minute to read the inspirational "Recipe for a Festive Story Time" on the inside front cover of the book and refer to the pronunciation guide in the back to learn any of the simple Spanish words you do not already know. Ages 3–8

Wheeler, Lisa. 2003. *One Dark Night*. San Diego, CA: Harcourt. As Mole and Mouse fearfully venture out into the dark woods, mystery and intrigue build when a beastly character is introduced. When the story reads, "He growled BEASTY growls," pause to ask the children what beasty growls would sound like. Give them time to try out their voices. When it says, "He stomped BEASTY feet," ask the children to show you what that might look like. The author builds up the climax, creating a high-interest story, but brings everything full circle to a reassuring end. Ages 3–8

Yee, Brenda Shannon. 2001. *Hide & Seek*. New York: Orchard Books. Mouse plays hide-and-seek with the house owner, but it is up to the reader to decide which one is more scared of the other. Ages 3–6

MUSIC AND MOVEMENT WITH VOICES

Sing Along: "Look Out!"

Sung to the Tune: "Mexican Hat Dance"

Look Out! Look Out!
Run as fast as you can!
Look Out! Look Out!
Run as fast as you can!
Poor mouse he is having a bad day!
An unlucky, terrible sad day!
But he thinks he's having a glad day!
So let's help him to keep it that way!
Look Out! Look Out!
Run as fast as you can!
Look Out! Look Out!
Run as fast as you can!
The cat wanted mouse for his lunch!
The mouse wanted cheese to munch!
But me—I have my own hunch,
Cat's paw's getting ready to SCRUNCH!
Look Out! Look Out!
Run as fast as you can!
Look Out! Look Out!
Run as fast as you can!
Mouse is safe, and he's taking a nap!
Cat's looking to set a new trap!
So next time you hear a snap!
Make sure that the cat's in your lap!
Look Out! Look Out!
Run as fast as you can!
Look Out! Look Out!
Run as fast as you can!
LOOK OUT!

Directions

Read through the song first and let the children echo you when you yell "Look Out!" If puppets are available to share, pass them out and let the children yell "Look Out!" with a puppet. Play song #37 from the accompanying *The Sound of Storytime* CD. This fast-paced song is sure to be another storytime hit!

ADDITIONAL SONGS TO SHARE

Palmer, Hap. *Rhythms on Parade.* Hap-Pal Music Inc., 1995. Compact Disk. HP102E AC633. Play song #2, *The Mice Go Marching.* Lead the children in a parade around the room, marching to the rhythm in this song. Have the children imitate the sounds and movements the mice and monster make.

STORYBOARD

Mouse's Hungry Walk

Supplies Needed

Ellison die-cuts, mouse, cat #3, mutt, wolf #1, cow, pig #2, one of each

Tiny scrap of yellow construction paper

Scissors

Tape or self-adhesive material to attach items to storyboard

Directions

Prior to the activity, attach the mouse and all the other animals onto the storyboard. Cut the scrap of yellow construction paper to form a shape that resembles a tiny wedge of cheese. Attach the tape to the back of the cheese and hide it behind one of the animals. When you begin the activity, control which animals the children will make the sounds of and which they will look behind first, so as not to find the wedge of cheese too quickly. After you have gone through a couple of animals, let the children choose which animal they think is hiding the mouse's cheese. Remember to have them make the animal sound and shout "GIVE IT BACK!" before you remove the animal to reveal what might be hiding behind it. Another element to this activity, if you have time, is to hide funny pictures behind the animals that have nothing to do with a snack. When the children remove an animal, there will be something behind it, but not what they are actually searching for. Be prepared to repeat this easy activity, as once will not be enough. Children always love seek and find storyboard activities.

> Mouse took a walk but lost his snack.
> Can you help him get it back?
> One of the animals is hiding the snack,
> Make the animal sound and shout, "GIVE IT BACK!"

MAKE AND TAKE

Thumbprint Mice

Supplies Needed per Child

Construction paper or white copy paper, one each

Washable ink pads in red, yellow, and blue

Washable markers or crayons in assorted colors

Damp paper towels or wipes for cleaning up little thumbs

Directions

Help the children place their thumb on the ink pad(s) of their choice and then on the paper to make the colorful body of a mouse. Use the washable markers or crayons to draw a swirling tail, beady eyes, and little round ears. The children will have fun with this easy activity and will want to experiment by making several mice on their paper. Make sure to tell them to clean their thumbs well before using another stamp pad. A great resource book for thumbprint art is: Emberley. Ed. 2002. *Ed Emberley's Complete Funprint Drawing Book.* Boston: Little, Brown. This book is filled with easy, step-by-step techniques that show youngsters how to create their own thumbprint art.

LESSON 35

SHARKS

CURRICULUM TOPICS

Sharks, Ocean Life

FEATURED BOOK

Lloyd, Sam. 2003. *Yummy Yummy! Food for My Tummy!* Wilton, CT: Tiger Tales.

SUMMARY

Two monkeys wish to visit each other so they can share banana milk shakes and coconut cake, but the islands they live on are separated by shark-infested waters! The monkeys think of some very inventive ways to try to cross the water without getting eaten by the sharks. None of their ideas work. Finally, the discouraged monkeys climb to the tops of their coconut trees to think of a new solution when the problem miraculously fixes itself. Ages 3–8

ACTIVITY

Teach the children the repeating lines of this story, "Yummy, yummy, food for my tummy," by reading the title of the book and asking your audience to repeat the title after you. Explain that these are the words of the menacing sharks in this toothy tale. Ask the children to practice one more time but this time to say their part like a shark would. Tell the children they may sing out these words in their sharkiest voices every time the line appears in the story. Let your audience know you will point to them and say, "The sharks sang—" each time it is their turn. Sometimes the author has this repeating line before the cue words, simply rearrange the words as you tell the story. At the conclusion of the book, the monkeys indeed get to meet for banana milk shakes and coconut cake. The author does not put this line in, but as we finish reading this story, we like to add the line, "And then it was the monkeys that sang—yummy, yummy food for my tummy!" Say this last line slowly, emphasize the words "and then" and "monkeys." If you pause after the word "sang" and put your hand up to your ear, the children will know to chime in with you. Every one likes to be in on a joke, and this always brings laughs to a group of youngsters.

FEATURED BOOK

Sharratt, Nick. 2002. *Shark in the Park.* New York: David Fickling Books.

SUMMARY

Timothy Pope has a brand new telescope. He takes his new toy to the park, but close up some things look surprisingly different. Children love the rhyme and repetition of this crafty story. Round cut-outs in the pages reveal what Timothy sees through his telescope. Ages 3–8

ACTIVITY

Tell the children that you are going to read the title of the next book you are about to share and that you want them to repeat the title after you. Calmly read the title of the book to the children. When they mimic you, look like you are pondering something and say, "Shark in the park? If there really were a shark in the park, is that how you would tell somebody?" Of course it isn't. Ask the children to say the title as if there really, truly was a shark swimming around the park. Explain that the audience will get to say this repeating line with you each time it appears in the story. To have even more fun with this book, prop the book on an easel and act out the part of Timothy playing with his telescope. Each time the book repeats that Timothy looks at the sky, at the ground, to the left and right, and all around, make a telescope with your two hands held to one eye as you close the other eye. Act out all these actions as you read, and encourage the children to make their own pretend telescopes and imitate you. Fun!

ADDITIONAL BOOKS TO SHARE

Axworthy, Anni. 1998. *Guess What I Am*. Cambridge, MA: Candlewick Press. This guessing-game storybook reveals clues through die-cut holes and peculiar facts about unusual animals. The shark is included among five other animals. Ages 2–7

Davies, Nicola. 2003. *Surprising Sharks*. Cambridge, MA: Candlewick Press. Now that you have spurred an interest in sharks, display or booktalk this nonfiction picture book for check-out to take home and read. This colorful book is full of curious shark facts and unusual witty comparisons. Encourage children to check out this book as well as others from your nonfiction collection. Make a quick book display by decorating the area with plastic ocean animals, real seashells, and starfish the children can touch and explore. Ages 3–8

Galloway, Ruth. 2003. *Smiley Shark*. Wilton, CT: Tiger Tales. Smiley Shark's toothy grin frightens away all the other creatures in the sea, leaving the poor shark very lonely. Then, one day Smiley gets the opportunity to rescue the other fish from the fisherman's trap and net some new friends too! Ages 3–7

Garrett, Ann, and Gene-Michael Higney. 2000. *What's for Dinner?* New York: Dutton Children's Books. Open the mouths of five animals to see what they eat. This story is told in humorous rhyme. You will learn the fun facts about these odd creatures. Each large, colorful illustration, including one of a shark, covers a full two-page spread, making this a good choice for reading to large groups. Ages 2–7

Griff, Andrew. 2000. *Shark-Mad Stanley*. New York: Hyperion Books for Children. Stanley loves all kinds of creatures, especially sharks. When Stanley discovers his pet goldfish is much like a shark, he ponders the idea of getting a pet shark too. Join Stanley as he investigates and learns everything there is to know about sharks. We love the retro-styled illustrations that show Stanley researching sharks in library books and making picture collages and scrapbooks of his discoveries. Stanley will inspire your young audience to do some ocean exploring of their own. A CD-ROM is included. Ages 3–8

Mahy, Margaret. 1989. *The Great White Man-Eating Shark*. New York: Dial Books for Young Readers. Norvin poses as a shark in order to scare off the other swimmers and have the popular swimming hole all for himself. His plan seems sound until a female shark reveals her romantic intentions toward Norvin. Ages 4–8

Martin, Rafe. 2001. *The Shark God*. New York: Arthur A. Levine Books. In this adaptation of a traditional Hawaiian tale, two children save a wounded shark and then are saved in return. Ages 5–8

MUSIC AND MOVEMENT WITH VOICES

Sing Along: "Shark Watching!"

Sung to the Tune: "When Johnny Comes Marching Home"

The sharks are swimming round and round! WATCH OUT! WATCH OUT!
They know how not to make a sound! WATCH OUT! WATCH OUT!
The water's deep, the sharks are out,
Circling for food and they're about to GET YOU!
You better WATCH OUT! WATCH OUT!
The sharks are swimming round and round! WATCH OUT! WATCH OUT!
They know how not to make a sound! WATCH OUT! WATCH OUT!
The sharks are hungry, there's no doubt,
They're coming closer and they're about to GET YOU!
You better WATCH OUT! WATCH OUT!
The sharks are swimming round and round! WATCH OUT! WATCH OUT!
They know how not to make a sound! WATCH OUT! WATCH OUT!
Their teeth are sharp, they have big fins,
I think the sharks are about to WIN!
So you better HURRY OUT! WATCH OUT!

Directions

Play song #38 from the accompanying *The Sound of Storytime* CD. Keep this song lively and spirited! Sing in a suspenseful, worried voice. At each "WATCH OUT!" shout it out, as if it really is happening and you are very concerned.

JUST FOR FUN

Let's Go Fishing!

Supplies Needed

Ellison die-cut fish #2, in bright colors, one each

Blue tablecloth

Children's-size fishing poles or dowel rods (3' long), two

Fishing line

Small magnets, two

Glue gun

Paper clips

Tape

Directions

If using a dowel rod, tie the fishing line around the dowel rod securely and reinforce by taping over the line. Finish by tying or hot gluing a magnet to the end of the line. If using a child's fishing pole, attach the magnet in the same way to the end of the fishing line. Spread the blue tablecloth onto the floor. Attach a paper clip to the mouth of each fish. Then spread the fish out on the blue tablecloth. Let each child take a turn trying to catch a fish with the fishing pole. If you have a variety of fish colors to choose from, suggest a specific color of fish each child could try to catch as they take their turn. This activity offers hand and eye coordination as well as fun! Pass out prepackaged fish-shape snack crackers to the children as a "great catch" reward after the activity!

ADDITIONAL SONGS TO SHARE

Scelsa, Greg, and Steve Millang. *Big Fun.* YoungHeart Music, 1997. Compact Disk. YM-016 CD Play song #2, "Silly Willies." Dance and sing along with this silly movement song.

Disney's Silly Songs. Walt Disney Records, 1988. Compact Disk. 60819-7. Play song #15, "Three Little Fishies," while the children are entering storytime and during craft time.

STORYBOARD

Little Fishy's Lucky Day

Supplies Needed

Ellison die-cut shark, one

Ellison die-cut tiny fish, one small in a bright color

Tape or adhesive material to attach items onto storyboard

Optional Enrichment: Make stick puppets of Little Fishy and the Shark. Make one of each for every child. Attach the Ellison die-cut tiny fish and shark to individual small craft sticks with tape. Pass them out and let the children join the activity of the Shark circling Little Fishy and diving down.

Directions

Read through the storyboard story and become familiar with the movements needed to make with Shark and Little Fishy. Add Shark and Little Fishy at the appropriate times. Read the story with enthusiasm and concern. The end of the story asks, ". . . but when his mom finds out what will she say?" Use this opportunity to discuss whether Little Fishy should have challenged Shark. The children will enjoy sharing this story and brainstorming what Little Fishy should have done.

Hungry Shark was waiting for a bite, *(add Shark)*
Circling around the water looking for a fight!
Along came Little Fishy as happy as could be, *(add Little Fishy)*
He looked at Shark and said, "Bet you can't catch me!"
Shark said, "Just you wait, and watch and see,

You'll be eaten before the count of three!"
Shark circled and he circled and circled some more, *(Shark circles Little Fishy)*
Poor Shark got dizzy and sunk to the ocean floor! *(lower Shark on board)*
Little Fishy dove down to the ocean floor! *(lower Little Fishy on board)*
He looked at Shark and said, "do you want some more?"
Proud Little Fishy won the challenge that day,
If he knows what's good for him, he better stay away!

ADDITIONAL STORYBOARD

Benton, Gail, and Trisha Waichulaitis. 2003. *Ready-to-Go Storytimes: Fingerplays, Scripts, Patterns, Music, and More.* New York: Neal-Schuman Publishers. Play #10, *We Dove in the Ocean* on the book's accompanying CD-ROM. Enrich this lesson by using this song and activity.

MAKE AND TAKE

Ocean Picture

Supplies Needed per Child

Construction paper, 12" × 18" in size, blue, one

Ellison die-cuts—shell #3, clam shell, sea horse, tiny fish, fish #2, shark—assorted colors, five

Glue stick

Washable markers or crayons

Directions

Let children make an ocean picture out of the Ellison die-cuts you have available for them. Have them glue the ocean die-cuts onto their paper. They can also use washable markers or crayons and add other sea creatures or ocean life to their picture. Children never tire of using their little hands to create individual masterpieces.

LESSON 36

SNORING

CURRICULUM TOPICS

Nighttime, Bedtime Rituals, Snoring, Grandparents

FEATURED BOOK

Long, Melinda. 2000. *When Papa Snores*. New York: Simon & Schuster Books for Young Readers.

SUMMARY

A girl's nana and papa snore so much that they rattle the lamp and shake the dishes. How will she ever get to sleep with all that noise? Ages 3–8

ACTIVITY

Divide the group by girls and boys. When the story reads, "Papa snores, HONNKK SHOOOOO, HONNKK SHOOOOO," the boys get to make the sound effects. When the story reads, "Nana snores, CARRROOSH, CAR-RROOSH," the girls get to make the sound effects. You can make up different snores if you prefer; just as long as each is distinct. We like to make Nana's snore a sweet little, "HONNKK, MEEE, MEEE, MEEE, MEEE, MEEE." If you have the equipment, give the boys shakers to play when the book reads, "the lamp at his bedside rattles and shakes." Give the girls bells or tambourines to play when the story reads, "the blinds on the window clink-clank together." The children have a blast making all the snoring noises.

FEATURED BOOK

Wood, Audrey. 1984. *The Napping House*. San Diego, CA: Harcourt Brace Jovanovich.

SUMMARY

In Granny's house numerous creatures sleep peacefully, stacked one on top of another, until a wakeful flea causes a great commotion. Ages 3–7

ACTIVITY

Every time this cumulative tale repeats, "on a snoring granny," the children make snoring sound effects.

ADDITIONAL BOOKS TO SHARE

Alda, Arlene. 2005. *The Book of ZZZs*. New York: Tundra Books Heartwarming, real-life photographs depict people and animals catching some zzz's. A stretched-out goat, a seal on rocks, and twin baby girls, one sleeping and one smiling, are a few of the adorable photos included in this book. Ages 2–7

Bogan, Paulette. 2003. *Goodnight Lulu*. New York: Bloomsbury Children's Books. Lulu's mother tucks her into bed and reassures her little chickadee that there is nothing to fear of bears, tigers, and alligators. The illustration of this kind and gentle mother hen transforming into a ferociously protective beast who bites tigers on the tail and chases bears is hysterical. Ages 3–7

Faulkner, Keith. 1999. *The Big Yawn*. Brookfield, CT: The Millbrook Press. Die-cut pages reveal bigger and bigger animals that open their mouths to yawn before closing their eyes to go to sleep. Encourage children to make the sound effects of the yawning animals. Ages 2–7

Hamm, Diane Johnston. 1992. *Rock-A-Bye Farm*. New York: Simon & Schuster Books for Young Readers. The farmer rocks his baby, dog, hen, sheep, pig, cow, horse, and mouse to sleep. Farm animals are the subject of numerous children's picture books. Over the years we have accumulated puppets and stuffed animals of about every farm or jungle animal imaginable from garage sales and thrift stores. These props come in very handy. Make it a point to watch for these items for your own collection. Make this story interactive by passing out to all of the children stuffed animals or puppets of farm animals. Let the children rock their animals to sleep as you read the story to them. Ages 2–6

Hendry, Diana. 1999. *The Very Noisy Night*. New York: Dutton Children's Books. Night noises frighten Little Mouse. Big Mouse tries to reassure Little Mouse, but Little Mouse will not be satisfied until Big Mouse invites him to share his bed. Big Mouse does not want Little Mouse to sleep with him because he wiggles too much and his paws are cold. Will either of them get any sleep on this long night? Charming illustrations detail lots of common household items the mice have resourcefully used to create their colorfully decorated home. Ages 3–7

Markes, Julie. 2005. *Shhhhh! Everybody's Sleeping*. New York: HarperCollins. This brightly illustrated book shows community workers sleeping in a way children may actually think they sleep. One page has a librarian peacefully sleeping with a book in one hand and her glasses in another, with her bed near shelves of books. Another page shows a policeman sleeping near a busy street. The story briefly assures the reader that community workers might be peacefully sleeping, but their specific tasks are completed for the day. This is a soothing, restful story to read to all ages. In the end, there is a small, bright-eyed child whom a mother cuddles and wishes would sleep as well. Ages 2–8

Roth, Carol. 2004. *Who Will Tuck Me in Tonight?* New York: North-South Books. It is bedtime and Woolly lamb can't find his mother. One at a time all the other farm animal mothers try to tuck Woolly in and reassure him until his mother returns. But no one can do it like his mom. Create a pathetic little voice for Woolly the lamb by speaking like you have a cold or by holding your nose. Ages 2–7

Whybrow, Ian. 2000. *Where's Tim's Ted?* Hauppauge, NY: Barron's Educational Series. When Tim loses his teddy bear at his grandparent's farm house, Tim and the farm animals venture out in the night to try to find it. Ages 2–7

Wild, Margaret. 2000. *Nighty Night!* Atlanta, GA: Peachtree. All the animal children on the farm are wide awake and want to play past their bedtime. The children play tricks on their animal parents by switching beds. Ages 3–7

Wilson, Karma. 2002. *Bear Snores On*. New York: Margaret K. McElderry Books. One by one, friends come in from the cold and gather in bear's cave. While bear sleeps through the cold winter, the friends enjoy food and festivities. The story repeats the line, "But the bear snores on." Each time you start to say this phrase, pause after the word "But" and let the children join in. Encourage them to end the line with a loud snore. Parachute play is a very popular activity at storytime. If you have access to one, read the story then get out the handled parachute and play. Make a cave by raising the parachute overhead. Then pull the chute down behind your back and sit down on the floor underneath the parachute. Pretend to be snoring bears in a cave. Next, say "1, 2, 3, *Wake up bears! It is springtime, come out and see!*" Ages 2–7

Ziefert, Harriet. 2000. *Clara Ann Cookie, Go to Bed!* Boston: Houghton Mifflin. It is bedtime for Clara Ann Cookie, but she does not want to go to bed. When she breaks the unwelcome news to her dolls and toys, they all obey and go right to sleep. That is, all but Popcorn, her teddy bear. Clara dutifully administers all the nighttime rituals as a good mother should, but the little bear is still defiant. Clara must even resort to putting Popcorn in time out. Symbolic of the reconciliation Clara makes with her own resentful feelings about bedtime, the two finally call a truce, climb into bed, and fall asleep. Ages 3–7

MUSIC AND MOVEMENT WITH VOICES

Sing Along: "Oh, Please Don't Snore Anymore!"

Sung to the Tune: "My Bonnie Lies Over the Ocean"

My papa, he snores very loudly!
My mama, she snores worse than that!
My brother and sister make strange sounds.
Now, the only one left is the cat!
Don't snore! Oh, don't snore!
Oh, please don't snore anymore! *(Make snoring sounds)*
Don't snore! Oh, don't snore!
Oh, please don't snore anymore! *(Make snoring sounds)*
My papa, he claims he quit snoring!
My mama says she never did!
My brother and sister ignore me!
Because I'm the littlest kid!

Don't snore! Oh, don't snore!
Oh, please don't snore anymore! *(Make short snoring sounds)*
Don't snore! Oh, don't snore!
Oh, please don't snore anymore! *(Make snoring sounds)*
My family all say they quit snoring,
and making strange noises at night!
I hardly believe what they're saying,
cause me and the cat know we're right!
Don't snore! Oh, don't snore!
Oh, please don't snore anymore! *(Make snoring sounds)*
Don't snore! Oh, don't snore!
Oh, please don't snore anymore! *(Make snoring sounds)*

Directions

Play song #39 from the accompanying *The Sound of Storytime* CD. Have the children replace the word "snore" while making the snoring noise throughout the song! This activity will keep everyone on their nose . . . we mean toes!

ADDITIONAL SONGS TO SHARE

The Best of the Best Preschool Play Songs! Madacy Kids, 2001. Compact Disk. WW 24398. Play song # 11, "Roll Over." Children can stand up and turn around in place on the words "roll over." On the words "one fell out," everyone claps and then squats down. Get back up and start again on every verse. Keep track of the numbers on your fingers.

Scelsa, Greg, and Steve Millang. *Kids in Action.* Greg & Steve Productions, 2000. Compact Disk. Play Song #4, "Goin' on a Bear Hunt." This is one of our favorite versions of this traditional movement chant. The male voice accompanied by the children echoing the lines makes for a perfect blend. The artists have added a brilliant musical element throughout this movement activity.

STORYBOARD

Five SNORING Bears

Supplies Needed

Ellison die-cut bear #1, five
Construction paper, 12" × 18" in size, black, one
Scissors
Tape or adhesive material to attach bears onto the storyboard

Directions

Cut the large sheet of black construction paper to resemble the shape of a cave. Feel free to embellish it any way you like. Attach it to the storyboard prior to the activity. Add one bear to the cave each time you are prompted by the verse. As you add the bears, ask the children to put their palms together and put them to the side of their faces as if they are napping. Have them make the snoring sound of the bear. Begin by having the children help softly snoring with one bear. As you continue to attach the bears onto the board, prompt the children to snore louder with each added bear. At the end, when they shout "WAKE UP!", have the children use their hands or feet or both and make a running sound on the floor as if they are running to get away from the wild bears they just woke up!
Recite the following verses:

(Put one bear onto black cave)
One lazy bear sleeping in a cave alone,
Another bear crept in, and was tired to the bone. *(Add second bear)*
Two tired bears snoring loud and long,
Another bear crept in, and joined the snoring song! *(Add third bear)*
Three tired bears snoring up a storm,
Another bear crept in, to dry off and get warm! *(Add fourth bear)*
Four tired bears snoring and shaking the ground,
Another bear crept in when he heard the snoring sound! *(Add fifth bear)*

Five tired bears snoring until springtime comes!
The spring is here, let's wake them up!
(Let children shout) WAKE UP!
NOW LET'S ALL GET READY TO RUN!!

MAKE AND TAKE

Edible Sleeping Bear Cave

Supplies Needed per Child

Paper plate, small size, one

Graham crackers, two

Canned cake frosting, approximately ½ cup for each craft table

Gummy Bears, three

Craft sticks, one

Moistened paper towels or wipes for clean up

Directions

Always have the children wash their hands before starting a food craft. Give each child a small paper plate. Next, take two graham crackers and lean them together to form a tent. Secure the top with the cake frosting, reminding the children to use their own craft stick to apply the frosting. Place three gummy bears inside the graham cracker cave. The children are sure to love this edible and unique take-home craft, if they have anything left to take home!

LESSON 37

WILD ZOO ANIMALS

CURRICULUM TOPICS

Jungle Animals, Zoo, Wild Behavior, Tigers, Monkeys, Elephants, Crocodiles, Parrots

FEATURED BOOK

Taylor, Thomas. 2002. *The Loudest Roar*. New York: Arthur A. Levine.

SUMMARY

Clovis, a small tiger, likes to sneak up on the other jungle animals and surprise them with a loud roar. The animals soon get tired of Clovis's mischief and join their voices to teach him a lesson. Ages 3–7

ACTIVITY

Before storytime, make picture flash cards of the jungle animals in this story. One fourth of the cards will be parrots, one fourth elephants, one fourth monkeys, and one fourth crocodiles. You will need one card for each participant at storytime. Pass out the cards before reading the story. The children are going to assume the role of the animal character on their card. Ask the children to look at their cards and think about what sounds their animal makes. Call on volunteers to demonstrate their animal's sound. Then encourage all the children with that same character to practice together. Ask the children, "If all the jungle animals made their sounds at once would be very noisy?" Give them an opportunity to try out their sounds in one loud chorus. Point out and discuss the title on the cover of this book. Explain to the children that they may use their voices to roar each time they see the title word "ROAR" printed in bold letters throughout the book. Next, show them the page from the story where all the jungle animals sneak up on Clovis to surprise him. Explain, when they see this page, that they are to play the part of their animal and call out their wildest jungle animal sound.

ADDITIONAL BOOKS TO SHARE

Campbell, Rod. 1982. *Dear Zoo*. New York: Little Simon. When a child writes to the zoo and requests that it send him a pet, a series of mysterious packages arrive in the mail. Repeating lines and simple lift-the-flaps reveal the tale of one child's quest for the perfect pet. As you read, ask the children to guess what they think might be in the package. For some storyboard fun, make a big cage with bars for your board. Before the story, pass out Ellison die-cut jungle animal pieces of an elephant #1, giraffe #1, lion #2, camel, snake #1, monkey #2, and frog #2. Each time the book reads, "I sent him back," the child with the appropriate animal brings their piece to the board and puts them back in the zoo. Ages 2–7

Cimarusti, Marie Torres. 2003. *Peek-A-Zoo*. New York: Dutton Children's Books. The animals at the zoo are playing peek-a-boo with you. Full-page characters inhabit this guessing-game book. Ages 1–5

Fox, Mem. 2000. *Harriet, You'll Drive Me Wild!* San Diego, CA: Harcourt Brace. Sometimes little kids can be as wild as zoo animals. Parents and children alike will relate to this endearing story of one child's sincere yet futile attempt to not try her mother's patience and one mother's sincere yet futile attempt to keep her patience. Ages 3–7

Freeman, Tor. 2002. *Roar!* Cambridge, MA: Candlewick Press. Throughout the day, Lotte pretends to be the animals her mother reads to her about in her story books. Ages 3–7

Faulkner, Keith. 2002. *Guess Who? At the Zoo*. New York: Barron's. This is a fun guessing book for the younger children. One big, bright page has an easy-to-solve riddle about a zoo animal. The next page has a larger-than-life lift-the-flap with a huge picture revealing the animal. Children love guessing games, and this is a must-read for storytime. Ages 2–6

Hendrick, Mary Jean. 1996. *If Anything Ever Goes Wrong at the Zoo*. San Diego, CA: Harcourt Brace. Leslie and her mother visit the zoo every Saturday. Each week, Leslie offers to keep the animals at her house, if ever anything should go wrong at the zoo. The zoo keepers graciously decline the invitation, but when an unthinkable rain floods the zoo, Leslie saves the day and gets her wish. Ages 3–7

Levin, Bridget. 2004. *Rules of the Wild: An Unruly Book of Manners*. San Francisco: Chronicle Books. Do your mom and dad let you stay up as late as you want? Father Fruit Bat lets his children stay up all night! The rules of the wild are probably very different from your own house rules. Explore the strange habits of various wild animals, and stir a child's wonder with this playful science adventure. As you read each rule of the wild, ask the children to explain the animals' behaviors and why they might have that rule. Some are harder than others. Be prepared to offer explanations for the ones the children do not already know. Ages 4–8

Martin, David. 2005. *We've All Got Bellybuttons!* Cambridge, MA: Candlewick Press. Wild animals demonstrate all the body parts we have in common with them. Can you clap your hands like the monkeys and stretch your neck like a giraffe? Animals invite the children along for some wild play in this colorful story book. Ages 2–7

Paxton, Tom. 1996. *Going to the Zoo*. New York: Morrow Junior Books. Read or sing this families zoo adventure. Encourage the children to interact by playing along with the animals as they clap, roar, hop, swing their trunks, scratch like monkeys, and fly in circles. The musical tune to the verse of this story is provided on the cover of the book. Ages 3–7

Weeks, Sarah. 2004. *If I Were a Lion*. New York: Atheneum Books for Young Readers. When a little girl's wild behavior lands her in the time-out chair, she contemplates how wild she would be if she were an animal. Given time to think about her actions, she decides she prefers to behave like the sweet, polite little girl she is. Both parents and children delight in this rhyming story. To help the children better understand what is happening in the story, we add the repeating line "I'm not wild" after every couple pages. Ages 3–7

Wilson, Karma. 2004. *Never, Ever Shout in a Zoo*. New York: Little, Brown. This rhyming tale shares the calamity of consequences that transpired from shouting in a zoo. Encourage the children to help tell the story. Every time you read "Uh-oh," have the audience say the repeating line, "Don't say I didn't warn you!" Ages 3–7

Winthrop, Elizabeth. 2003. *Dancing Granny*. Tarrytown, NY: Marshall Cavendish. Children are sure to love this endearing book about a little girl and her granny. The young girl decides she and her granny need to take a nighttime trip to the zoo where the animals have prepared a fabulous party. Granny does not want to go, but with affectionate coaxing, she simply cannot resist her sweet little granddaughter's invitation. They share an unforgettable night at the zoo! Ages 3–8

MUSIC AND MOVEMENT WITH VOICES

Sing Along: "Jungle Sounds"

Sung to the Tune: "Froggie Went A-Courtin'"

Can you roar like a lion can?
ROAR! ROAR!
Can you roar like a lion can, and be the King of jungle land?
ROAR! ROAR!
Can you make a monkey sound?
Oooo, Oooo! Eeee, Eeee!
Can you make a monkey sound, scratch your head, jump up and down?
Oooo, Oooo! Eeee, Eeee!
Can you snap like a crocodile?
SNAP! SNAP, SNAP!

Can you snap like a crocodile? Show your teeth and lazy smile!
SNAP! SNAP, SNAP!
Can you make all three sounds?
ROAR! OOOeee! SNAP, SNAP!
Can you make all three sounds, so they'll be heard for miles around?
ROAR! OOOeee! SNAP, SNAP!
Now you're the King of jungle land!
HOORAY!
Now you're the King of jungle land, you're jungle sounds were really grand!
HOORAY! HOORAY!

Directions

Play song #40 from the accompanying *The Sound of Storytime* CD. Before beginning the song, let the children practice making jungle animal sounds. Ask which animals live in the jungle and what each of them sound like. Explain to the children that in the song they are getting ready to sing, they will be asked to roar like a lion, oooo-eeee like a monkey, and snap like a crocodile. Give them time to practice these three sounds. What child does not like to make animal sounds? While they are practicing the three animal sounds, tell them you can't hear them. Give them the opportunity to get louder and louder. They will be "roaring" to go by the end of the practice session. When they make the monkey sound, remind them to scratch their head and jump. Show the children how to place the heel of their palms together as they make the snapping sound of the crocodile while shouting, "Snap! Snap, Snap!"

ADDITIONAL SONGS TO SHARE

Scelsa, Greg, and Steve Millang. *Kids in Motion*. YoungHeart Music, 1987. Compact Disk. YM 008-CD. Play either song #3, "Animal Action I" or song #10, "Animal Action II." Play along as the song directs. You can also use this song to perform an easy, nonspeaking puppet show. Gather puppets to represent the characters in the music. Set up a puppet stage and have a puppet musical. Manipulate the puppets to pop their heads up and dance around as their animal characters begins to sing. The children can perform the animal actions during the song. An additional leader should be on the outside of the puppet stage directing the children.

STORYBOARD

A View at the Zoo

Supplies Needed

Ellison die-cut zoo animals, monkey #2, giraffe #1, lion #2, bear #1, elephant #1, hippo and tiger #1—seven in total

Ellison die-cut ice cream cone

Tape or adhesive material to attach items to storyboard

Directions

As you chant the following verses, attach the appropriate zoo animal to the storyboard. Hold up the animal you are getting ready to place on the board so the children know ahead and can chant the verses along with you. The leader can say, "I went to the zoo, and what did I see?" Prompt the children to say the line, "I saw a *zoo animal* looking back at me!" as you hold up the zoo animal and attach it to the storyboard.

> I went to the zoo, and what did I see?
> I saw a *monkey* looking back at me!
> I went to the zoo, and what did I see?
> I saw a *giraffe* looking back at me!
> I went to the zoo, and what did I see?
> I saw a *lion* looking back at me!
> I went to the zoo, and what did I see?
> I saw a *bear* looking back at me!
> I went to the zoo, and what did I see?
> I saw an *elephant* looking back at me!
> I went to the zoo, and what did I see?
> I saw a *hippo* looking back at me!
> I went to the zoo, and what did I see?
> I saw a *tiger* looking back at me!
> I went to the zoo, and what did I see?
> I saw an *ice cream cone* looking back at me!
> So what did I do?
> I ate that ice cream cone at the zoo!

When finished with the storyboard, point to each animal and let the children call out the different sounds they make.

MAKE AND TAKE

Lion Masks

Supplies Needed per Child

Paper plate, one

Craft stick, large size, one

Yarn, 2" pieces, yellow (optional), approximately 100 per craft table

Glue stick

Washable markers or crayons in brown and yellow

Safety scissors (adult use preferred)

Stapler or strong tape (adult use preferred)

Directions

You will need to precut two holes for the lion's eyes in each paper plate with a sharp cutting tool, large enough for the children to see through. Additionally, precut or ask the parents or caregivers to assist the young children with the safety scissors in cutting 1" to 2" slits all around the outer edge of the paper plate to make the lion's mane. Let the children draw the lion's nose, mouth, and whiskers on the paper plate with the washable markers or crayons. They can color in the lion's face and add eyelashes or whatever they want. Let them glue yarn around the perimeter of the plate to add the lion's mane. When finished with the mask, help the children attach their masks onto the large craft stick using strong tape or a stapler. If you want the children to use the mask with any of the books listed above, make this craft at the beginning of the storytime session.

PART VII

ENCORE MEDLEY

❦

ASSORTED INSTRUMENTS

CURRICULUM TOPICS
Construction, Counting, Family Life, Houses, Tools

FEATURED BOOK
Shulman, Lisa. 2002. *Old MacDonald Had a Woodshop*. New York: G. P. Putnam's Sons.

SUMMARY
This story puts a new spin on the classic children's song "Old MacDonald Had a Farm." By transforming the traditional farm into a woodshop, and the animal sounds into the many tools used for building, the author creates an imaginative story perfect for introducing a unit on building and construction. The text and pictures are bright and splendidly simplistic. Ages 3–7

ACTIVITY
There are many wonderful ways this book can be expanded. We have included a few ideas for accommodating both small and large groups of children. Collect quality pictures of tools from a hardware catalogue, sale flyer, or Ellison die-cut tool set, if you have access to them. Display the pictures on small poster boards. Begin the activity by discussing tools—the ways we use them, what sounds they make when you operate them, and what they do for us. Pass out the posters to the children. Encourage them to bring their picture up one at a time as they identify the sound their tool makes. Have the children add their piece to the storyboard. If you have any toy tools available, they would be fun to share as well. Always be aware of safety issues before sharing real tools. A simple alternative to the storyboard activity is using a nonfiction book with quality pictures of tools. Have the pictures in the book identified and ready to share. Whether using either of these methods, remember to highlight the tools that are in the featured book: a saw, drill, hammer, chisel, file, screwdriver, and paintbrush.

For a very young or particularly large group, simply pass out the sand blocks and have the children make the first repeating sound of the saw. Show them how to rub the two wood pieces together to make the "zzt, zzt" sound. This sound repeats in every verse, and on every turn of the page.

Another fun, but slightly more difficult method is to divide the group in half. You could split the group by girls and boys, or simply draw an imaginary line down the middle. Give one half of the children the sand blocks to play the part of the saw. Give the rest of the children the rhythm sticks to create the sound of the hammer. Everyone chants the part of the drill. The instruments you select need to imitate the sounds of the tools that appear early in the story. This allows the children plenty of opportunity to perform their part in the subsequent verses.

For a smaller group of five to twenty children, you can orchestrate a full band! Here are some ideas for additional instruments:

"Zztt, zztt" of the saw—sand blocks
"Rurr, rurr" of the drill—chant or use kazoos
"Tap, tap" of the hammer—rhythm sticks or sand blocks hitting together
"Chip, chip" of the chisel—triangle, bells
"Scritch, scratch" of the file—sand blocks or shakers

"Squeak, squeak" of the screwdriver—chant
"Swish, swash" of the paintbrush—paint brushes, sand blocks, or shakers

ADDITIONAL BOOKS TO SHARE

Crum, Shutta. 2003. *The House in the Meadow*. Morton Grove, IL: Albert Whitman. A couple gets married and their ten best friends attend. The couple wants to build a house. In the year following their marriage different-size crews of construction workers build a house for them, from nine strong diggers to one inspector. This cleverly written rhyming book has great illustrations as well as a cute storyline. Ages 3–8

Dahl, Michael. 2004. *One Big Building*. Minneapolis, MN: Picture Windows Books. From one plan to twelve stories, this counting book follows the construction of a building. There are hidden numbers on the pages that the children will enjoy trying to find. Ages 2–7

Fleming, Denise. 2000. *Where Once There Was a Wood*. New York: Henry Holt. This book is about all the wild animals, meadows, and creeks that once were, but now are gone. Many houses have been built and have changed the landscaped habitat of the formerly quiet community. The clearly illustrated pictures in this book are expressive and revealing. Ages 3–8

Katz, Karen. 2003. *Daddy and Me*. New York: Little Simon. While the young son helps him out, Daddy is making something special for Henry the dog. This is a sweet lift-the-flap book that helps a young child identify different tools used to build. At the close of the book, a dog house has been constructed by the daddy and son. Ages 3–6

Lewis, Kevin. 2001. *The Lot at the End of My Block*. New York: Hyperion Books for Children. Children will delight in reciting the words in this cumulative rhyming book. With the turn of each page, something new has been added to the lot at the end of the block. This book shows the steps in constructing a new building in a fun and witty way. Ages 3–7

Merriam, Eve. 1998. *Bam, Bam, Bam*. New York: Henry Holt. This is a rhyming account of a construction site and all of the different noises that you might hear at one. Make sure when reading the story to make all of the construction noises and then ask the children to help you to make them even louder! Ages 2–6

Rockwell, Anne, and Harlow Rockwell. 1971. *The Toolbox*. New York: Macmillan. This is a great descriptive book about tools. It is the next best thing to owning a toolbox full of "real" tools. The illustrations are lifelike, and the easy-to-read text is a perfect introduction to tools for any youngster. Ages 3–6

Sawicki, Norma Jean. 1989. *The Little Red House*. New York: Lothrop, Lee & Shepard Books. Pages of this book unfold a series of colorful toy houses, each one containing another slightly smaller house. The smallest house reveals a surprise inside. Ages 3–6

Suen, Anastasia. 2003. *Raise the Roof!* New York: Viking. Starting with expressive cartoon-type illustrations, this book captures the details around the construction site as a busy family lends a hand (and sometimes a paw!) to help build their dream house. Ages 3–8

Wallace, John. 1996. *Building a House with Mr. Bumble*. Cambridge, MA: Candlewick Press. Mr. Bumble and his friends are going to build a house but need help choosing the proper tools. Inside are clues to what type of tool is used to complete the task. Along with pictures of tools, there are other silly items from which to choose. Young children will enjoy helping to select the correct tool. Ages 3–5

Zimmerman, Andrea Griffing, and David Clemesha. 2004. *Dig!* Orlando, FL: Harcourt. Mr. Rally and his dog Lightning love to dig! Mr. Rally drives a big yellow backhoe. In this story the hardworking pair shares five different digging jobs. The tasks in this story are moving dirt and rocks on a bridge, making a drain for the rain, removing a load on the road, digging a hole for a pool at the school, and leveling a site for "a zoo, all brand new." The text reinforces counting skills as the words and the numbers are both presented. Each time another task is completed, Mr. Rally and Lightning compliment each other. The book conveys pure joy for a job well done. The illustrations are simple, colorful, and just enough to make this a perfect storytime read. Ages 3–7

MUSIC AND MOVEMENT WITH ASSORTED INSTRUMENTS

Sing Along: "Worker's Song"

Sung to the Tune: "Ten Little Indians"

Workers won't you get your hammers! *(Rhythm sticks)*
Workers won't you get your hammers!
Workers won't you get your hammers!
Let's pound, pound, pound those nails!
Workers won't you get your saws! *(Sand blocks)*

Workers won't you get your saws!
Workers won't you get your saws!
Let's saw, saw, saw that wood!
Workers won't you get your brooms! *(Shakers)*
Workers won't you get your brooms!
Workers won't you get your brooms!
Let's sweep, sweep, sweep this mess!
Workers do you hear that sound? *(Tambourines)*
Workers do you hear that sound?
Workers do you hear that sound?
It's time to take a break!
Workers do you hear that ring? *(Bells)*
Workers do you hear that ring?
Workers do you hear that ring?
It's the truck that brings ICE CREAM! Let's GO!

Directions

Divide the children into five groups and pass out equal amounts of the following instruments: rhythm sticks, sand blocks, shakers, tambourines, and bells. Play song #41 from the accompanying *The Sound of Storytime* CD. In this song, several instruments are used to imitate the sounds made by the construction workers on the job site. Keep the five groups somewhat separated. When it is their turn to make their sound, it will be easier for them to do so in unison. Explain to the children that each group will get the opportunity to use their instruments as the song progresses. At the end of the song, have the children shout "Let's GO!" Let the children exchange instruments and play the song again.

ACTIVITY

Sing Along: "The Percussion Medley"

Sung to the Tune: "The Mulberry Bush"

I love to strike my tambourine!
Tambourine? Tambourine!
I love to strike my tambourine, all day long!
I love to ring my jingle bell!
Jingle bell? Jingle bell!
I love to ring my jingle bell, all day long!
I love to tap my rhythm sticks!
Rhythm sticks? Rhythm sticks!
I love to tap my rhythm sticks, all day long!
I love to make my shaker shake!
Shaker shake? Shaker shake!
I love to make my shaker shake, all day long!
I love to rub my sand blocks!
Sand blocks? Sand blocks!
I love to rub my sand blocks, all day long!
When we play them altogether,
Altogether, altogether!
When we play them altogether!
This is how we sound!
Repeat the rhythm of the song by using the percussion instruments in unison

Directions

Pass out assorted instruments and play song #42 from the accompanying *The Sound of Storytime* CD. Have the children sit down and keep their instrument quiet until it is their turn. Direct the children to listen to the music and stand up and play their instruments as the song directs. Ask them to be seated again when their turn is over. At the end of the song have all of the children stand and play in unison. Plan to repeat this song and allow the children time to develop their musical skills, as they enjoy and clearly understand the activity much more the second time around.

ADDITIONAL SONGS TO SHARE

Palmer, Hap. *Rhythms on Parade.* Hap-Pal Music Inc., 1995. Compact Disk. HP102E AC633. Play song #22, "I'm A Little Wood Block." Pass out sand blocks, bells, tambourines, rhythm sticks, and shakers. Each child has one instrument part to play. Children play along when they hear their instrument described. On the first verse clap the sand blocks together or tap one rhythm stick to one block.

Scelsa, Greg, and Steve Millang. *We All Live Together,* Vol. 5. Silverlake Sound, 1994. Compact Disk. YM-014-CD. Play song #9, "Rock'n'Roll Rhythm Band." Pass out assorted instruments and play according to the prompts in this action-packed, jazzy song.

Wiggles. *Dance Party.* Lyrick Studios, 2001. Compact Disk. LYR 1160-00. Play song #19, *Joannie Works with One Hammer.* Children can pretend to hammer with one hand, then two, then add one foot, the other foot, and lastly their head. This cute adaptation changes the gender of the traditional song from Johnny to Joannie.

STORYBOARD

Five Little Nails

Supplies Needed

Five real nails

Construction paper, 12" × 18" in size, brown, or a large brown paper sack cut open and the bottom removed (to look like a wall made of wood)

Washable marker, dark brown

One small toy hammer or one rhythm stick

Tape or adhesive material to attach paper wall and nails to the storyboard

Rhythm sticks (two per child)

Directions

Using strong tape, attach the large sheet of brown construction paper or large grocery sack to the storyboard. Draw lines on the paper with the dark marker to imitate wood grain. Slide all five nails slightly into the top of the paper, placing the nails evenly across the top of the paper wall. When you begin the chant, point at the nails standing straight and tall, then get your hammer ready and gently pound them down the wall one at a time. Try to make it look like you are pounding very hard, while using a light touch to slide the nails down into the paper wall. Continue pounding each nail with the toy hammer or end of a rhythm stick until all five are in the wall. Pass out two rhythm sticks to each child. Have them hold one stick in a vertical position and the other in a horizontal position to imitate the hammer and a nail. Let the children practice slightly gripping the bottom portion of the rhythm stick. Using the horizontal stick as a hammer tap the top of the vertical stick. By using a light grip, the vertical stick will slip down their little hand as if it were a nail being hammered into place. Repeat the following rhyme with the children:

Five little nails, standing straight and tall,
Workers get your hammers ready—let's pound one in the wall!
POUND! POUND! POUND! POUND!
Four little nails, standing straight and tall,
Workers get your hammers ready—let's pound one in the wall!
POUND! POUND! POUND! POUND!
Three little nails, standing straight and tall,
Workers get your hammers ready—let's pound one in the wall!
POUND! POUND! POUND! POUND!
Two little nails, standing straight and tall,
Workers get your hammers ready—let's pound one in the wall!
POUND! POUND! POUND! POUND!
One little nail, standing straight and tall,
Workers get your hammers ready—let's pound one in the wall!
POUND! POUND! POUND! POUND!
No more nails standing straight and tall!
Good job workers! You've finished building the wall!

MAKE AND TAKE

This Is the House That [insert child's name] Built!

Supplies Needed per Child

Ellison die-cut house, assorted colors, five

Glue stick

Stapler, one per craft table (with adult assistance)

Sale circulars from discount, home improvement, or lumber stores (Select household items from ads, and precut them for the craft)

Washable markers in assorted colors, several for each craft table

Directions

Introduce this activity by reading any version of the book *This Is the House That Jack Built*. Staple the houses together to form a book. Write the title of the book on the cover page, using the child's name to replace the name Jack. Have the children select from the precut pictures things they would want in their house. Direct them to glue the items onto the individual pages of the house.

LESSON 39

FEATHERS

CURRICULUM TOPICS

Ducks, Chickens, Feathers, Foxes, Wolves, Turkeys, Thanksgiving

FEATURED BOOK

Silverman, Erica. 1998. *Don't Fidget a Feather!* New York: Aladdin Paperbacks.

SUMMARY

Duck and Gander are having a contest, but duck swims faster and gander flies higher. They decide to have a freeze-in-place contest and the winner will be champion of champions. The duck and gander are being careful not to fidget, not even a feather, when along comes a host of visitors including the dreaded fox. Ages 3–7

ACTIVITY

Supplies Needed per Child

Ellison die-cut feather, one (natural or craft feathers work well, too)

Directions

Pass out one feather to each child before you begin to read the book. Explain to the children that you are going to read a book about a duck and a gander. Ask them to lay their feathers in their laps until you direct them to pick them up. Begin reading the book. When you get to the page where the duck and gander begin their freeze-in-place championship game, ask the children to pick up their feather and hold it very, very still—do not move them even a little bit, do not even "fidget a feather." Continue to read the rest of the story while the children are holding their feathers as still as they can. This is a fun activity for the leader as well as each participant. It is a fulfilling and magical experience when you have the audience "captured in suspense." This is one book that holds the children's attention as they hold their feather without fidgeting, and they love it!

ADDITIONAL BOOKS TO SHARE

Brown, Ken. 2001. *The Scarecrow's Hat.* Atlanta, GA: Peachtree. Chicken admires Scarecrow's hat and would like to have it. Scarecrow agrees but only if she can trade it for a walking stick. Chicken does not have a walking stick, but she knows who does—Badger. She visits Badger and he tells her he will gladly give up his walking stick but only for a ribbon to tie open his door. Chicken knows who has a ribbon, so she sets out to visit crow to see if she can talk him out of the ribbon. Crow will give up the ribbon in exchange for some wool to make a nice, soft nest. The story continues with one trade after another until chicken finally comes full circle and becomes the proud owner of Scarecrow's hat. The illustrations are adorable, bright, and airy. The children will love chicken's problem-solving adventures. Year after year, this story is one of our favorite books to share in our storytimes. Ages 3–7

Church, Caroline. 2003. *One Smart Goose.* New York: Orchard Books. All the other geese tease the one dirty goose that likes to bath in the mud until they figure out that he is the only one that isn't chased by the fox. Ages 3–7

Crum, Shutta. 2002. *Fox and Fluff.* Morton Grove, IL: Albert Whitman. Fluff, a baby chick, thinks Fox is his papa and follows him everywhere. Fox tries to remove himself from the responsibility of being Fluff's papa, but Fluff will not let him go that easily. A series of heartwarming events take place as Fox tries to rid himself of the sweet baby chick. There is a happy ending to this delightful book. Ages 3–7

Ginsburg, Mirra. 1991. *Across the Stream.* New York: Mulberry Press. Mother Hen and her chicks are helped across the stream by a duck and her ducklings and away from the fox in their dream. Ages 2–5

Grindley, Sally. 2002. *Where Are My Chicks?* New York: Phyllis Fogelman Books. When Mother Hen loses track of her chicks, Mother Goose scolds that she should have taken better care of her chicks. All the other animals help to find the chicks, but when they have four babies too many, the lesson is for Mother Goose. For some storyboard fun, color photocopy the four chicks and four goslings on the inside back cover of the book. Number the chicks from one to four. Number the goslings from five to eight. Laminate the pieces and add tape on the back. Pass out the pieces to the children in your audience. As you read the story, ask children to bring the appropriately numbered character to the storyboard and place in order on the storyboard. Ages 3–7

Hindley, Judy. 2002. *Do Like a Duck Does.* Cambridge, MA: Candlewick Press. There's a hairy-scary stranger tagging along after Mama Duck and her babies, claiming to be a big brown duck. He can waddle and he can strut like a duck, but is he a duck? Mama Duck thinks she knows the truth, and she also knows a way to beat him at his own game. This is a cleverly written book. Ages 3–7

Johnston, Tony. 2004. *10 Fat Turkeys.* New York: Scholastic. This is a silly countdown story of ten fat turkeys on a fence and the adventures they have as they are eliminated from the fence one by one. There is a repeating line on every page, "Gobble gobble wibble wobble." Let the children help count down from ten to none and recite the silly repeating line as you lead. Ages 2–6

Kasza, Keiko. 2003. *My Lucky Day.* New York: G. P. Putnam's Sons. When a young pig knocks on a hungry fox's door, the fox thinks dinner has arrived. In a witty twist, pig has other plans. Ages 3–7

Kasza, Keiko. 1996. *Wolf's Chicken Stew.* New York: Putnam & Grosset Group. More than anything in the world, the wolf loves to eat. One day he spots a chicken who seems just right when he has a terrible craving for stew. He begins to think about how much more stew there would be if he could fatten her up before eating her. When he finally visits Mrs. Chicken to collect his meal, a big surprise is in store for the wolf. Ages 3–7

Nikola-Lisa, W. 2004. *Setting the Turkeys Free.* New York: Jump at the Sun/Hyperion Books for Children. A young boy makes his own hand print from paint on a piece of paper. He realizes his hand print looks like a turkey. He begins to make more and embellish them with sequins, toothpicks, feathers, and anything he can think of. He loves them so much, they soon take on a life of their own. He makes a pen out of craft sticks to keep his turkeys safe. A fox enters the picture and tries to get in the turkey pen. A series of events transpires before the young artist devises a plan to set the turkeys free. Ages 3–7

Roddie, Shen. 1991. *Hatch, Egg, Hatch!* Boston: Little, Brown. Mother Hen tries everything she can think to get her little egg to hatch, but nothing happens. Worn out from all her efforts, Mother Hen puts her egg under her warm feathers, falls asleep, and then wakes up to a surprise! Ages 2–7

Shannon, George. 2003. *Tippy-Toe Chick, Go!* New York: Greenwillow Books. In this story, a mother hen and her three chicks enter a garden daily for their favorite treat. When a barking dog interferes with their tasty treats, the littlest chick devises a way to get back into the garden. There is a repeating line in the book, "tippy-toe, tippy-toe." Let the children repeat the word using a high-pitched voice. Ages 2–7

MUSIC AND MOVEMENT WITH FEATHERS

Sing Along: "Feather Day"

Sung to the Tune: "Looby Loo"
Supplies Needed per Child

One Ellison die-cut, natural, or craft feather

Let's all stand up and play, and have a feather day!
Feathers are so much fun! Is everyone holding one?
Put your feather in, put your feather out,
Give your feather a shake, shake, shake and turn your self about!
Oh! Feathers are so much fun, I'm glad that I have one!
There's so much that we can do, and they're tickly, wickly too! *(Tickle your tummy)*

Raise your feather up, lower your feather down,
Place your feather on your head and turn yourself around!
Oh! Feathers are so much fun, I'm glad that I have one!
There's so much that we can do, and they're tickly, wickly too! *(Tickle your chin)*

Touch your feather on your leg, touch your feather on your knee,
Touch your feather on back, and now touch all three!
Oh! Feathers are so much fun, I'm glad that I have one!
There's so much that we can do, and they're tickly, wickly too! *(Tickle your foot)*
Hold your feather in your hand, and sit down on the floor,
take a breath, blow it out, and watch your feather soar!
Oh! Feathers are so much fun, I'm glad that I have one!
There's so much that we can do, and they're tickly, wickly too! *(Tickle your nose)*

Directions

Pass out one feather to each child. Read through the song with the children and let them have a practice session before you actually add the music. This is an easy way to introduce a new movement song to a group of young children. After the children are comfortable with the movements, explain to them that when the music starts, they will follow your lead and move their feather as instructed. Play song #44 from the accompanying *The Sound of Storytime* CD. Be sure and remember to let the children tickle their tummy, chin, foot, and nose at the end of the chorus. This will be their favorite part of the song!

STORYBOARD

Would You Fidget a Feather?

Supplies Needed

Ellison die-cuts—toy boat, goat, pick up, duck, house and mouse—one of each

Ellison die-cut, natural, or craft feather, one per child
Tape or self-adhesive material to attach items onto the storyboard

Directions

Give one feather to each child. Ask the children to hold their feather as still as they can during the song. Play song #43 from the accompanying *The Sound of Storytime* CD and place the corresponding die-cut on the storyboard as the song directs throughout each verse. When the song asks, "Would you fidget your feather in a . . . ?" Have the children shout, "NO! NO!" while holding their feather still.

Sing Along: Would You Fidget?

Sung to the Tune: "She'll be Coming Round the Mountain"

Would you fidget your feather in a boat? *(Leader)*
NO! NO! *(Children)*
Would you fidget your feather in a boat? *(Leader)*
NO! NO! *(Children)*
Would you fidget your feather, would you fidget your feather,
would you fidget your feather in a boat? *(Leader)*
NO! NO! *(Children)*

Continue singing or chanting, changing the lines to the following:

> Would you fidget your feather with a goat? NO! NO!
> Would you fidget your feather in a truck? NO! NO!
> Would you fidget your feather with a duck? NO! NO!
> Would you fidget your feather in a house? NO! NO!
> Would you fidget your feather with a mouse? NO! NO!

MAKE AND TAKE

Duck and Gander Picture

Supplies Needed per Child

Construction paper, 9" × 12" in size, light colors, one

Ellison die-cut, natural, or craft feather (optional), two

Washable markers or crayons

Glue

Directions

Using the construction paper and markers or crayons, have the children draw a picture of the duck and gander during their staring contest from the featured book, *Don't Fidget a Feather*. When the children are finished drawing, let them glue one feather on the gander and one feather on the duck.

MAKE AND TAKE 2

Handprint Turkeys

Supplies Needed per Child

Construction paper, 9" × 12" in size, assorted colors, one

Washable markers or crayons in assorted colors

Glue stick

Craft feathers, four to eight each

Craft sticks, small, ten each

Directions

Enlist the parents or helpers to get the children started with this activity. Trace around one of their hands with a washable marker or crayon onto the construction paper. Show the children how the hand can make a picture of a turkey by using their traced thumb for the head and neck, their palm for the body, and their fingers for the tail feathers. Next, let the children color the turkey, adding the turkey's feet, an eye, and a beak, and don't forget to color in the turkey's red wattle underneath the beak. After the turkey is colored, have the children glue on their feathers. Next, glue the craft stick fence over the top of the picture. The children can draw an entire picture around the turkey. It is so much fun to see the creative juices flowing from their little minds. Make sure to read *Setting the Turkeys Free* so children can better enjoy the experience. Thanksgiving is a good time to make this craft, but do not be afraid to use it other times of the year. Children will not care the season this craft is made. They love creating this original masterpiece any time of the year.

LESSON 40

❧❦❧

LIBRARY VOICES

CURRICULUM TOPICS

Library Etiquette

FEATURED BOOK

Bruss, Deborah. 2001. *Book! Book! Book!* New York: Arthur A. Levine Books.

SUMMARY

When all the children who live on the farm go back to school, the farm animals are bored. They have no rides to share, no one to scratch their ears, and nothing to do. They are so bored, they decide to go to town to see if they can find something to do. They end up in front of the public library. They see people with happy faces coming out of the building. They decide they want to be where the happy faces are, so this must be the place to ask for something to do. The hen wants to go in first, but the horse tells her that she is too small; and so, he is the first to go. The horse clip-clops in and politely asks the librarian for something to do, but she can't understand him. One by one, each animal makes their way into the library, but the librarian does not understand what they want. Finally, the frustrated little hen decides it is her turn. She flaps herself into the library and clucks out "Book!" The librarian replies, "What's that noise?" "Book, Book, Book!" clucks the hen. The librarian finally understands and goes to the shelf and hands the hen three books. The farm animals take the books and go back to the farm very satisfied. The last page has a cute little frog and a funny ending. We have read this book many times at our library, and each time the children giggle and laugh throughout the story. This is a must-read library story. Make sure when reading "Book, Book, Book!" to make the sound of a hen clucking. Practice makes perfect! Ages 2–7

ACTIVITY

Each time you read the repeating line, "All she heard was . . ." put your hand to your ear as if listening for something. Then, pause long enough for the children to supply the appropriate animal sounds in the story. Beckon the children to participate through your body language.

ADDITIONAL BOOKS TO SHARE

Bertram, Debbie, and Susan Bloom. 2003. *The Best Place to Read.* New York: Random House. A young boy is excited to have a new book to read and is looking for just the right place to enjoy it. He tries his little chair, but finds he has outgrown it. He tries his Grammy's soft cozy chair, but can't get the dog to move off it. He continues to move from room to room inside the house and then tries the outdoors. He simply cannot find anywhere comfortable to read. He is ready to give up when he sees his mother sitting alone in her chair. He proceeds to ask her if he can sit in her lap and share his new book with her. At last he finds the most comfortable chair in the whole world, his mother's lap. The children will relate to this story and agree that Mom's lap is the best! Before reading the story, ask the children where they think the best place to read a book would be. Tell them you absolutely know the best place, and they will too after you share this book with them. Ages 2–7

Craig, Paula M. 2003. *Mr. Wiggle's Book.* Columbus, OH: Waterbird Books. Mr. Wiggle's is a small inch worm who describes different ways careless readers destroy books. This is a great book to teach young children to love and respect their books—whether they are library books or their own personal collection. Take your time as you go through the pages to let the children see the destruction on each page. After the story, continue the discussion by recapping the problems found in the book. Ask the children if they can think of other things that could damage a book and ways to keep their books safe. When daycares and preschools visit, we use this book as an introduction to the proper care of library books. Ages 2–7

Fraser, Mary Ann. 2003. *I. Q. Goes to the Library*. New York: Walker. The class pet, a mouse, visits the school library during "Library Week." Each day of the week he enjoys his visit as he looks through all the videos, CDs, DVDs, audiocassettes, magazines, puppets, newspapers, fiction books, and nonfiction books. Most of all he wants to get his own library card and check out the funny story the librarian read to them on the first day. Can a mouse get a library card? Ages 4–8

George, Kristine O'Connell. 2001. *Book!* New York: Clarion Books. A young boy unwraps a flat gift and discovers a book. He takes the book with him throughout his day. He thinks of all kinds of things he can do with his wonderful book. He can read it to the cat, or wear it like a hat, and even take it on a wagon ride. He can give it a hug and take it to bed with him to snuggle. This is a sweet picture book that captures the simple joy of a small child's first encounter with a book. This read-aloud is an excellent introduction to books and reading with simple and bright illustrations. Ages 2–6

Heap, Sue. 2003. *Four Friends Together*. Cambridge, MA: Candlewick Press. It is storytime and Seymour the sheep, Rachel the rabbit, and Florentina, the great big flowery bear, are ready. Mary Clare, their fourth friend, is asleep and has the book wrapped tightly in her arms. The three friends are patiently waiting for Mary Clare to wake up and read to them. Florentina, the great big flowery bear, needs to find a seat and get comfortable. She finds herself a chair but it is much too small for her to sit in. Florentina then tries to be smaller by squeezing her arms into her body. Her friends giggle at the sight and the noise wakes up Mary Clare. It is finally time to read, but all three friends cannot see the book at the same time. As Mary Clare attempts to read, her friends continue to interrupt the storytime, complaining about the view. They try moving around but nothing seems to work. They finally work out a way for everyone to see the pictures as Mary Clare reads to them. They snuggle in Florentina's big flowery lap and all four friends are finally happy. Large, bold text teamed with simple but colorful illustrations makes this a must for the younger storytime children. Ages 2–6

Herman, Gail. 2003. *Sam's First Library Card*. New York: Grosset & Dunlap. A young boy named Sam takes his first trip to the library with his mother. He gets a library card and is allowed to check out books. The librarian gives him special instructions about taking good care of his books and returning them on time. Sam browses the library and gets to take a huge stack of books home. He reads some to himself and enlists his mom and dad to read a few to him as well. One day his mother announces that they will have to return the library books the following day. Sam can't bear to part with the books he has read and read over again. He decides to return most of them, but he hides a few of his favorites under his pillow. That night Sam feels really bad about what he has done and finally wakes up his mother to confess. The following day they return the three books and Sam apologizes to the librarian and pays his fine. The librarian talks to Sam about renewing his books the next time he would like to keep them a bit longer. Sam learns a lesson in library etiquette and leaves happy. This is a cute little book to read to children when orientating them to the library. Ages 3–7

Sierra, Judy. 2004. *Wild About Books*. New York: Alfred A. Knopf. A librarian accidentally drives the bookmobile into the zoo and makes herself at home. She begins reading aloud and the animals begin to check out the whole reading thing. Before long, all the animals are going wild for books. Giraffes want tall books while pandas demand more books in Chinese. Otters ask for waterproof books and geckos want stick-to-the-wall books. Not only do the animals learn to read, but some also take up writing. Hippo's memoir is given the Zoolitzer Prize. This is an adorably amusing rhyming book, large in size, with strong illustrations. The story ends with the animals building their own Zoobrary. Ages 4–8

MUSIC AND MOVEMENT FOR STORYTIME

Sing Along: "Are You READY?"

Sung to the Tune: "London Bridge"

Let's get ready for storytime, storytime, storytime!
Let's get ready for storytime! Are you READY?
Are your pockets on the floor? On the floor? On the floor?
Are your pockets on the floor? Are you READY?
Are your hands in your own lap? Your own lap? Your own lap?
Are your hands in your own lap? Are we READY?
YES, we're READY!! *(Children shout this line)*

Directions

Play song #45 from the accompanying *The Sound of Storytime* CD. Sing this song before beginning storytime to capture the children's attention and get their focus. Are their pockets on the floor? Are their hands in their own lap?

Are they ready? It is good to start out storytime with the same song. After a few sessions, the children will begin to hear the music and start settling in for the session on their own.

ACTIVITY

Sing Along: "Sit Your Pockets on the Floor Once More!"

Sung to the Tune: "If You're Happy and You Know It!"

Sit your pockets on the floor once more! CLAP! CLAP!
Sit your pockets on the floor once more! CLAP! CLAP!
Sit your pockets on the floor, sit your pockets on the floor,
Sit your pockets on the floor once more! CLAP! CLAP!

Directions

Play song #46 from the accompanying *The Sound of Storytime* CD. Sing this song when the children are restless and are starting to squirm. It is a fast little song with a catchy tune. By using this song to regroup, the children will soon familiarize themselves with the tune. When they hear it, they will quickly readjust back into their sitting position. After you learn the tune of this song, feel free to sing it a cappella to save time.

ADDITIONAL SONGS TO SHARE

Arthur and Friends: The First Almost Real Not Live CD (or Tape). Rounder Kids, 1998. Compact Disk. 11661-8084-2. Play song #2, "Library Card," when children are entering storytime or during craft time.

Palmer, Hap. *Can a Jumbo Jet Sing the Alphabet?: Songs for Learning through Music and Movement.* Hap-Pal Music Inc., 1998. Compact Disk. HP 110. Play #11, "The Bean Bag." Pass out bean bags and follow the directions. The children will enjoy throwing bean bags in the air, catching them, turning around, and stamping their feet in this fun-filled CD.

Scelsa, Greg, and Steve Millang. *Big Fun.* YoungHeart Music, 1997. Compact Disk. YM-016 CD. Play #10, "The Magic of Reading," when children are entering storytime or during craft time. This is another fun option for creating a positive atmosphere in the library as well as a clever way to introduce library cards to young children.

STORYBOARD

Book Review

Supplies Needed

Ellison die-cut open book, one per child

Magazine cut-outs, small pictures of items children could identify in a book

Tape or adhesive material to attach items to the storyboard

Directions

Prior to the activity attach the Ellison die-cut open books onto the storyboard. If you are not sure how many children to plan for, prepare for more than you think you will use. Place on the storyboard enough open books for one per child. Put the precut magazine pictures in a container and let each child pick one. Tell the children the library has books about everything we can imagine. Explain to the children that they will get to come to the storyboard one at a time to place their item on an open book cut out. They will also tell everyone what their book is about. For example, if they pick a dinosaur, they will face the audience and say, "The library has books about dinosaurs!" (Have tape available to help the children tape their item onto their book.) Every child will take a turn and enjoy coming up and adding their item onto their own book. When everyone has had a turn, take a moment to ask the children if they can think of other things besides books that are in the library. Ask the children if they knew the library had books about all of the different items on the board. Show excitement and enthusiasm as you speak to the youngsters.

MAKE AND TAKE

Bookworm Bookmarks

Supplies Needed per Child

Ellison die-cut worm cut out of heavy white card stock, one

Washable markers or crayons

Directions

Give the children one worm each and let them color them any way they like. Remind them of the story *Mr. Wiggle's Book* and how we need to take good care of our books. Tell them they can use this worm as a bookmark in their library book and a reminder to take good care of their library books.

LESSON 41

PAINT BRUSHES

CURRICULUM TOPICS

Paint, Colors, Rain, Rainbows, Warthogs, Mice, Cats

This series of lessons was inspired by the marvelous little action song, "Dippin' in the Paint Box," from the book *Ready-to-Go-Storytimes*. The authors of this book recommend giving each child a paper paint brush and encouraging them to pretend to paint an imaginary picture as the song directs. Our patrons and children enjoyed this activity so much we began to look for other ways to incorporate paint brushes into our storytimes.

For their durability, we decided to purchase real paint brushes. From the paint department at our local discount store, we bought twenty-five 2" paint brushes with wooden handles. The cost was approximately fifty cents each. The handles were then spray painted in a primary color. A clean paint can with the label removed, creating a shiny tin pail, was used as storage for the paint brushes. The props turned out great. If this option is not available, paper paint brushes also work perfectly fine.

When the song and activity was introduced to the young children at our library, they were wild about it. The children's movements were fascinating to watch, and the activity generated lots of imaginative discussion. We would act silly and pretend to paint our faces like a clown using Mom's makeup. We discussed other pictures we would like to paint. Months went by after these sessions, and the children were still begging to "paint" again. We began to include more paint brushing activities at our storytime sessions. The following lessons are a few of our favorite paint brush storytimes.

FEATURED BOOK

Edwards, Pamela Duncan. 2001. *Warthogs Paint: A Messy Color Book*. New York: Hyperion Books for Children.

SUMMARY

The Warthogs spend a rainy day painting the house. Through many messy spills and calamities, they learn about mixing colors. Ages 3–7

ACTIVITY

When directed by the story, you will need one paint brush for every child. Divide the group into thirds. Give one third of the group the red paint brushes, one third the blue paint brushes, and the last third yellow paint brushes. Read the first few pages of the story. After the line "Everyone rushes to find the paint and fetch the brushes," say something like, "Where are the brushes? Oh! Yes, here they are!" Pass out the paint brushes and get to work. Resume the story. The repeating line in this story goes, "Splish! Bend low. Splash! Stretch tall!" As the children say this line with you, have them stand up and paint from their toes to as tall as they can stretch themselves. With younger two- and three-year-old children, encourage everyone to participate each time regardless of their paint brush color. Older groups learning about mixing colors could be led to "paint" only, when their paint brush color is being painted or is part of the color blend being painted in the story. Encourage all ages to say and play the repeating lines with you.

FEATURED BOOK

Root, Phyllis. 2001. *Soggy Saturday*. Cambridge, MA: Candlewick Press.

SUMMARY

In the rainy month of April, we like to talk about rain, rainbows, and colors of the rainbow at storytime. One of our all-time favorite "rainy day" books is *Soggy Saturday*. In this story, a rainstorm washes the colors out of everything on the farm and a little farm girl has to paint all the animals and farm landscape back to their true colors. This adorable book lends itself perfectly to the idea of pretend play with the paint brushes. Ages 2–7

ACTIVITY

Pass out the paint brushes before you begin to read the story. We prefer to read the first half of the story and then pass out the paint brushes. After the line, "So Bonnie got busy with the brushes and buckets," turn to your audience and say, "She has so much work to do, could all of you help, too?" Quickly pass out the paint brushes and let the children get to work. Resume the story. As you read, lead the pretend play. Pretend to paint the speckles on the chickens by showing the children how to dot, dot, dot with their paint brushes. Paint the cow with long, horizontal brown strokes. Paint the pig pink, and don't forget his curly tail! To do this, make swirling motions with your brush. When the little farm girl, Bonnie, climbs the ladder to paint the blue back into the sky, have the children stand up and pretend to climb the ladder too. Next, have them stand up on their tippy toes and stretch high in the sky. The kids will take to the activity like "ducks to water."

FEATURED BOOK

Walsh, Ellen Stoll. 1995. *Mouse Paint.* San Diego, CA: Harcourt Brace.

SUMMARY

Three white mice discover three jars of paint. One jar is red, one is blue, and the other is yellow. They have a lot of fun mixing colors and painting themselves. There is a pesky cat in the plot that the mice have to keep away from. In spite of all the colors of paint the mice mix and enjoy, in the end the white mice devise a plan to "blend in" in order to keep the cat from spotting them. Ages 3–7

ACTIVITY

Pass out one Ellison die-cut paint brush #2, or a real paint brush to each child. Divide the group of children into thirds. Give one third of the group the red paint brushes, one third the blue paint brushes, and one third the yellow paint brushes. Preread the story and familiarize yourself with the line "So they washed themselves down to a nice soft white." Then you, the storyteller, add the line, "Got out their paint brushes." You could say, "Okay, little mice, get out your paint brushes—let's see what you learned about mixing colors!" When everyone is settled, resume the story with the line, "They painted one part red." Direct everyone with a red paint brush to lift their brushes in the air and pretend to paint. (Be sure to show them how to paint, starting high in the air, using long strokes, and slowly brushing in a downward motion.) Repeat with the yellow paint brushes, and then the blue paint brushes. When the story gets to the colors of orange, green, and purple, ask the children, "What colors did they mix to paint the orange part?" (Only red and yellow should be painting.) Repeat the question for green and purple. When you get to the last page of the story, hush the children and wait until they are all perfectly still. Then, in a whisper, read, "But they left some white because of the cat!" If you have a young audience of two- and three-year-olds, this activity should be slightly modified to be less specific by allowing everyone to paint at each opportunity. Four- and five-year-olds are ready to follow more specific directions and should enjoy the challenge in this lesson.

ADDITIONAL BOOKS TO SHARE

No Author. 2003. *Are Lemons Blue?* New York: DK Publishing. This novelty series of books asks such funny questions as "Are eggs square?" and "Are elephants tiny?" Ages 2–4

Barry, Frances. 2004. *Duckie's Rainbow.* Cambridge, MA: Candlewick Press. Follow Duckie on her colorful walk home to a big, bold surprise. Ages 2–4

Beaumont, Karen. 2005. *I Ain't Gonna Paint No More!* New York: Harcourt. A little boy loves to paint in this defiant story. The trouble is, he does not know when to stop. After making a huge mess, he is caught by his mother. She hides his paints and exclaims, "Ya ain't a-gonna paint no more!" The naughty little boy can't resist. So he climbs up in the closet and retrieves the hidden paints. He paints and paints and paints from his head to his toes and everywhere between, all the while chanting, "Now I ain't gonna paint no more." This book is sure to cause giggling in storytime. This book lends itself perfectly to face painting. Get some washable, nontoxic paint or washable markers and have some face painting fun. Make sure to have a mirror available for children to see their face after it is painted. Ages 3–7

Dodd, Emma. 2001. *Dog's Colorful Day: A Messy Story about Colors and Counting.* New York: Dutton Children's Books. A little dog always manages to be underfoot when someone makes a mess with red jam, blue paint, pink ice cream, and orange juice—the history of his day splattered on his white coat. By evening, there are ten colorful spots for readers to count. Ages 3–7

Dunbar, Polly. 2004. *Flyaway Katie.* Cambridge, MA: Candlewick Press. Feeling a little gray, Katie cheers herself up by donning brighter clothing and colorful paint. Ages 2–7

Lionni, Leo. 1997. *A Color of His Own.* New York: Alfred A. Knopf. Chameleon is in search of his own color but finds something even more special. Ages 2–7

Lloyd, Sam. 2004. *What Color Is Your Underwear?* New York: Scholastic. Readers can lift the flaps to see animals in their crazy, colorful underwear. Ages 2–7

Martin, Bill Jr. 1983. *Brown Bear, Brown Bear, What Do You See?* New York: Henry Holt. A boldly colored frog, cat, horse, and duck parade across the pages. Ages 2–6

Tashiro, Chisato. 2003. *Chameleon's Colors.* New York: North-South Books. The jungle animals are envious of Chameleon's ability to change colors. The animals soon learn that changing their original appearance causes problems they never expected. Ages 3–7

Ziefert, Harriet. 2003. *Lunchtime for a Purple Snake.* Boston, MA: Houghton Mifflin. Jessica's grandpa is an artist. She loves to visit him in his studio so she can paint with him. In this painting session, Grandpa encourages Jessica to turn her "mistake" (and accidental blob of paint on the page) into "something good." They paint together. As Jessica learns about mixing colors together to achieve yet another color, she paints a purple snake while her Grandpa adds to the picture by painting a bug and so on. This is a sweet story that teaches us we all make mistakes but some can be turned into good. Ages 3–7

MUSIC AND MOVEMENT WITH PAINT BRUSHES

Sing Along: "I'm Painting a Sunny Day"

Sung to the Tune: "Clementine"

Will you help me paint a picture on this very rainy day?
We can paint sunny pictures, so the rain will go away!
Dip your paintbrush in the green paint, paint some green grass here and there,
Move your paintbrush up and down, and put trees everywhere!
Dip your paintbrush in the blue paint, paint some blue birds way up high!
Can you hear them singing birdsongs, how they love the clear, blue sky!
Dip your paintbrush in the yellow paint, paint a circle—round and round.
Paint a great big yellow sunshine, this will help to dry the ground!
We need a rainbow! Yes, a rainbow! Let's splash some colors in the air,
Pretty colors, lots of colors! Look! There's rainbows everywhere!
Now we're finished with our painting, and in just the nick of time,
The rain has stopped and we can play now—in the warm sunshine!

Directions

Pass out one Ellison die-cut paint brush or real paint brush to each child. Before the music starts, tell the children they are going to paint a picture in the air. Ask them if they know how to paint grass, trees, bluebirds, sunshine, and a rainbow? Practice with the children so they can see how you move the paint brush. Play song #47 from the accompanying *The Sound of Storytime* CD. Tell the children to follow along painting everything they practiced when directed in the song.

ADDITIONAL SONGS TO SHARE

Benton, Gail, and Waichulaitis, Trisha. 2003. *Ready-to-Go Storytimes: Fingerplays, Scripts, Patterns, Music and More.* New York: Neal-Schuman Publishers. This is an excellent resource book with a music CD that includes the song "Dippin' in the Paint Box."

Directions

Pass out one Ellison die-cut paint brush or real paint brush to every child. This song leads its audience to paint an imaginary picture. It is a huge hit in all of our storytime sessions. Enjoy the fun without all the mess!

STORYBOARD

Picture Guessing

Supplies Needed

Construction paper—red, orange, yellow, green, blue, indigo, and violet—one each

Scissors

Tape or adhesive material to attach items to the storyboard

Directions

Cut the construction paper in 1" half-moon-shaped, strips making an arch to form a rainbow. Each arch should grow smaller in size. When assembled, they will fit together just like a rainbow. Have the children help you create a rainbow on the storyboard. Begin by announcing that the group is going to create a picture on the storyboard. Do not give away what the picture is to become. Place the largest red arch on the board and ask the children to tell you what color it is. Repeat with all the subsequent colors, pausing each time to allow the children to tell you the color of each arch as you attach it to the storyboard. At the end ask, "What did we make a picture of?" The correct answer is a rainbow! Discuss with the children when rainbows appear and what makes a rainbow. After the children are familiar with this activity, but before you present the next piece, ask your audience to guess what color comes next. Another variation of this activity is to pass out the colored arches to the children and, as you call the individual colors, have them place them on the board one at a time.

MAKE AND TAKE

Crayon Rainbows

Supplies Needed per Child

Construction paper, 9" × 12" in size, light color, one

Crayons in each color of the rainbow—red, orange, yellow, green, blue, violet—one set

Tape or rubber band

Directions

Tape or rubber band together the rainbow color set of crayons for each child. Have the children color a rainbow by making a big arch on their paper. They can add animals or other characters from the stories highlighted in this lesson.

LESSON 42

SCARVES

CURRICULUM TOPICS

Wind, Kites, Ribbons, Scarves, Rainbows, Sunshine, Rain, Weather

FEATURED BOOK

Hooper, Patricia. 1995. *How the Sky's Housekeeper Wore Her Scarves*. Boston: Little, Brown

SUMMARY

In this fantastic fable, an old woman wears one of seven colorful scarves each time she goes out to polish and straighten all the splendid entities of the sky. On the days the sun and the rain are both out at once, she ties all her scarves to the fence post so she will not get lost in the dreary sky while she is hard at her work. The fable explains that this is why we see a rainbow when the sun comes out after a rain. Ages 3–7

ACTIVITY

Pass out scarves in the seven bright colors listed in the book. Duplicate the colors as many times as you need so every participant has a scarf. Each time the story mentions one of the old woman's colored scarves, have the children with the appropriate color wave their scarves in the air pretending to be the old woman working and flying through the sky. Make up actions to do with the scarves for the different kind of work she does each day of the week. For instance, when she polishes the sun, show the children how to make circular, polishing motions with their scarf. When she winds up the comets, show the children how to wind up their green scarf. When she sews the clouds back together, show them how to use their violet scarf like a needle and thread.

ADDITIONAL BOOKS TO SHARE

Emmett, Jonathan. 2003. *Someone Bigger*. New York: Clarion Books. When you are a kid, it seems there is always something you are too small to do. When Sam's father takes him out to fly the kite they made, it seems this is the case for Sam too. Sam asks to hold the kite string first, but his dad replies, "This kite needs someone bigger." This line repeats throughout the story. After a few repetitions, children will enjoy filling in these words for you. Sam's dad launches the kite. Before you know it, he is pulled up into the sky with it! The adventure begins as more and more townspeople grab on to the kite string to help pull dad back down to the ground. As each person, and even a few zoo animals, is whisked away, they continue to call for someone bigger. The boy pleads to be given a chance to help, but they all say he is too small. In the end, Sam becomes the hero when he, indeed, is just what they need to pull the kite back down. This story is a favorite at storytime and is so much fun to tell. Each time a character calls down from the sky, hold your hand to your mouth and call the lines out as if you are looking down from above. Each time Sam replies, put both hands to your mouth and call out the words looking up to the sky. Ages 3–7

Munsch, Robert N. 1999. *Ribbon Rescue*. New York: Scholastic. Jillian's grandmother makes her a beautiful dress with grand flowing ribbons. The dress does not stay beautiful for long. Jillian assists several people with emergencies and her dress becomes the biggest mess of all. This story has a sweet ending that will bring a smile to everyone's face. Ages 3–8

Pittar, Gill. 2003. *Milly, Molly and the Secret Scarves*. Gisborne, New Zealand: MM House Publishing. Two friends work very hard to make special gifts for each other. Unbeknownst to the other, they both end up making the same gift: a knitted striped scarf. They both love their gifts and decide to wear them all the time. Ages 3–7

Root, Phyllis. 1996. *One Windy Wednesday*. Cambridge, MA: Candlewick Press. The wind blows so hard that it blows the moo right out of the cow and the quack right out of the duck. After the wind dies down, all the animals on the farm are making the wrong sounds. Bonnie Bumble has to work hard to put everything back the way it belongs. Have the children make the animal noises and imitate the blowing wind with you as you are reading. When the duck says "moo," pause and make a funny, surprised face. Ages 2–6

Schaefer, Carole Lexa. 1998. *The Squiggle*. New York: Crown. A school teacher leads her class on a field trip to the park. The last girl in line spies a "squiggle" on the ground. She picks it up and begins to enjoy the imaginary designs she can make. The "squiggle" is a small red piece of string. The little girl is in a world of her own enjoying the new found treasure. She finally realizes she has fallen behind and yells for the group to wait! Everyone turns around, and with her captive audience the little girl makes a dragon, a wall, an acrobat, fireworks, and many other spectacular designs she has created with one little "squiggle." In the end she shares her "squiggle" with all the children to grab on, as they finish walking to the park. Pass out the scarves following the story and let the children use their imagination to make a few unique squiggles of their own. Ages 3–7

Watson, Richard Jesse. 2005. *The Magic Rabbit*. New York: Blue Sky Press. In this magical story, a white rabbit jumps out of a black hat and finds he can perform magic tricks. He performs amazing tricks like pulling colorful scarves tied one to another from his hat and making a picnic with his favorite foods. The white rabbit becomes lonely. He discovers there is another hat inside his magic hat where another rabbit lives inside! For an additional enrichment, learn an easy scarf trick and dazzle the audience. Ages 3–7

Wisdom, Jude. 2002. *Whatever Wanda Wanted*. New York: Phyllis Fogelman Books. Wanda is a spoiled, overindulged bratty girl who gets whatever she wants whenever she wants. Her parents give her anything and are too busy to spend time with Wanda. One day she goes shopping with her mother. Wanda discovers a new store she has never been to before. She is enamored by a huge colorful kite hanging high in the shop. She wants that kite badly. The shopkeeper informs Wanda that it is not for sale, but Wanda stomps her foot and demands the shopkeeper give it to her. Wanda wins and is whisked away by the huge colorful kite and learns many valuable lessons. She learns one in particular, "There's more to life than things!" Every time we read this book to a group of children, they sit captivated by the ugliness of Wanda. This is a good lesson for all ages about being materialistic. Ages 3–8

MUSIC AND MOVEMENT WITH SCARVES

Sing Along: "Grandma's Magic Scarf"

Sung to the Tune: "Polly Wolly Doodle"

I found some scarves in my grandma's drawer, and she said I could take just one!
So I picked a scarf, placed in on my head, and then the magic begun!
It went up, it went down, and it twirled me around and around!
It went up and down and all around, and then dropped to the ground!
Well, I picked it up and I shook it hard, and I moved it to and fro!
It wrapped itself around my waist and it wiggled my hips just so!
Well, I pulled—that scarf—right off my waist you see,
And then it dropped down to my toes—and back up to my knees!
I twirled and twirled and giggled and played with the magic scarf that day,
Then I folded it up, put it back in the drawer—so it wouldn't get away!
Next time—you're at grandma's, and you're looking for something to do,
Ask her if she has a scarf, and show her a trick or two!

Directions

Familiarize yourself with the movements in this song prior to acting it out. Get ready to move! Pass out the scarves and follow along with song # 48 from the accompanying *The Sound of Storytime* CD. This has a catchy little tune, and some fast movement the children will enjoy. The more you repeat the song and actions, the more fun the song will be. The children will not only be doing the actions, but singing the song with you! Don't forget to imitate pulling out the drawer and choosing the scarf, and then pulling the drawer back out, folding the scarf and placing it in the drawer.

ADDITIONAL SONGS TO SHARE

Palmer, Hap. *Hap Palmer's Can a Cherry Pie Wave Goodbye?* Hap-Pal Music Inc., 1990. Compact Disk. HP103. Play song #8, "Parade of Colors." Get all the children to line up for a parade! Pass out the scarves, begin the song and march around the room waving colored scarves. When the bell sounds during the song, everyone freezes until the music begins.

Piggyback Songs: Singable Poems Set to Favorite Tunes. Kimbo, 1995. Compact Disk. KIM 9141CD. Play song #24, "My Kite." Pass out the scarves. On the words "my kite is up so high," children wave their scarves in the air. On the words "my kite is falling down", bring scarves to the ground and wave kites low. When the song says "the wind has caught my kite" toss scarves in the air and yell "wheee!"

Scelsa, Greg, and Steve Millang. *We All Live Together*, Vol. 5. Silverlake Sound, 1994. Compact Disk. YM-014-CD. Play song #6, "Rainbow of Colors." Pass out red, yellow, blue, green, white, brown, orange, and black colored scarves. When the song asks participants to show a particular color, audience members with the appropriate color wave the scarf in the air. Simple scarves can be made from fabric remnants by cutting squares with pinking shears or by surging the edges. Bandanas can also be used in place of scarves. Bandanas are inexpensive and can be purchased in all of these colors at a local discount store.

Stewart, Georgiana. *Musical Scarves & Activities.* Dubway Studios, 2002. Compact Disk. KIM 9167CD. This entire CD is comprised of activities to play with scarves.

Summer Dance Party. Sony Music, 1996. Compact Disk. A 26911. Play song #9, "Limbo Rock." Tie colorful scarves together in place of a limbo stick. Have the children form a line and two leaders or parents hold each end of the scarf rope. Explain to the children that they are to go under the scarves trying not to touch them with any part of the body. When each child has had a turn in line, lower the scarves. When we play this game, everyone continues playing until the game is over regardless of whether they touch the scarves. You may have to play the song a few times to make sure everyone has enjoyed the activity.

STORYBOARD

Just Me, Myself and I

Supplies Needed

Ellison die-cut kite—red, yellow, green, blue, white—one each

Markers or stickers

Tape or adhesive material to attach the kites onto the storyboard

Curly ribbon, bright colors (optional)

Directions

Decorate the white kite with bright markers or stickers to make it really special. This is the kite the child in this story makes for herself. It needs to be very eye-catching and unique. Add a little colorful, curly ribbon for the tail to really jazz it up. Attach tape or adhesive material to the back of each kite. Place the kites on the board as the story directs:

My brother had a red kite that flew high in the air,
I wanted to fly it, but he wouldn't share! *(Add red kite)*
My sister had a yellow kite that flew high in the air,
I wanted to fly it, but she wouldn't share! *(Add yellow kite)*
My cousin had a green kite that flew high in the air,
I wanted to fly it, but he wouldn't share! *(Add green kite)*
My friend had a blue kite that flew high in the air,
I wanted to fly it, but she wouldn't share! *(Add blue kite)*
Soooo, I made me a kite and I flew it really high,
And I flew it by myself, just me, myself and I! *(Add unique, one-of-a-kind kite)*

MAKE AND TAKE

Bright Kites

Supplies Needed per Child

Construction paper, 12" × 18" in size, assorted colors, one each

Washable markers or crayons in assorted colors, several for each craft table

Stickers or scraps of construction paper (optional)

Glue stick

Hole punch

Tape

Yarn, precut two to three feet in length, any color, one

Crepe paper streamers or ribbon in bright colors, precut in 12" strips, five

Directions

Precut the construction paper into diamond shapes and using the hole punch, punch a hole at the bottom point of each diamond. Precut 12" strips of crepe paper or ribbon to use for the kite tails. Let the children color their kites as well as glue decorate with construction paper scraps or stickers. When they are finished creating their kites, using a glue stick or tape, attach the ribbons or crepe paper to the bottom of their kite for the flowing tail. Assist the children with threading the yarn into the hole-punched area and tying. Adding tape onto the bottom point of the kite before using the hole punch may reinforce the construction paper to better support the yarn.

THE SOUND OF
STORYTIME RESOURCES

Source A: Library Collection Suggested CD and Song Title List

Action, California. Greg and Steve Productions. Distributed by Youngheart Music. Recorded at Worlds Tallest Music Studio, Mad Hatter Studios. Greg and Steve Recording.

The Ants Go Marching. Macacy Entertainment, 2002. Compact Disk. MK2 5083isk. #3, "The Ants Go Marching"

Arnold, Linda. *Make Believe.* Ariel Records, 1986. Compact Disk. YM 121-CD #2, "Tick Tock"; #7, "Bathtub Song"

Arthur and Friends: The First Almost Real Not Live CD (or Tape). Rounder Kids, 1998. Compact Disk. 11661-8084-2. #2, "Library Card"

Atkinson, Lisa. *The Elephant in Aisle Four and Other Whimsical Animal Songs.* 2000. Compact Disk. GW1061. Albany, NY: A Gentle Wind, 2000. Performer: Lisa Atkinson. Recorded, Mixed and Mastered by Donald Person at Windy Acres Studio. #3, "Puppy Kisses"

Baby's First Playtime Songs. St. Clair Entertainment Group, 1999. Compact Disk. BFM44472. #4, "We're Going on a Bearhunt"

The Best of the Best Preschool Play Songs! Madacy Kids, 2001. Compact Disk. WW 24398. #11, "Roll Over"

Birthday Party! Singalong. Little Buddha Studios, 2001. Compact Disk. R2 74261 #2, "The Balloon Game"; #5, "The Freeze Dance"

Cedarmont Kids Singers. *Toddler Action Songs.* October Sound and Mattinee Studio, 2002. Compact Disk. 84418-0137-2. #2, "The Ants Go Marching"; #5, "Baby Bumblebee"; #13, "John Brown's Baby"

Chapin, Tom. *Great Big Fun for the Very Little One.* Sundance Music, 2001. Compact Disk. R2 78361. #6, "The Parade Came Marching"

Chenille Sisters. *1-2-3 for Kids.* Red House Records, 1989. Compact Disk. RHR CD 33. #1, "Singing in the Tub"; #5, "I'm Being Swallowed by a Boa Constrictor"

Chenille Sisters. *Teaching Hippopotami to Fly!* CanToo Records, 1996. Compact Disk. CTR CD 01. #1, "Deepest Africa"

Disney's Silly Songs. Walt Disney Records, 1988. Compact Disk. 60819-7. #8, "Pizza Pie Song"; #9, "A Peanut Sat on a Railroad Track"; #10, "It Ain't Gonna Rain No More"; #15, "Three Little Fishes"; #17, "Bill Grogan's Goat"

Feldman, Jean R. *Dr. Jean & Friends.* Progressive Music, 1998. Compact Disk. DJ-DO2. #2, "Monkeys and the Alligator"; #11 "Tooty Ta"

Gang, Goanna. *Kids Dance and Play*, Vol. 2. Soundhouse, 2002. Compact Disk. CRG 191032. #3, "Monster Mash"; #8, "The Chicken Dance"; #9, "The Locomotion"

Harper, Jessica. *Nora's Room.* 4th Street Recording Studio, 1996. Compact Disk. ALA 2005. #1, "Nora's Room"

Hickman, Sara. *Toddler.* Sleeveless, 2001. Compact Disk. PMB 431. #2, "Ten Little Bubbles"

Moricz, Michael. *Time to Sing!* Anything Audio Multimedia, 2000. Compact Disk. 113SING. #1, "Wheels on the Bus"; #24, "Five Little Monkeys"

Most Amazing Dinosaur Songs. Dragonfly Studio, 2004. Compact Disk. R2 78987. #8, "Going on a Dino Hunt"; #12, "Hokey Pokeysaurus"

Most Amazing Truck, Train & Plane Songs. Dragonfly Studio, 2004. Compact Disk. R2 76567. #8, "Wheels on the Bus"

100 Sound Effects, Vol. 2. Premium Music Collection, 1998. Compact Disc. PMC60802.

Palmer, Hap. *Can a Jumbo Jet Sing the Alphabet? Songs for Learning through Music and Movement.* Hap-Pal Music Inc., 1998. Compact Disk. HP110. #11, "The Bean Bag"

Palmer, Hap. *Hap Palmer's Can a Cherry Pie Wave Goodbye?* Hap-Pal Music Inc., 1990. Compact Disk. HP103. #8, "Parade of Colors"

Palmer, Hap. *Rhythms on Parade.* Hap-Pal Music Inc., 1995. Compact Disk. HP102E AC633. #2, "The Mice Go Marching"; #3, "Woodpecker"; #10, "Tap Your"; #12, "Bean Bag Shake"; #17, "Stuff It in the Closet"; #18, "Slow and Fast"; #20, "Play and Rest"; #22, "I'm a Little Wood Block"

Peter, Paul, and Mary. *Peter, Paul & Mommy, too.* Warner Brothers, 1993. Compact Disk. 9 45216-2. Song #7, "I Know an Old Lady Who Swallowed a Fly"

Piggyback Songs: Singable Poems Set to Favorite Tunes. Kimbo, 1995. Compact Disk. KIM 9141CD. #11, "Never Play with Matches"; #16, "Time to Pick Up the Toys"; #20, "Toes Are Tapping"; #24, "My Kite"; #35, "Housework Song"

Playhouse Disney. *Bubble-O Popple-O.* Walt Disney Records, 2001. Compact Disk. 60695-7.

Raffi. *Let's Play!* Shoreline Records, 2002. Compact Disk. 11661-8108-2. #9, "If You're Happy and You Know It,"

Raffi. *The Singable Songs Collection.* Shoreline Records, 1996. Compact Disk. 8051. #3, "Brush Your Teeth" (from the CD *Singable Songs for the Very Young*)

Ready-To-Go-Storytimes: FingerPlays, Scripts, Patterns, Music, and More. New York: Neal-Schuman Publishers, 2003. Song #12.

Reid-Naiman, Kathy. *Tickles and Tunes.* Merriweather Records, 1997. Compact Disk. M9701. #18, "See the Ponies"; #24, "I'm Passing out the Sticks/Tap and Stop"; #25, "When You're One"; #26, "Time To Put Away"; #29, "Criss Cross Applesauce"

Scelsa, Greg, and Steve Millang. *Big Fun.* YoungHeart Music, 1997. Compact Disk. YM-016 CD. #2, "Silly Willies"; #3, "In My Backyard"; #10, "The Magic of Reading"

Scelsa, Greg, and Steve Millang. *Kids in Action.* Greg & Steve Productions, 2000. Compact Disk.

Scelsa, Greg, and Steve Millang. *Kids in Motion.* YoungHeart Music, 1987. Compact Disk. YM 008-CD. #3, "Animal Action I"; #4, "The Freeze"; #10, "Animal Action II"

Scelsa, Greg, and Steve Millang. *We All Live Together,* Vol. 5. Silverlake Sound, 1994. Compact Disk. YM-014-CD. #2, "The Number Game"; #6, "Rainbow of Colors"; #8, "Get Up and Go"; #9, "Rock'n'Roll Rhythm Band"

Silverstein, Shel. *Where the Sidewalk Ends.* Sony Music Entertainment, 1992. Compact Disk.

Stewart, Georgiana. *Musical Scarves & Activities.* Dubway Studios, 2002. Compact Disk. KIM 9167CD.

Summer Dance Party. Sony Music, 1996. Compact Disk. A 26911. #9, "Limbo Rock"

Tallman, Susie. *Children's Songs.* Rock me Baby Records, 2004. Compact Disk. RMBR91005-2. Song #4, "Bingo"

Toddler Trio: Silly Favorites. Little Buddha Studios, 2000. Compact Disk. R2 76675. Song #18, "Who Stole the Cookies!"

Twenty-Five Toddler Songs. Straightway Music, 2003. Compact Disk. 7243 5 82858 2 SWD 82858. #20, "Brush Your Teeth"

Wiggles. *Dance Party.* Lyrick Studios, 2001. Compact Disk. LYR 1160-00 #19, "Joannie Works with One Hammer"

Wiggles. *Yummy Yummy!* Lyrick Studios, 1999. Compact Disk. 9206. #2, "Shaky Shaky"; #13, "The Monkey Dance"; #15, "Shake Your Sillies Out"

Source B: *The Sound of Storytime* CD Index

1 "Poor Little Kitty"
2 "Feather Fun"
3 "Cookies to Share"
4 "Fire, Fire, Fire!"
5 "The Fire Truck"
6 "Let's Make a Pizza Pie"
7 "Is It My Turn Yet?"
8 "The Ring-a-ling Song"
9 "I Spied an Apple"
10 "The Birthday Knock"
11 "My Tick-Tocking Clock"
12 "The Billy Goats Ballad"
13 "Tap with Me 1-2-3"
14 "Two Sticks"
15 "Woodpecker Tap!"
16 "I Love to Scrubba-dub"
17 "Do You Wanna Be a Crocodile?"
18 "Shaggy Dog"
19 "Ole Pesky Fly"
20 "A Hairy Problem"
21 "I Love to Brush!"
22 "Them Old Brittle Bones"
23 "Shim-Sham-Shoo"
24 "Rainy Day Blues"

25 "Snakey Tail"
26 "Hurry Back Train!"
27 "The Alphabet Tree"
28 "My Messy Room!"
29 "Wake Up, Farm!"
30 "Tambourine Action!"
31 "The Hippo Groove"
32 "Jungle Drum Echo"
33 "Boom, Boom, Crash!"
34 "Waa! Waa! Waa!"
35 "Have You Ever?"
36 "You & Me"
37 "Look Out!"
38 "Shark Watching!"
39 "Oh, Please Don't Snore Anymore!"
40 "Jungle Sounds"
41 "Worker's Song"
42 "The Percussion Medley"
43 "Would You Fidget a Feather?"
44 "Feather Day"
45 "Are You READY?"
46 "Sit Your Pockets!"
47 "I'm Painting a Sunny Day"
48 "Grandma's Magic Scarf"

Source C: *The Sound of Storytime* Book/Author Index

Source D: *The Sound of Storytime* Subject Index

About the Authors

Tiara Dixon has been working in libraries since her early teens. She holds a BA from Park University, from which she graduated Magna Cum Laude. In addition to serving as the mother of four children, she currently works at the Mid-Continent Public Library of Liberty, Missouri, where she coordinates storytime programs for toddlers and babies.

Paula Blough is now in her twentieth year as assistant branch manager at the Mid-Continent Public Library, where she plans and administers programs for the young. As a mother of four and grandmother of four, she is pleased to share her years of storytelling experience with a growing community. She is currently planning and presenting baby storytime, and assisting with toddler and preschool storytimes as needed.